WATERFRONT
DUNCAN McNAB

GRAFT, CORRUPTION AND VIOLENCE
– AUSTRALIA'S CRIME FRONTIER
FROM 1788 TO NOW

Every effort has been made to acknowledge and contact the copyright holders for permission to reproduce material contained in this book. If anyone has further information, please contact the publishers.

Published in Australia and New Zealand in 2015
by Hachette Australia
(an imprint of Hachette Australia Pty Limited)
Level 17, 207 Kent Street, Sydney NSW 2000
www.hachette.com.au

Copyright © Duncan McNab 2015

This book is copyright. Apart from any fair dealing for the purposes of private study, research, criticism or review permitted under the *Copyright Act 1968*, no part may be stored or reproduced by any process without prior written permission. Enquiries should be made to the publisher.

National Library of Australia
Cataloguing-in-Publication data:

McNab, Duncan, author.
Waterfront/Duncan McNab.

ISBN 978 0 7336 3251 8 (paperback)

Political corruption – Australia.
Crime – Australia.
Criminals – Australia.
Waterfronts – Social aspects – Australia.
Harbors – Social aspects – Australia.

364.13230994

Cover design by Luke Causby
Cover photographs: *Top* FXT 269999, Fairfax Syndication. *Bottom* NSW Police Forensic Photography Archives, Justice and Police Museum, Sydney Living Museums
Text design by Bookhouse, Sydney
Typeset in 11.8/16 pt Simoncini Garamond Std by Bookhouse

CONTENTS

Prologue — v

1. Land ho! — 1
2. Rum and the lash — 7
3. The Campbells are coming! — 23
4. Bounty and mutiny — 30
5. Rebels and revenge — 39
6. The new broom — 52
7. The adventures of Batman — 60
8. Boom times — 68
9. Solidarity forever — 77
10. Strike! — 89
11. The contenders — 100
12. Enter the Push — 109
13. Plague! — 122
14. A nation united – sort of — 133
15. Australia goes to war – again — 141
16. Mr Hughes goes travelling — 151
17. A spot of pillage — 161
18. Snorts and rorts — 172
19. Slash — 182
20. It's all in the timing — 193
21. The Hungry Mile — 203
22. The bounty of war — 214
23. Accidental incentives — 225
24. Silk stockings — 233
25. Mr Big's big break — 241
26. Squirrel grip — 252
27. It's only a crime if you're caught — 259
28. The underbelly — 268
29. Oceans of cash — 277

30	Here comes the judge(s)	283
31	Demise of the dinosaurs	301
32	Skulduggery	306
33	Some things change, some remain the same	313
	Epilogue	321

A note on sources		325
Acknowledgements		330
Index		331

PROLOGUE

'Crime is rife,' thundered Justice Lukin of the Queensland Supreme Court, referring to the Brisbane wharves. Down in Sydney it was a similar story with the *Sydney Morning Herald* reporting the city was 'Coping with the evil' of waterfront crime. Royal Commissioner William Macfarlane presented his report to the Federal Government, delivering the dismal news that the nation's waterfront was stricken with 'pillaging carried out to a serious extent' and that having a criminal record for dishonesty was no bar to employment on the docks. Stronger penalties for waterfront crimes were called for, and screening of employees' criminal pasts was recommended. Today's news? No – this was the early 1920s.

Almost a century later and we're still reading similar headlines. In September 2009, the *Sydney Morning Herald* declared, 'Australia's docks are still fertile territory for crime networks'. It was an understatement. The ensuing publicity caused the government to react and announce a parliamentary inquiry. Nearly three years later, the *Sydney Morning Herald* brought its readers some results, and inadvertently channelled Justice Lukin, reporting 'Crime groups rife at ports – inquiry claims'. Three days later, *The Age* added to the story, reporting 'Secret files show the underworld's grip on the dock' and 'but much of the information about the corruption at the Port of Melbourne uncovered by State and Federal Police inquiries over the past decade has never been adequately investigated'.

Inevitably, promises to tighten up security and vetting of waterside and airport employees were made, crackdowns were ordered, emotively named task forces formed, and stern-faced police officers fronted media conferences to trumpet infrequent successes. Nothing much seems to have changed in spite of royal commissions, task forces, parliamentary inquiries, world wars and decades of firm assurances.

The high-rating television program *Border Security: Australia's Frontline* gives its audience some titillation as shifty-looking Australians and visitors begin to sweat as Customs officers inspect their baggage after a cute little beagle has signalled the possibility of drugs inside. Swabs are slipped into a machine, and moments later we know if the subject of the search is edgy because they're trafficking drugs, or just suffering from a decent-sized hangover. Schapelle Corby and her boogie board bag stuffed full of weed captivated the nation with a similar story – our fellow humans bringing piles of drugs across borders.

As an island with vast amounts of unpopulated coastline, most people seem to think that the creatively minded crook in a large yacht, motorboat, tramp steamer or the like can just sidle up to a remote inlet or small port, or for those with a plane, a piece of flat earth in the middle of nowhere, and merrily unload crates of drugs or weapons. It's happened, but for the professionals, there are much easier, less risky and more profitable ways.

The Australian Crime Commission's *Illicit Drug Report 2010/2011* reported that 'six sea cargo detections accounted for 69.3 per cent of the total weight of heroin detected at the Australian border that year'. Cocaine was similar, with six detections, mainly sea and aircraft cargoes, accounting for the bulk of the 701.8 kilograms found that year – a disturbingly low figure when members of Mexico's Sinaloa Cartel brag of flying in cargoes of 500 kilograms. Joining these two staples are 'amphetamine type stimulants' better known as 'ecstasy', 'crystal meth' and 'ice'. The import market is growing rapidly because of cheap production of the finished product in the 'meth labs' of Southeast Asia. Why risk blowing yourself up in a meth lab in the southeast Queensland hinterland when you can get a keenly priced and decent product in bulk?

All of these drug imports have a common thread – they arrive in quantity and slip easily through Customs on Australia's docks and airports. They're joined by other products that are part of the organised crime list – weapons, wildlife and cash – with the last two leaving Australia in the shipping containers and planes that brought their profitable products across the border. You'd have to wonder what would happen if the vigour applied to 'turning back the boats' of refugees was applied to dealing with crime at our gateways.

The sad truth is that since the First Fleet dropped anchor in Sydney Harbour, crime on the nation's waterfront, and more recently airports, hasn't been a priority for law enforcement and their political masters. Victoria Police in 2013 estimated that 90% of their 'top end gangsters' have ties to the waterfront. The problem bobs up occasionally, like something undesirable in a punchbowl, and is dealt with using well-tried political set piece moves like a task force or commission of inquiry, or harsher penalties – useless unless someone is caught! – and then the agenda moves on. As in many areas of public life, we deal with the symptoms not the disease. This neglect is a bonus for crooks – it gives them opportunity to organise, network and thrive.

Australia's major ports have been the birthplace of the nation, home to the tight-knit communities that were pivotal in the birth of the union movement and the Australian Labor Party, as well as to 'colourful identities' and empires of the criminal underworld. The waterfront is our greatest asset and our greatest vulnerability, but we've given it cavalier treatment.

1
LAND HO!

The British, when talking to or about Australians, can't help quip about the nation's convict past. But Britain kept the worst offenders at home – sentenced to long years in vile prisons or a quick trip to the scaffold. By comparison, those souls transported to Australia were often economic refugees – pushed into petty crime by the simple need to feed themselves and their families.

The idea of using Australia as penal colony wasn't a British idea – the French beat them to it. Charles de Brosses wrote in his 1756 *Histoire des Navigations aux Terres Australes* that Australia would be the perfect spot to dump French felons and the like.

The notion of Australia as a penal colony gathered impetus in Britain because of the American Revolutionary War from 1775 to 1783. Transportation to the former American colony was no longer possible, and with about 1000 prisoners per year usually transported, British prisons and the hulks on the Thames, which were used as makeshift gaols, were overflowing.

The laws of the time were harsh, and brought with them mandatory penalties – a concept that remains popular in spite of its lack of success. Around 150 crimes including murder, arson, rape, shoplifting goods worth over 5 shillings, pickpocketing over 1 shilling, etc, brought with them a mandatory death sentence.

Crimes like bigamy, manslaughter, stealing fish from a river (presumably owned by a member of the aristocracy or the like), were dealt with more leniently by transportation, whipping and imprisonment. Transportation was preferable to years spent in gaols full of diseases like smallpox, venereal diseases, and various plagues.

The prison reformer John Howard wrote in his 1777 book *The State of the Prisons in England and Wales* that 'the men are put at night into dungeons; one seven feet square for three prisoners; another, the Great Hole has only one little window. In this I saw six prisoners, most of them transports, chained to the floor. In that situation they had been for many weeks and were very sickly.'

The poor souls on the rotting hulks in the Thames were in equally miserable conditions. James Hardy Vaux, a one-time draper, law clerk, unsuccessful thief and later author of what was probably the first autobiography and dictionary written in Australia, spent time on the hulks before being transported to Sydney in 1801. Vaux also has the dubious distinction of being transported to Australia on three occasions – twice for theft and once for forgery. Vaux wasn't a competent criminal but he was busy. In 1811 his *Memoirs of the First Thirty-Two Years of The Life of James Hardy Vaux, A Swindler and Pickpocket; Now Transported for the Second Time, and For Life, to New South Wales* were published. In 1819, he wrote of his experience in the hulks that 'there were confined in this floating dungeon nearly six hundred men, most of them doubly ironed [chained]; and the reader may conceive the terrible effects arising from the continuing rattling of chains, the filth and vermin naturally produced by such a crowd of inhabitants, the oaths and execrations [cursing] constantly heard among them'.

In 1783, both Joseph Banks and diplomat James Mario Matra – shipmates on the *Endeavour* – spoke of the opportunity of using Australia as a penal colony and a place of commercial opportunity. Matra drafted *A Proposal for Establishing a Settlement in New*

South Wales, which was sent to Lord Sydney, then Secretary of State for the Home Department. Banks had been a fan earlier when he suggested to a House of Commons committee that Botany Bay would be a good location 'from whence . . . escape might be difficult, and where, from the fertility of the soil [colonists] might be enabled to maintain themselves, after the first year, with little or no aid from the mother country'. He also said there were 'no beasts of prey' and he didn't expect much resistance from the indigenous population.

The point that really got the committee's attention was Banks' observation that 'if the people formed among themselves a civil government, they would necessarily increase, and find occasion for many European commodities; and it was not to be doubted that a large tract of land such as New Holland, which was larger than the whole of Europe, would furnish matter of advantageous return'.

And then nothing much happened. In 1784, the British government were again pondering the prospect of 'a colony of disgracefuls at some very distant part of the earth'.

It took Edmund Burke, the Irish-born British politician and one of the ideological fathers of today's Conservative party, to strike the nerve that stimulated some action. He told the House of Commons in April 1785 that the gaols were 'crowded beyond measure' and quipped that the population of Newgate Prison was now 558 members – around the same number as the House. Burke said, 'public safety, no less than a humane regard to the individuals in question, called for interposition of Parliament'. The point was made and something had to be done, and Australia was looking like the most promising way of dealing with the overcrowding.

Politicians are seldom quick to act, unless it's in self-interest, so it was over a year after Burke's comments that Lord Sydney, in August 1786, asked the Admiralty to provide escorts for a fleet of convict-carrying ships bound for Botany Bay. On 12 May 1787, the 'First Fleet' under command of Captain Arthur Phillip and comprising nine merchant ships carrying convicts and two Royal

Navy ships, HMS *Sirius* and HMS *Supply*, gathered off the Isle of Wight, to begin their 24,000-kilometre voyage.

Phillip was described by Lucy Turnbull in *Sydney: Biography of a City* as a 'man of forty-nine with an uninspiring but honourable record as a naval officer'. The *Australian Dictionary of Biography* concurred, saying that he was 'a man of mature years whose attainments, though not particularly outstanding, were solid'. A safe pair of hands.

Of the convicts piled on board the First Fleet, historian Dr Frederick Watson estimated that around 83% were minor offenders and offered 'does not this not largely falsify the illiberal reproaches on the beginnings of a nation, unmerited odium given birth to in the eighteenth century and thriving still at the end of the nineteenth. Whatever vices the transportees sowed in the new colony must largely have been due, not to any inherent tendencies, but to the hardships endured, the seeming utter hopelessness of their future and consequent abandonment.'

By transporting the convicts to the other side of world and putting them in a place that offered better weather but a similar social environment, the British had only increased the chances of convicts resorting to repetitive behaviour.

William Ullathorne, a young Catholic priest who arrived in Sydney in February 1833, wrote in his 1837 pamphlet *The Horrors of Transportation* that 'the poverty and distress which have urged these men, I grant it, have been great, but the misery and degradation [of transportation] which they have now, in their ignorance, brought up on themselves is such to make their former lot, being compared, an earthly paradise'. He also wrote that 'with my own eyes I have seen how transportation sinks the soul of a man into, beyond all imagination, blacker and fouler perdition, than the first crimes which cause all his misery'.

Ullathorne thought that 'the transported convict becomes a slave', and observed, 'the Governor shall have a property in the services of the convict for the term of his transportation with the power of transferring such property to the inhabitants.' He noted slaves fared better, saying, 'the West Indian owner of negro slaves is as careful of his people as he is of his horses, because they cost a great deal of money, and fresh ones are not easily procured. But the owner of the convict slave has not the same cause for care. On receiving him he pays the sum of one pound for the clothes on his back, this is all. And when one is worked out, another may be easily had for the asking.'

One naval officer, Captain Bertram, wrote in 1806 that women convicts onboard the transport ships had their own particular slice of misery. 'The captain and each officer enjoy the right of selection. Thus they continue the habit of concubinage until the convicts arrive at Sydney town. Each sailor and soldier is allowed to attach himself to one of the females.' For the women who refused to acquiesce, Bertram said 'consent was won by scourging [whipping with a belt or similar], and the lash was applied without unnecessary ceremony.'

Transportation wasn't about rehabilitation. It was about alleviating the overcrowding in British prisons and taking the prisoners to the other side of the world, out of Britain and away from the public's view. The added bonus was it provided cheap labour to start a new colony.

On 19 January 1788, the fastest of the eleven ships of the First Fleet arrived in Botany Bay. Two days later, Phillip wasn't dazzled by Botany Bay, fearing 'the openness of this bay and dampness of the soil' would see his charges 'rendered unhealthy'. On 21 January, he set sail, heading north to have a look at Port Jackson – a bay mentioned by James Cook. Phillip was keen to find a suitable location as quickly as possible so the convicts could disembark for the first time in eight months. Just after lunch, he entered Port Jackson – 'the finest harbour in the world,' he thought. Captain David Collins of the Marines wrote in his *Account of the English Colony in New South Wales* published in 1798, that Port Jackson was 'this noble and capacious harbour, equal if not superior to any yet known in the world'. The official record noted 'here all regret rising from the former disappointment [at Botany Bay] was at once obliterated'.

Phillip and his colleagues beached their vessels at what is now Camp Cove where they camped for two nights and spent the days exploring. The preferred site was one 'which had the finest spring of [fresh] water, and in which ships can anchor so close to the shore that very small expense quays may be constructed where the largest vessels may unload. In honour of Lord Sydney, the Governor distinguished it by the name Sydney Cove.'

The site of Australia's first European settlement, and birthplace of the Australian waterfront, had been found.

2
RUM AND THE LASH

Captain Arthur Phillip returned to Botany Bay on 24 January 'having sufficiently explored Port Jackson and found it in all respects highly calculated to receive such a settlement as he was appointed to establish'. The next day, he was back in HMS *Supply*, anchoring in Sydney Cove. The long summer afternoon was spent clearing some of the dense timbered area for a camp site near the Tank Stream, the best supply of fresh water in the colony.

Sirius and the other ships arrived on 26 January 1788 and joined *Supply* in Sydney Cove. Freemen, seamen and convicts got their first glimpse of their new home on the other side of the world. The Union Jack was hoisted, not only for ceremony but perhaps to make a point to Jean François de Galaup, better known as the Comte de Laperouse, who had been tasked by Louis XVI to continue Cook's expeditions. Laperouse and his ships had arrived off Botany Bay on 24 January but bad weather prevented them entering. They made it in on the 26th, just as the remainder of the First Fleet, under the command of Captain John Hunter, were about to set sail for Port Jackson. Despite the frequent clashes and simmering rivalries of Europe, their meeting was amicable with Hunter and his men assisting Laperouse to anchor.

Around 1030 people sailed on the First Fleet, of which 778 (reports vary slightly) were convicts, including a boy who had been a chimney sweep and was just nine years old. The journey, via Tenerife, Rio de Janeiro and Cape Town was remarkably safe for the time, with only twenty-three convicts dying in the cramped conditions below decks.

By 27 January 1788, the convicts were on the ground and, though many were in poor health, they set to work, clearing camp sites, erecting tents and unloading supplies – Australia's first wharfies. Phillip ordered that both convicts and captors cast fishing nets into the harbour and share the catch.

Of the first days, David Collins – the colony's first deputy judge advocate, wrote,

> the confusion that ensued will not be wondered at when it is considered that every man stepped from a boat literally into a wood. Parties of people were everywhere heard and seen variously employed; some in clearing ground for the different encampments, others in pitching tents or bringing up such stores as were more immediately wanted; and the spot which had so recently been the abode of silence and tranquillity was now changed to that of noise, clamour and confusion; but after a time order gradually prevailed everywhere. As the woods were opened and the ground cleared, the various encampments were extended, and all wore the appearance of regularity.

One of the first tasks was to build Government House – a canvas structure pre-fabricated in England – on the eastern side of Sydney Cove, still the location favoured by Sydney's politicians, bureaucrats and the commercial elite. A camp site for the marines was placed in the middle of the cove near the Tank Stream, and convicts were sent to the western side, an area that would become the hub of Australia's early maritime infrastructure, and for many years home to Sydney's waterside workers and their families.

The conditions were miserable with violent storms, plenty of rain, and the first taste of Australian wildlife. Lieutenant Ralph Clark wrote that he'd never had worse sleep 'with the hard, cold ground, spiders, ants and every vermin that you can think of crawling over me'.

The need for the community to become self-sufficient was a priority, and while Phillip had planned on the colony being reliant on imports for the first four years, an outbreak of dysentery and scurvy within days of landing – both treatable with an improved diet including fresh fruit and vegetables – provided an impetus to get farming underway as quickly as possible. However, there was the small problem of skilled labour: there wasn't any. The convicts weren't selected for the journey for their skills. One of the few men with any farming knowledge was Arthur Phillip, who'd picked up some basics on his farm at Lyndhurst in Hampshire, but more by observation than getting his hands dirty.

Phillip also had a management problem. The marines believed their role was to keep the peace, not as overseers of convict work gangs, or to do any building or farming work themselves. The matter was further complicated because Phillip's commission didn't include the power to grant land to the marines, so their enthusiasm for farming was further dampened by lack of opportunity for profit.

The marines' attitude led to Australia's first workplace demarcation dispute, which was resolved by negotiation rather than confrontation. The convicts were divided into gangs under the supervision of a convict handpicked for the task, and put to work. The marines could continue with their peacekeeping duties.

Fortunately for the new arrivals, the local inhabitants were initially both intrigued and friendly. On 28 January, Hunter, along with Lieutenant William Bradley who was also a cartographer, and James Keltie, the Master of the *Sirius*, began to survey Sydney Harbour. The survey took two weeks. Bradley reported that 'on a point of land between Middle Head and Bradley Point' they'd met a group of natives who were 'quite sociable, good humours and pleased with us'. That wouldn't last.

On 7 February 1788, the day following the return of Hunter's survey party, the first government in Australia was formalised. Captain David Collins, the Judge Advocate General, read the commission appointing Phillip as 'Captain-General and Governor in Chief over the territory of New South Wales and its dependencies'. Phillip's power was absolute. The nineteenth-century British author Samuel Sidney wrote

> all the labour of the colony was at his disposal, all the land, all the stores, all the places of honor and profit, and virtually all the justice. His subjects consisted of his subordinate officers – for, as captain-general, the commandant of the troops was under his orders, of the few who resorted to New South Wales to trade, whose profits were at his disposal, and the convicts, outcasts without civil rights . . . there was no publicity and no public opinion to restrain the despotism, which was the only possible government in such a penal colony.

Lieutenant Clark observed that 'I never heard of any single person having so great a power invest'd in him as the Gov' has'. The convicts were mustered for the event and ordered to sit while the marines marched in a circle around them, playing drums and fifes, after which Phillip addressed them. It wasn't to welcome them to their new home. Daniel Southwell, a midshipman on HMS *Sirius*, recalled Phillip pointed out that some crimes would be treated more severely than in England. He said Phillip told the convicts, 'in England, thieving poultry was not punished with death, in consequence of them being so easily supplied, but here a fowl was of the utmost consequence to the settlement, as well as other species of stock, as they were reserved for breed, therefore stealing the most trifling article of stock or provisions she'd be punished with death'. Phillip finished his address, saying 'you have my sacred word of honor that whenever ye commit a fault you shall be punished, and met severely. Lenity [leniency] has been tried; to give it further trial would be [in] vain.'

It didn't take long for Phillip to make good his threat. One of the first construction tasks was the frame used to whip the convicts – Ullathorne described these constructions as 'the gory triangle'. It would have plenty of customers.

On 11 February, just four days after the Criminal Court had been established, three convicts appeared: one charged with assaulting a marine; one with stealing a biscuit; and one with stealing a plank of wood. The 'gory triangle' was put to use.

A little over two weeks later, on 27 February, convicts Thomas Barrett, Henry Lovell, Joseph Hall and John Ryan appeared before the court, charged with stealing bread, pork and peas from the government store. Ryan cut a deal, offering evidence against the other three in return for leniency. He was sentenced to 300 lashes, and the other three sentenced to death by hanging.

Barrett, though a young man, was described by Watkin Tench, a marine captain, as 'an old and desperate offender' and Phillip believed him to be the mastermind of the gang. Barrett had been sentenced to death in 1782 for stealing a watch, but the sentence was commuted and instead he'd been earmarked for transportation to America.

Shortly after embarking on the ship *Mercury,* bound for America, the convicts overpowered the crew, landed and escaped into the countryside near Devon, UK. Barrett was one of the ringleaders and when caught, was tried and sentenced to death, which was again commuted. He ended up on a hulk for three years before heading to Australia – where he wasn't third time lucky.

At 6.30 pm on 27 February 1788, on what is now the corner of Essex and Harrington Streets, Thomas Barrett became the first European executed in Australia. His body was left to dangle from the tree that had been used as the gallows for an hour. Phillip was determined to make a very clear point with the execution and had all the convicts present. As a precaution, a full battalion of marine guards was there to ensure the convicts remained firmly under control. The marines had one other task that night – finding a man to carry out the grisly task of executioner had been difficult and there were no volunteers. Barrett's partner in crime, John Ryan, was the executioner after the marines had to threaten to shoot him to get him to carry out his task. The other two offenders, Lovell and Hall, were granted a twenty-four hour reprieve, but had to watch. They returned to the gallows the next day, and were given another reprieve.

Two days later, Daniel Gordon and John Williams were convicted of stealing wine, and the following day, John Freeman and William Sheerman were convicted of stealing seven pounds of flour – the weekly ration for everyone in the colony. Phillip pardoned Williams, saying he was an 'ignorant black youth'. Sheerman received 300 lashes, and Gordon and Freeman the death penalty. Along with Lovell and Hall, now making their third visit, they were taken to the gum tree used as the gallows. As the four were prepared for execution, and the crowd readied themselves for the day's promised grisly spectacle, Major Ross – the lieutenant governor – arrived and announced that Phillip would grant a pardon but there were conditions. Hall and Lovell had to agree to transportation to another settlement and Freeman must become the colony's first official hangman – a position he accepted 'after some little pause'. The major then delivered Phillip's message that 'upon his word of honour that nothing in future would save a thief'. Lovell was sent to Norfolk Island and Hall and Gordon to the island in the harbour now known as Fort Denison.

Lieutenant Clark, who'd witnessed Barrett's execution and Phillip's attempts to make a point, observed, 'I think after his goodness they ought to behave well, but I am certain before I am a fortnight older, some of them will be brought to trial for capital offences'. Clark was wrong on the timing – the next execution was on 2 May – but right on the effect of Phillip's largesse. Confronted with opportunity, motive and the potential for profit, brutal punishments don't work – criminals believe they won't get caught.

Phillip's need to make a point extended to crimes that didn't incur the death penalty. Charles White, in his 1889 book *Convict Life in New South Wales and Van Diemen's Land*, wrote, 'one man who was caught by the solitary clergyman in the settlement stealing potatoes from a garden was sentenced to 300 lashes, to have his ration of flour stopped for six months, and to be chained for that period to two others who had been caught robbing the Governor's garden'. Phillip was even-handed in his approach to justice, and when six soldiers were arrested in January 1789 for conspiring to steal from the government stores, they were tried, found guilty and swiftly executed. For Phillip, justice had to be done, and be seen to have been done.

The colony grew rapidly and in July 1788, Phillip reported his plan for the new township back to his superiors in London. He said that cottages were being built for himself and his lieutenant governor, huts for the convicts had been built, an observatory was under construction and bricks were being made at Long Point, the current site of Darling Harbour and the Haymarket. The bricks were lugged down to what is now George Street by the convicts. The First Fleet had been short on things like spades and wheelbarrows, and animals to do the heavy dragging, so the convicts, gathered in groups of twelve, had to haul five loads of 350 bricks per day. Phillip also reported that 'principal streets are placed so as to admit a free circulation of air and are two hundred feet wide'. The first wharves were just rocky landing points on both sides of Sydney Cove, but in 1789 the Government Wharf was built on the eastern side, and followed by the Hospital Wharf in 1790. A storehouse made of local bricks was opened on the shore behind a landing point behind Hospital Wharf.

Phillip knew the essential development of the waterfront meant it would also bring a growth in crime, and the major issue was the stealing of precious stores in a colony precariously close to starvation. The problem was brought into focus when, in March 1789, the six marines were executed for stealing stores. The solution came from a convict – John Harris – who approached David Collins with his plan. In turn Collins took it to Phillip, proposing 'that a watch be established for the preservation of public and private property', and a guard began on Saturday 8 August 1789. In the early days marines, along with handpicked convicts, patrolled the shores of Sydney Cove on foot and by boat. They were known as the Night Watch and Row Boat Guard – and along with preventing pilfering they were tasked to prevent convicts stowing away on First Fleet ships returning to London. The watch was a success, with Phillip reporting to Lord Sydney in February 1790 that the 'institution of the Night Watch to control robberies (particularly of vegetables and poultry) was immediately effective' with 'no robbery in three months'.

The prospect of more fleets arriving, the beginnings of trade, and the grumbling of the marines who had to play 'policeman', signalled the need for a permanent police presence. In August 1789, Phillip formed the colony's first police force of twelve men – all convicts who had proven themselves trustworthy and sober.

One of the copper's early tasks was to deal with Australia's first celebrity criminal, John Black Caesar, better known as just 'Black Caesar'. He was of African parents, rumoured to be an escaped slave from America, and transported on the First Fleet after being convicted of burglary. In April 1789 in Sydney he was convicted of theft and had his sentence extended to transportation for life, but he didn't get the message. A few weeks after his conviction, he stole a musket and a cooking pot and fled into the bush. He was captured on 6 June 1789 and David Collins wrote that Caesar was 'Incorrigibly stubborn . . . his frame was muscular and well calculated for hard labour; but in his intellects he did not very widely differ from a brute'. Instead of hanging – which Collins believed 'would not have the proper or intended effect' – Caesar was placed in chains. In December 1789, while working at Garden Island, he again stole weapons, and this time, a canoe. The nation's first major manhunt followed, but Caesar was more of a city boy than explorer and returned to the colony on 31 January 1790 after nearly starving to death and being speared after unsuccessfully trying to standover some Aboriginals and steal their food. Watkin Tench had a compassionate view and wrote of this escapade that Caesar approached the Aboriginals 'with a wish to adopt their customs and live with them: but he was always repulsed'.

Phillip decided to remove the thorn in his side and in March 1790 sent Caesar to Norfolk Island where he met Anne Power and the couple had a daughter in 1792. He got the message at last, and was given an acre of land to farm, and had his convict work reduced to three days a week. Family life suited Caesar, but only briefly – a year later he left them and headed back to the colony, where he once again ran off and again was captured shortly after. According to Collins, he was severely punished but cried out defiantly, 'all that would not make him better!'

It wasn't an idle boast and in December 1795 he escaped again, this time joining up with a group of other escapees and becoming the leader of Australia's first criminal gang, and the 'usual suspect' for numerous crimes – Collins wrote 'every theft that was committed was ascribed to him'. The gang was armed with muskets stolen from the arsenal – a theft only realised after the commissary had done an audit. The governor at the time, John Hunter, troubled that Caesar was becoming a celebrity, offered a reward of five gallons of spirits – thus stimulating the currency in rum – for his capture, and two weeks later, on 15 February 1796, Caesar was shot to death at Liberty Plains (now Strathfield in Sydney's inner west) by John Wimbow, another armed convict wandering the bush. Wimbow later claimed the shooting was in self-defence, but it was more likely a chance to claim the reward without the risk of capturing the man.

The convicts on the Second Fleet, which arrived in Sydney during June 1790, didn't fare as well as those on the First. Of the 1017 who'd embarked in Britain, 278 died on the voyage from starvation and disease, and around 500 arrived seriously ill, some close to death. Blame was laid at the feet of the private contractors who'd provided the provisions and ships, and skimped on basics like food. The *Sydney Cove Chronicle* of 30 June 1790 reported:

DIABOLICAL CONDITION OF THE CONVICTS THEREON
278 died on the fearsome journey to Sydney Cove

The landing of those who remained alive despite their misuse upon the recent voyage, could not fail to horrify those who watched. As they came on shore, these wretched people were hardly able to move hand or foot. Such as could not carry themselves upon their legs, crawled upon all fours. Those, who, through their afflictions, were not able to move, were thrown over the side of the ships; as sacks of flour would be thrown into the small boats. Some expired in the boats; others as they reached the shore. Some fainted and were carried by those who fared better.

Herbert Evatt, in his 1938 book *Rum Rebellion,* observed the worst was yet to come, and wrote 'many of the convicts who escaped with their lives from the horrors of the voyage out became brutalized and irreclaimable'. Welcome to Australia.

In spite of the hardship of the journey and the less than warm greeting on their arrival, the convicts on each subsequent fleet found themselves in a colony growing steadily and one in need of their skills and ability to drive that growth. John Macarthur, a lieutenant in the newly formed New South Wales Corps, arrived on the Second Fleet and was soon to play a major role in the Rum Rebellion and later the sheep industry. Along with Macarthur was another free settler D'Arcy Wentworth, a medical student who'd been charged with highway robbery. After being found 'not guilty' of the charges, Wentworth decided the voyage would be an opportunity to make his fortune and also avoid any further run-ins with law who had obviously 'marked his cards'. Wentworth worked his way as an assistant surgeon. The pair's timing was perfect, as they arrived when the government was handing out tracts of land to promote free settlers. Wentworth's son William Charles went on to explore the Blue Mountains, and began a dynasty that included journalists and politicians. Macarthur was the father of Australia's greatest early export – wool.

After the appalling death toll on the Second Fleet, improvements were made and when the Third Fleet arrived between July and October 1791 it carried over 1800 convicts, of which 182 perished during the voyage – still a staggering number when compared to the First Fleet. The subsequent fleets were dispatched twice each year, carrying sufficient stores for both the passage and the colony. The British Government also arranged for supplies of grain to be sent from India and livestock from America. Along with the scheduled arrivals, merchants had realised a new and captive market had emerged; so well-stocked ships were sent to Sydney to see what deals could be done.

The first merchant ship to arrive was the US ship, *Philadelphia,* on 1 November 1792. Popular among the cargo was a white spirit from India, called 'rum' in the colony. While it wasn't 'rum' in the usual sense, it had a similar impact and a strong market. The colony loved it.

When Phillip left for England in December 1792, there were around 1200 people living in Sydney, and 1600 at the newer settlement in Parramatta – decentralisation at work. Around two-thirds of the total population were convicts.

Phillip wasn't immediately replaced and instead his Lieutenant Governor, Major Francis Grose, was appointed as acting governor. Grose was a soldier who'd been appointed as lieutenant governor in 1789, and Commandant of the New South Wales Corps, later known, with just a hint of derision, as the 'Rum Corps'. Grose had been instrumental in raising the corps, and the success of that venture saw him back in full employment.

The corps was a nice little earner for Grose. Owing to the relative peace in Europe he'd been on half pay for the preceding six years, and when he heard the British government were keen to bring the marines home from the colony, Grose saw an opportunity and stepped forward with a plan. He'd spent two years working in recruiting, knew all the wrinkles and had a fine contact book – he knew where to find men and how much he'd have to pay to appeal to his potential foot soldiers. He gave the government an undertaking to raise a force of 300 men, and in return, the government gave him the right to sell the position of officer in the corps for any price he cared to set. The government also offered to pay him three guineas for each enlisted man, and Grose was permitted to keep the difference between that sum and what he paid them for signing on. The first company of the corps sailed for Sydney with the Second Fleet.

Grose remained in Britain and successfully lobbied for a second tranche – 200 men and one additional major who paid £200 (nearly A$18,000 currently) for his commission. One contemporary critic of the scheme described the corps as 'blacklegs or blackguards' [scoundrels]. Grose arrived in Sydney in February 1792. To build his corps, the marines in the colony who'd been offered a discharge and land grants to encourage them to remain were offered an incentive of £3 (around A$260 today) and a further land grant to enlist in the corps. It was an offer many found too good to refuse, and Grose's corps quickly grew to 886 officers and men. One marine officer tempted by the deal was George Johnston who became a captain and would later be a pivotal player in the 'Rum Rebellion'.

Irish rebel leader Joseph Holt, who'd fought the British in County Wicklow and was transported in 1799, said the corps were men 'who have been considered disgraceful to every other regiment in His Majesty's service' and were 'thought of as fit and proper recruits for the New South Wales Corps'. Dr John Lang, the clergyman, educator and politician, agreed with Holt and wrote in his *History of New South Wales,* published in 1834, that he'd seen the corps in action and they were men 'banded together on every suitable occasion to maintain by violence and injustice what they had obtained by the sacrifice of honour'.

Grose, in spite of the dim views of his corps, was an easy-going man, with a ready smile and plenty of charm – the forerunner of some of today's smooth-talking, well-connected lobbyists perhaps – and arrived in Sydney with a keen eye for opportunities, and a desire to reduce his workload and line his pockets. When Phillip departed and Grose became acting governor, he rearranged the colonial administration to suit his plans. He replaced the civilian magistrates with military officers, delegated responsibilities and appointed John Macarthur as Inspector of Public Works – giving him control of the colony's resources and infrastructure development. Grose also increased the weekly food ration for the military. For the first time since 1788, they had more than the convicts. He won further hearts and minds by increasing the number of land grants and making them easier to get – a move that stimulated the westward growth of Sydney, and encouraged those in Britain contemplating life on the other side of the world as a free settler. Macarthur was one beneficiary, receiving grants of prime farmland near Parramatta that became Elizabeth Farm.

Grose stimulated his own fortunes as well, joining his officers in chartering ships filled with a variety of cargo they knew they could sell in the colony. One of their first ventures was in 1792 when Macarthur led a consortium that chartered the *Britannia* for £2000 (around A$350,000 today) to sail to the Dutch-controlled Cape of Good Hope with £2200 in cash to buy goods and livestock for the colony. The deal upset Sir Francis Baring, Chairman of the East India Company, which believed it had the monopoly on trade with the colony. Baring, on hearing of Macarthur's venture, commented he was 'the serpent we are nursing at Botany Bay'.

The first whiff of corruption was in the air, and Grose added to it by turning a blind eye to his officers' other commercial activities. On his watch, they were allowed to buy entire cargoes and charter ships, with alcohol a favourite product, and set the price in the market. The officers of the corps used funds pooled from their fellow members, and on arrival it was distributed according to the size of each member's investment. Prices for onward sales to merchants and farmers were also at rates fixed by the cartel. Rum reportedly attracted a mark-up thirty times its original price, and tobacco – another popular import – was reportedly sold for fifteen times its landed cost. Adding to the problem was Macarthur's appointment as paymaster, which meant that imports were controlled by the corps along with the supply of money and labour.

The result was that, in the 1790s, Sydney was run by a small clique of military men who kept trouble to a minimum and had a commercial and judicial system that worked to their advantage. Setting an example to the convicts wasn't on the agenda. Convict labourers on the waterfront could see opportunity coming their way as well and seized it when they thought no one was looking. Cases of rum – twenty-two gallons of the liquor were stolen from a waterfront warehouse on Christmas Eve 1791, thus ensuring a jolly time for the thieves and their clients – food, dry goods and anything else readily portable and saleable was stolen; either for personal use or to sell to merchants disgruntled by the military's price fixing, or to members of their tight-knit waterfront community where luxuries were scarce and out of the reach of most. It was done in the taverns, secluded laneways and dingy dwellings of The Rocks, and was the birth of a market in stolen and contraband goods that would thrive over the ensuing centuries.

Lucy Turnbull writing in *Sydney: Biography of a City* said that 'it was during his [Grose's] term in office that the moral and administrative rot in the colony really set in'. Grose left Sydney in December 1794, returning to Britain and his military career.

Governor John Hunter arrived in 1795 but had little impact on the stranglehold the officers of the corps and their cronies had on the commercial life of the colony. Hunter had a low opinion of the new colony and was not committed to the task of being its governor. Herbert Evatt noted it would have been easier for him to have founded an entirely new settlement 'than to have attempted the recovery of one so shamefully plunged in Profligacy and Licentiousness . . . a mere sink of every species of infamy'.

One area Hunter did succeed in was the next major step in Sydney's development as a port. One of his early worries was the lack of a competent boat building and repair facility to maintain the smaller craft needed to keep open supply and communication lines with the settlements that were developing in places like the Hawkesbury River. Boats were the lifeline for the settlers. Shortly after his arrival, Hunter reported to London that,

> The Boats of the Settlement by which our principal Communication between this Place and other Districts is to be kept up, having also fallen to Ruin & Decay, it becomes a very essential Concern, to have them rebuilt, or repaired, as without them we cannot convey the necessary Supplies of provisions or other Stores from one Place to the other; no Time must therefore be lost in putting them in such a State, as to render them safe & useful.

The colony's first official boat builder, Daniel Paine, had arrived with Hunter and his first task was to source timbers appropriate for boat building, but he didn't last long. His friendship with Scottish Martyrs who had been transported in 1794, and their support for the very French notion of 'liberty, equality and fraternity' that was a cornerstone of the Revolution currently in that country, would prove to be his downfall. The Martyrs were Australia's first political prisoners, but were treated far better than the convicts and not put to hard labour.

Paine lasted only eleven months and was replaced by Thomas Moore. Moore was no stranger to the colony, having first passed by as the ship's carpenter on *Britannia*, and after four years at sea in the Pacific and Indian Oceans, he returned as free settler and took up the position of master boat builder.

The dockyard was situated on the western side of the cove, opposite the hospital and gaol, well away from the Tank Stream. The rocky foreshore and small sandy beaches were ideal. Building began in 1798, first with sheds for the boats, sheds for the sawyers, a 'steamer' to season the planks and a fence around the site. By 1800, a 'commodious stone house' – a two-storey home with a mansard roof on a high rocky point just to the north of the dockyard – had been added as Moore's home.

The dockyard brought a commercial focus to the western side of Sydney Cove, and the beginnings of a community of convicts and ex-convicts to work as stevedores, labourers, and warehousemen. Ocean-going ships, along with smaller craft, were built in the dockyard and in the smaller yards established later in Woolloomooloo and on the Hawkesbury River. By 1804, fifteen of the twenty-one 'schooners and sloops belonging to individuals in his Majesty's territory of New South Wales' had been locally built. Schooners were the trade link between Sydney and Botany Bay, and the Georges River as far as Bankstown and Liverpool, with smaller craft working the trade between Sydney and Parramatta.

It also brought opportunity for entrepreneurs and one man was soon to arrive who would shake the whole place up.

3
THE CAMPBELLS ARE COMING!

Robert Campbell turned Sydney's fledgling commercial scene on its head. He was born in Greenock, Scotland, in 1769, one of ten children, and after an unspectacular business career in his homeland, headed to Calcutta to join Campbell Clarke & Co, a trading company set up by his older brother John in 1790. Their main business was importing wine and spirits. In 1797, the Campbell Clarke company was expanding into the export business and sent its first cargo of spirits and general merchandise to Australia on the *Sydney Cove*, which went aground on 8 February near Preservation Island in Bass Strait. Sixteen of its crew set off in a longboat to get help in distant Sydney. Unpredictable and appalling weather took its toll on the men in the longboat and only three made it to Sydney three months later. It took two trips to rescue those who'd remained with their ship and the cargo that could be salvaged.

Robert Campbell left India, bound for Sydney, in April 1798 on board the company's ship *Hunter*. When he arrived in Sydney, he found that, in spite of the military cartel running the colony's commercial scene, there was plenty of opportunity for a man with cash, ideas and the ability to deliver the goods that were keenly sought.

Campbell arrived around the time of the discovery of what was to become a major export industry: coal. Lieutenant John Shortland, sent north to track escaped convicts, sailed into 'a very fine river', and exploration revealed significant coal deposits around the area where Newcastle is now situated. Collins described the find: 'in this harbour was found a very considerable quantity of coal of a very good sort, and lying so near the water side as to be conveniently shipped; which gave it, in this particular, a manifest advantage over that discovered to the southward'.

Within a few years King's Town – named after Governor King who oversaw the colony after Governor Hunter – was settled by convicts and freemen, to work the coal deposits and to fell timber that was more suitable for boat building than the timber around Sydney Cove.

Before heading back to India in August 1798, Campbell bought a sweeping parcel of harbourfront land at Dawes Point near the western tip of Sydney Cove, and on his return in February 1800 commissioned the building of a warehouse and private wharf. On the ridge behind the warehouses, the former convict John Leighton, known later as 'Jack the Miller', built three windmills to grind corn – a task that led to the name 'Millers Point', home for generations of dock workers.

Campbell had come to stay this time, and his arrival marked the beginning of Australia's maritime trade. Campbell made another wise decision in 1801 when he married Sophia Palmer – the sister of the NSW Commissary John Palmer who'd arrived on the First Fleet and was one of the early success stories. It was a marriage made in commercial heaven for the young entrepreneur.

The commissary was responsible for buying all the colony's supplies and thus a handy man to know for an aspiring merchant. Palmer was also one of the magistrates appointed by Grose, and one of the largest landholders and most successful men in the land. He built a grand residence on a grant and called it Woolloomooloo – most likely the anglicised version of an Aboriginal word. For Campbell, his connection to Palmer meant government contracts came his way, and he had an insight into the businesses of others dealing with Palmer – blood, albeit acquired by marriage, was thicker than water.

Within four years, Campbell's warehouses were complete and had an estimated £50,000 worth of goods from India stacked inside (around A$90 million these days). He'd also become a major supplier of livestock from India – selling into both the Sydney and Van Diemen's Land markets. Van Diemen's Land – better known as Tasmania after 1 January 1856 when it gained self-government and stopped being part of the colony of New South Wales – had only been settled in 1803 and primarily as a penal colony. The livestock was essential to feed the prisoners, soldiers and smattering of free settlers who'd arrived in the new outpost, and to kick-start the growth of their own livestock industry.

Sydney's free settlers were also Campbell fans, primarily because he was fair in his dealings and provided an alternative to Macarthur and his cronies. In 1804, 200 settlers wrote to Campbell to express their support and gratitude, saying, 'but for you, we had still been a prey to the Mercenary unsparing Hand of Avarice and Extortion'.

However, Campbell had two main problems – the first was the need to deal with the military cartel led by Macarthur that controlled the Sydney market. Macarthur in particular had been growing in power and affluence. In 1803 he'd been in England showing samples of merino and crossbred wool from the original stock sent from the Cape of Good Hope in 1796. He appeared before the Privy Council, advocating the potential of a wool industry in Australia and it was timely as the Napoleonic Wars had dramatically reduced wool supplies from Spain – Britain's traditional supplier. Lord Camden, who became Secretary of State for War and Colonies in 1804, had been sufficiently impressed to order a grant of 10,000 acres to Macarthur in what is now Camden. Macarthur bought a ship, *Argo*, and returned to Australia in 1805, along with two ewes and three rams from the stud of King George III. The wool industry that would drive Australia's exports, and the expansion of Sydney's and later Victoria's docklands, was about to get serious.

Campbell's second problem was the need for a local product to fill the ships for their return to India and Britain. Australia had yet to become a primary producer, the wool industry was in its infancy, but Campbell knew of one product that Europe wanted and he and his colleagues like Palmer could supply: seals. Their oil was considered superior to whale oil to lubricate the new machinery of Europe's industrial revolution and their skins were used for clothing and furnishings. China was also a potential market, at that time buying from the United States.

The sealing industry had begun under Phillip in 1791 when two ships from the Third Fleet, the *Mary Ann* and *Matilda*, unloaded their convicts and headed south in search of whales or seals. Whaling was already established as a profitable venture in Van Diemen's Land after it was discovered the Derwent River was a breeding ground for the southern right whale and Bass and Flinders found seal rookeries on their explorations of southern Australia.

The seal trade boomed in the early 1800s, and there were hazards other than the unpredictable weather and seas. Escaped convicts and sealers, dubbed 'Sea Rats' by the *Sydney Gazette*, found that attacking ships and sealers' camps was easier than doing the capturing and processing seals themselves. And then there were the Americans. Sealers from the United States, on hearing rumours of bountiful pickings in the southern oceans, headed south and weren't keen on sharing with the locals. In December 1803, Captain Moody on the Sydney-based schooner *Governor King* encountered the *Charles* from Boston. In a clash over who had the rights to hunt seals in the Kent Group of islands in Bass Strait, the Americans, who outnumbered Moody and his men, asserted that might does make right. George Howe, writing in the *Sydney Gazette,* said, 'the greatest violence was offered to the schooner's people, some of whom were treated with unexampled inhumanity'. Moody made it back to Sydney with thirty-seven tons of seal oil and around 700 seal skins. The oil was worth between £35 to £42 per ton in London, and the skins sold for between 6 to 14 shillings – around A$250,000 in today's market.

In 1804, amid concerns the Americans were dominating the seal trade in local waters, building seal boats in the islands off Van Diemen's Land, and fears that their aggressive tactics could also wipe out the seal population, Governor Philip Gidley King stepped in. He issued a proclamation preventing Americans from settling in the sealing areas; Sydney was not to be used as a port for them to operate from; and their ships, should they call, were only cleared to return to their original destination – and not to head off seal hunting.

Around this time, Robert Campbell and his colleagues – Henry Kable, James Underwood and Simeon Lord – had around 180 employees working in the seal trade in the Bass Strait islands. Kable had arrived as a convict on the First Fleet and later became a merchant, shipowner, publican and constable; Underwood and Lord arrived as convicts on the Third Fleet, with Underwood becoming a prominent shipbuilder and merchant, and Lord a publican, merchant and magistrate.

The most significant problem facing Campbell and his colleagues in sending their seal skins and oil to the UK was the East India Company's trading monopoly on non–British government import/exports. Campbell decided the only approach was a frontal assault. His first move was to ask Governor King for permission to export, which was declined. The second step was more assertive and showed that Campbell had a nose for politics as well as business. When his ship *Lady Barlow* was ready to leave for London, carrying 264 tons of oil, 13,730 skins and 3673 feet of solid oak and beet wood, he wrote to King, saying, 'I duly understand that no responsibility for sending the ship there can be attached to your Excellency'. It was a gutsy move and a landmark moment for the young colony.

The venture hit its first hurdle when London's port authorities, acting under pressure from the East India Company, impounded *Lady Barlow* with Campbell onboard. Governor King, exercising his own political talents, later wrote to the Secretary for War and the Colonies, saying 'the proprietor and the whole colony had flattered themselves that this first proof of their industry would afford pleasure to their native country and be favourably received. That it did not is to be regretted'.

It took four months of negotiation, and finally the intervention of Sir Joseph Banks, to have the ship and her cargo released – but in return, the cargo was sold to the East India Company for re-export, and *Lady Barlow* sailed for India with a cargo of goods from the East India Company. It was a compromise, rather than victory for either side. Campbell stayed in London, lobbying the Board of Trade for a better deal, and by the end of 1806, he was close. The board suggested 'a plan suited to provide the inhabitants [of the Colony] with the means of becoming by degrees less and less burdensome on the Mother Country'.

While the hiatus in London had brought Campbell perilously close to financial disaster – he lost £7000 in the deal – he recovered and enthusiastically contributed to easing Britain's burden. Profitable contracts from the government to supply livestock from India to the colony resulted in him importing around 2000 cows between 1804 and 1810 – a sizeable number considering there was only a shade over 3000 cows in the colony at the time he began. Locals dubbed him 'King of the Wharf'.

Campbell's success marked one of the first steps in the decline of what historian Dan Snow has described as the East India

Company's 'Age of speculation and profit'. Baring's serpent had struck, and by 1813 the East India Company's monopoly had been cancelled by parliament, and in 1815 Sydney was declared a free port.

Dealing with the military cartel proved trickier. Campbell said, 'in 1798, the officers fixed the price of all articles of merchandise which I had then for sale. In 1800 and from that time till my departure in 1810, the governor fixed the price of spirits and wine; the other articles we were allowed to dispose of to the best advantage.' The profiteering meant mark-ups of 'spirits sometimes at 500 per cent, at least; on other articles generally about from 50 to 75 per cent'.

One commentator of the period, known only by his surname Bennett, said of King's stewardship of the colony that, 'the six years of Governor King's rule, notwithstanding the occurrence of serious civil disturbances and the prevalence of drinking habits to a degree probably never before witnessed in any community, were marked by a steady advancement in the development of the material resources of the colony. The sealing trade and whale fishery were carried on with energy and profit, the foundation of what proved a lucrative intercourse with New Zealand and the South Sea Islands was opened up, new settlements were formed.'

Enter Governor William Bligh.

4
BOUNTY AND MUTINY

The story of William Bligh's misadventures on HMS *Bounty* in 1789 – a compelling yarn of struggle, villainy and adventure – has been popular in films since the silent movie era. The first outing was a 1916 film *The Mutiny of the Bounty* by Raymond Longford and Lottie Lyell. Charles Chauvel made *In the Wake of the Bounty* in 1933, which was the debut appearance of Errol Flynn, then twenty-four years old, as the mutinous Fletcher Christian, and the English-born actor Mayne Lynton, then pushing fifty, as the crusty Lieutenant Bligh. The reality was that at the time of the mutiny Bligh was only thirty-four and Christian twenty-four, but from Chauvel's film onward, Bligh would always be portrayed as a much older man.

Hollywood arrived on the scene two years later. In the 1935 *Mutiny on the Bounty* he was played by Charles Laughton, who once quipped, 'I have a face like the behind of an elephant's'. His Bligh was described by Andre Sennwald writing in the *New York Times* on 9 November 1935, as 'a fascinating and almost unbearable portrait of a sadist who took rapturous delight in watching men in pain' and 'his penalties for minor offenses are the judgments of a maniac. From the swish of the lash he derives a lewd joy. Bligh's reign of terror on the *Bounty* is described with such relish that in time you discover yourself wincing under the lash and biting your mouth to keep from crying out.' Clark Gable, then a rising star in Hollywood, played Fletcher Christian. Bligh's image had been firmly cast by Hollywood. Herbert Evatt, writing in his 1938 book *Rum Rebellion*, said Bligh had suffered 'condemnation from Hollywood, the sentences of which have universal jurisdiction'.

In 1962 Trevor Howard, with stiff upper lip firmly in place, was Bligh. Marlon Brando, heart-throb of the time, mumbled his way through his role of Fletcher Christian. Dino De Laurentiis had a go at the story in his 1984 production, *The Bounty*, starring Anthony Hopkins as Bligh and Mel Gibson as Christian. The *New York Times* had a dim view of the new film, with critic Vincent Canby commenting that in the earlier Hollywood outings, Bligh was portrayed as either 'a sadist or a fool', and the new film 'attempts to rehabilitate Bligh's reputation'. It didn't.

Bligh walked into a hornet's nest when he arrived in Sydney on 6 August 1806 onboard the merchant ship *Lady Madeleine Sinclair*, and he was about to encounter experiences for which his career at sea hadn't prepared him. The wise heads of Westminster believed that appointing a man with Bligh's authoritarian reputation and low tolerance for fools would sort out the colony's problems they'd heard of from King and Hunter. What they didn't know was history was about to repeat.

Bligh's arrival coincided with a report written by the Reverend Samuel Marsden, who'd arrived in 1800 and was the principal chaplain to the colony. He was known as 'the Flogging Parson' because of his vigorous interest in stern punishments. Marsden wrote,

> The depravity and vice which pervades a large portion of the community does, by its preponderating influence, effect the whole, and gives to the individual habits and manners much to be deplored. Any attentive, humane observer, who might

visit the colony, would soon be convinced of the truth of these remarks; and when he beheld a rising generation of several hundred of fine children exposed to a contamination fatal to body and soul, he would tremble for their danger.

The *Sydney Gazette* reported that, as Bligh's ship entered Sydney Cove, it was 'roses, roses all the way' from the officers and citizens who met him. His embarrassing departure from HMS *Bounty* in the mid-Pacific hadn't been an impediment to a fine naval career, but there was plenty of turbulence ahead.

Bligh officially took the office of governor on 14 August, the day on which Philip Gidley King retired to his home at Parramatta. In the days before, Bligh and King had been busy at Government House, with King making land grants to the new arrival, one of which was 240 acres for him to build the house he later called 'Camperdown' and now the site of the suburb of the same name. He was also given a grant of 105 acres near Parramatta, and 1000 acres 'for a private residence between Sydney and the Hawkesbury' near Rouse Hill, which Bligh named 'Copenhagen'. On 17 January 1806, Bligh returned the favour, granting King's wife Anna Josepha 790 acres near Rooty Hill, which she called 'Thanks'.

What Bligh soon found was while King had given him a summary of the colony's position, he hadn't quite outlined the problems he was having with Macarthur and his colleagues and their almost monopoly of the waterfront and import and export trade. On the day Bligh took over, George Johnston, representing the military, John Macarthur for the free settlers, and Richard Atkins 'for the civil' sent a letter of congratulations. Atkins was a former army officer who'd arrived in 1792 and been appointed by Phillip as a magistrate and later as Registrar of the Vice-Admiralty Court. Atkins was well-known for being a drunk and a man who didn't pay his debts. The *Australian Dictionary of Biography* noted his social position 'enabled him to enhance the aura of influential prestige behind which he sheltered from existing creditors while engaging fresh credit locally on the security of his family name'. In spite of or perhaps, considering his cronies, because of his reputation, he prospered, becoming the Judge Advocate, the colony's senior judicial officer.

Five weeks after the men's greeting, Bligh got a second greeting, from other 'free' settlers who pointed out that Macarthur was the last person they'd authorise to speak on their behalf. These people, many from the new settlements near the Hawkesbury River, had been at the mercy of the military cartel. Fresh produce was still highly sought after, and so it was common for the cartel's agents to try to buy entire crops, using rum as payment instead of cash. The rum was arriving in boatloads through Sydney Cove, both as properly imported cargo, and clandestinely. It slipped through easily because officers and civil servants controlling the unloading and movement of freight were in on the deal. Local stills had also been set up, and the sale and distribution of the spirit, whether homegrown or imported, was controlled by the cartel.

The cartel's agents offered generous amounts of rum, often worth more than the crop, to the farmers for the crop that was still in the ground. Then came the truly insidious part. If the crop failed, was reduced or didn't meet the market value of the amount of rum advance, the cartel would move in and force the farmers off their land. Having mates in the judiciary helped speed the process.

Charles White wrote in his 1889 book *Convict Life in New South Wales and Van Diemen's Land*, 'spirits were, in fact, the currency of the colony. Almost all extra work was paid for in spirits, and the diligence of prisoners even, in unloading a vessel laden with Government stores, was stimulated by giving half a pint of rum to each. Among free and bond, drunkenness was a prevailing vice – a natural result of the system introduced under this military-*cum*-trading crowd, of officially making rum the currency.' One unnamed commentator pithily observed the cartel was 'sucking the life blood of the community, rendering it almost impossible for the few honest and laborious settlers to make a living'. Former convict and Scottish Martyr, Maurice Margarot, said, 'it consists, first of all, of monopoly, then of extortion; it includes all the necessaries of life which are brought to the colony'.

Bligh, after assessing his new command, decided the settlers from Hawkesbury were the future of the colony, not the cartel. Writing to Joseph Banks in October 1807, he made his purpose clear, saying, 'I am not here for my ease or comfort, but to do justice and relieve the oppressed poor settlers who must be the support of this country and are honester men than those who wish to keep them under'.

The Reverend Samuel Marsden concurred with Bligh. He later wrote, 'when Governor Bligh took the command many serious evils existed, and which had been gradually maturing for the whole of the thirteen years I lived in the Settlement. The greatest of these was the Barter of Spirits; all others were only Branches that sprung from . . .'

Bligh issued a General Order on 7 February 1807, declaring:

> His Excellency the Governor regrets to find, by his late visit through the colony, that the most calamitous evils have been produced by persons bartering or paying spirits for grain of all kinds, and the necessaries of life in general, and to labourers for their hire; such proceedings depressing the industrious, and depriving the settlers of their comforts. In order, therefore, to remedy these grievous complaints, and to relieve the inhabitants who have suffered by this traffic, he feels it his duty to put a total stop to this barter in future.

He also discovered the settlers weren't the only ones being rorted – soldiers were being paid in goods, including rum, rather than cash. Joseph Holt, still a convict at the time of Bligh's arrival, wrote that Captain Anthony Fenn Kemp, when approached by a soldier keen to get his month's salary was greeted by Kemp who said,

> 'Well, what do you want?' to which the soldier replied, 'I want to be paid sir.' Instead of cash, Kemp offered, 'I have very good tobacco, ten shillings the pound, and good tea at twenty shillings the pound, prints [fabric] at eight shillings a yard' and so on. If the poor soldier answered, 'Sir, I do not want any of your goods,' the Captain's comment was, 'You don't! You are a damned saucy rascal.' Perhaps then the soldier would say, 'Sir, if you please, give me half money and half goods.' But this proposal was equally out, 'Be gone, you damned mutinous scoundrel or I'll send you to the guardhouse, and have you flogged for your impertinence!'

The practice drove the soldier to sell the goods just to make some cash. Given the high prices forced on him by his superiors, the transactions were often at a loss. Holt also noted he'd seen some of the officers, 'draw goods from the public store to traffic them in their own private gain, which goods were sent out [to the colony] for the advantage of the settlers, who were compelled to deal with those huxter officers for such articles as they may require, giving them from fifty to five hundred percent profit, and paying in grain'.

One of Bligh's first actions was to pay the soldiers in cash, followed by moving to squash the cartel. Spurred on by the free settlers, he also looked for advice beyond the military, and formed a working relationship with Robert Campbell. Bligh respected Campbell's ability and integrity, and agreed with the settlers' views that Campbell had given 'the greatest services to the inhabitants . . . that the price of his merchandise was the same in time of scarcity as in abundance, that he had advanced a great sum of money, and protected the poor and distressed settler; and that in fact he was the only private pillar which supported the honest people of the Colony'. He gave him control of the colonial treasury and commissioned him as a naval officer. Campbell's public office didn't mean he had to give up his private enterprises, and in 1807, on the site of what is now the Royal Sydney Yacht Squadron at Kirribilli, he built the first commercial dockyard.

Bligh ordered Campbell, in his role as a naval officer, to seize the liquor stills he believed had been imported and run by Macarthur. It was one of those relatively minor actions that were a catalyst for something far more dramatic. C. Hartley Grattan, the US academic and Australian history expert, wrote in his foreword to Evatt's *Rum Rebellion* that Bligh was 'hot and short tempered, violent in language, "rude" in his relations with his associates, unjust in speech (but just in action), a severe disciplinarian, and strongly self-confident and self-righteous', and added that 'Bligh never learned how to manipulate fools to the end on which his attention was bent'. Of Macarthur, Grattan wrote he was 'very like Bligh in character. He too was of violent temper, though it was a "cold temper" that found release not in curses that died away as uttered, but in calculated vituperation that lived on.' As Bligh was soon to find out, Macarthur was also 'a man who could manipulate men to his own ends' and was both 'his opponent and vanquisher'.

Bligh reported in October 1807 that he was worried the military and their rum trading habits may result in 'a dangerous militia'. He was right and as Charles White wrote, Bligh 'applied the lancet to this social gangrene with better effect' than his predecessors. Bligh also wrote to Banks, noting that 'the most material thing to be done is to make everyone confident he will enjoy a just and upright Government – remove without delay the very unfit and very disgraceful Judge Advocate – Change the NSW Corps and send them to India'.

Bligh was busy on other fronts as well. Floods in the Hawkesbury were causing hardships for the farmers who'd settled there, and Britain's war against Napoleon was slowing the arrival of convicts for labouring, and supplies of food and equipment to support the settlers. In response to what he rightly believed was laxity in the ports, he issued new regulations to boost government control of operations, including the ships, their cargoes and crews. His general orders stated:

> No Vessel is to be built in the Colony without His Excellency's permission; and no Register will be given until the necessary Bond is executed on which it depends, before the Vessel is launched.
>
> All Masters of Vessels coming into this Port are to strictly forbid the leaving of any of Crews, their Officers, or Passengers on shore when they depart; and until that is certified no Clearance is to be granted: And all such respective individuals are likewise forbidden on any pretence whatever, remaining in the Colony without authority from His Excellency the Governor. Govt. House, SG 5 October 1806

In an effort to make Sydney a more cohesively developing town, and one complying with the vision and plans of Phillip, he moved against men like Johnston and Macarthur who he believed were illegally occupying sites in the settlement. Bligh challenged leases he thought might have been given improperly. Australia's first attempt at curbing the property developers added further risk to Bligh's tenure.

Bligh applied his lancet on 25 January 1808, and, based on Campbell's work, demanded Macarthur appear before the Judge Advocate Richard Atkins to be prosecuted for importing stills to produce liquor; inducing sailors from a ship he owned to come ashore and get rations without the governor's permission; and 'deceitfully, wickedly and maliciously contriving and abetting against William Bligh'. Macarthur's annoyance was heightened by his dislike for Atkins – they had fallen out over debts and were locked in litigation.

Macarthur responded to the charges in a speech to the courtroom condemning Atkins and making public his displeasure at being hauled before the court. Bligh ordered Macarthur be taken to prison for his comments – the catalyst for a drama already scripted by the governor's opponents. Being a wily politician, Macarthur had another plan well advanced – a petition signed by himself and around 100 notables, requesting Johnston, the lieutenant governor, remove Bligh from office.

Bligh and his supporters like Robert Campbell and the free settlers were about to get a lesson in the consequences of trying to remove power and profit from those who'd grown accustomed to having it. The scene was set for the Rum Rebellion.

5
REBELS AND REVENGE

On 26 January 1808, the 20th anniversary of the arrival of the First Fleet in Sydney Cove, Bligh's speculation about a 'dangerous militia' came true. Macarthur, later described by Bligh as an 'arch fiend', and the cartel fought back. It was the first day of the 'Rum Rebellion' and began in earnest when Johnston ordered Macarthur released and the arrest of Bligh and Atkins.

George Suttor, describing himself as a free settler from Baulkham Hills, was a Bligh supporter and gave an excited account of the day's events in a statement of 4 June 1808. He recalled:

> seeing the greater part of the New South Wales Corps under Arms with fixed bayonets marching down from the Barracks, I hastened with others to know the cause; and was informed that they were going to arrest the Governor; and on proceeding a short way with them, I distinctly heard Serjeant Major Whittle make use of these expressions, 'Men I hope you will do your duty and don't spare them.' The men replied, 'Never fear us.' And some person from the opposite side cried out, 'Hush! Hush!' I think it was John Macarthur Esqr. The Serjeant Major Whittle also said, 'Children, go out of the way, for some of you I expect will be killed.'

One unnamed member of the Corps, had a more lurid account and hedged his bets. He recalled:

> we shall never forget the evening and night of the ever memorable January 26, 1808. We perfectly remember the marching of our then little army from the barracks of the New South Wales Corps up to Government House, in the front and rear of which the troops were all drawn up, under the orders of the lamented and misled Colonel Johnston. We were in the midst of the search made after the unfortunate Governor, and were obliged to give admittance to Lieutenant Laycock to the little printing office, which, in those antique times, was attached as an appendage to Government House. The Lieutenant, after examining the loft, in descending from which he had nearly dislocated the principal joints in his body, discovered that no Governor was there, and shortly after, his unfortunate Excellency (the representative of Majesty) was found beneath a bed upstairs, to which he had flown for refuge from those adversaries, who have ever since continued the enemies of good government. The day following, the 27th was a day of immense business. The Governor was formally deposed, bonfires lighted up at the corners of almost every street, magistrates were dismissed, the Provost Marshall escorted to prison, the then sitting Criminal Court dissolved, troops harangued in the Bonapartian style, the old Judge Advocate relieved of his offices . . .

The story of Bligh hiding under the bed was reiterated by soldier John Dunn at Johnston's court martial in London in 1811. He said he'd found Bligh under the bed, but on cross-examination said the space between bed and floor was about one foot, with a downward bulge of about four to five inches. The attempt to paint Bligh as a coward was having a credibility issue.

Bligh, unsurprisingly, had a different view of the day's events, and particularly the 'found beneath a bed' part. He said:

Immediately after the order for the release of Macarthur, there followed an operation of the main guard close to the gate of Government House, and the regiment marched down from the barracks, led on by Major Johnston and the other officers, with colours flying and music playing as they advanced to the house. Within a few minutes after the house was surrounded; the soldiers quickly broke into all parts of it, and arrested all the magistrates, Mr. Gore, the provost-marshal; Mr. Griffin, my secretary; and Mr. Fulton, the chaplain. I had just time to call to my orderly-sergeant to have my horses ready while I went upstairs to put on my uniform, when on my return, as I was standing on the staircase waiting for my servant with my sword, I saw a number of soldiers rushing upstairs with their muskets and fixed bayonets, as I conceived to seize my person. I retired instantly into a back room to defeat their object, and to deliberate on the means to be adopted for the restoration of my authority, which in such a critical situation could only be accomplished by my getting into the interior of the country adjacent to the Hawkesbury, where I knew the whole body of people would flock to my standard. To this situation I was pursued by the soldiers, and after experiencing much insult was conducted below by Lieutenant Minchin, who told me that Major Johnston was waiting for me. We passed together into the drawing-room, every part being crowded with soldiers under arms, many of whom appeared to be intoxicated.

I then received a letter brought by Lieutenant Moore, and signed by Major Johnston, (calling himself Lieutenant-Governor), requiring me to resign my authority, and to submit to the arrest under which he placed me, which I had scarcely perused, when a message was delivered to me that Major Johnston wished to speak to me in the adjoining room, at the door of which he soon afterwards appeared, surrounded by his officers and soldiers; and in terms much to the same effect as his letter, he there verbally confirmed my arrest. Martial law was proclaimed, my secretary and my friends were prevented from seeing me, and I was left alone with my daughter and another lady.

By Major Johnston's orders several persons seized my cabinet and papers, with my commission, instructions, and the great seal of the colony. These were locked up in a room guarded by two sentinels, and several others were placed around the house to prevent my escape.

The rebels confined Bligh to Government House in Sydney for over a year after he'd refused their demand to sail directly for England if he was released. Johnston took charge of the colony, but as White wrote, 'the very men who had made a catspaw of him in leading the rebellion were the first to thwart his efforts to properly conduct public affairs. Macarthur was virtually the Governor, although only holding office as Colonial Secretary, to which position he had appointed himself.'

Revenge was high on the rebel's order of business, and one of their first acts was to prosecute former convict George Crossley who'd been a lawyer convicted of perjury and sentenced to transportation. He was a Bligh supporter who'd resumed his legal career and drawn up the charges against Macarthur. Crossley's trial by the rebels was little more than a formality and he was sentenced to transportation to Coal River (now Newcastle) but released after Governor Lachlan Macquarie's arrival on 28 December 1809. He later successfully sued some of the rebels for damages.

Robert Campbell didn't escape their attention, and both he and his brother-in-law and business partner John Palmer were briefly gaoled. The experience didn't curb Campbell's support for Bligh and the citizens opposing Macarthur and his colleagues.

With matters of revenge dealt with, the rebels offered congratulations for a job well done in the form of land grants for themselves and their supporters. One example was Alexander

Riley, a merchant and later pastoralist who followed his two sisters to Australia after their marriage to officers in the NSW Corps, and who was given 3000 acres of land, and 40,000 gallons (182,000 litres) of spirits. It was a very cosy arrangement and a precedent for NSW in the generations to follow.

Robert Campbell had further bad luck in the first half of 1808. Opportunity is one of the great stimuli for crime, and with politics in turmoil and the new management focused on their own plans rather than building the future of the colony, the creative crooks were presented with a chance. On the morning of Monday 16 May 1808, Campbell looked out the window of his home with its view of Farm Cove, expecting to see his brig *Harrington* at her mooring. The brig was fully provisioned in readiness to sail to Fiji later in the week, but instead of his ship he saw the empty space where she had been the night before.

Around 10 pm on the Sunday night, two men had roused Arnold Fisk, the ship's first mate, who was in a deep sleep in his cabin. One put the barrel of a pistol to Fisk's head and told him that if he made a sound he'd be a dead man. Fisk surrendered. Around fifty men, all convicts and many armed, had crept onboard, and quickly subdued the crew of twenty-three with threats of death. The *Sydney Gazette* reported, 'they had cut away both anchors, and towed the vessel out; and that about 7 in the morning, when upwards of 20 miles at sea, they had ordered Mr. Fisk and the crew to go on deck, one by one, in which order they were put into two boats and sent away from the vessel; and that after being 8 hours on the water they reached the shore.'

Leading the convicts was Michael Stewart, or Seymour or Robert Stewart – a man of many names, a fraudster and charming rogue who easily slipped into the persona of a gentleman or aristocrat as needed. He'd been sentenced to death at the Old Bailey in May 1801, but then transported for life to Sydney, arriving in 1803.

Campbell immediately alerted the authorities. A ship, believed to be the *Harrington,* was spotted off South Head and so the small vessel *Halcyon* with ten members of the NSW Corps under command of Sergeant Windsor, was towed down the harbour – there was no wind – followed by a flotilla of volunteers in other small boats. Piracy provided a welcome break from the routine of the colony. Unfortunately for the pirate hunters there wasn't a breath of air and when a breeze finally arrived with the onset of evening, *Harrington* was nowhere in sight. Two days later, *Pegasus,* chartered by the government, and with Campbell, Fisk, and twenty-four soldiers on board, set off in pursuit. They believed the pirates might have been heading to New Zealand's Bay of Islands to capture the US brig *Eliza* that had sailed from Sydney in April. However, the pursuers were out of luck, and sailed on to Fiji without sighting *Harrington. Pegasus* returned empty-handed on 22 July.

Stewart and his crew made it as far as Manila where *Harrington* ran aground. He and a few others were taken into custody, while the rest escaped into the jungle. Stewart was taken to India, and escaped.

Even in NSW, all good things reach their use-by date. Britain was in the middle of fighting the Napoleonic Wars, but Viscount Castlereagh, the Secretary of State for War and the Colonies and former Chief Secretary for Ireland, wasn't tolerant of insurrection. Lieutenant Colonel Joseph Foveaux, who'd first arrived in Sydney in 1792, and who'd been Lieutenant Governor of Norfolk Island, was ordered back to Sydney to take over as Lieutenant Governor. He arrived in July 1808, and was followed by William Paterson.

Foveaux did nothing to relieve Bligh's misery – he was still confined – and instead moved onto positive matters like building the town. Bligh finally relented and on 17 March 1809 sailed for Van Diemen's Land in command of the *Porpoise* after giving his word that he'd return to England, but it was just a ruse, as Bligh believed that because it was given under duress he wasn't obliged to honour it. In Van Diemen's Land, he found the Lieutenant Governor David Collins unwilling to denounce the rebels. Their relationship deteriorated rapidly, and on 17 January 1810, after Governor Lachlan Macquarie's arrival in Sydney, Bligh returned, lingered until 12 May, and then sailed for England. He didn't endear himself to Macquarie during his stopover.

Shortly after Bligh had sailed for Van Diemen's Land with his cunning plan in mind, Johnston was sent to England for court martial. Macarthur, Johnston's chief defence witness, also headed the same way, but stopped in Rio de Janeiro for a bit of trading business, and met with Lachlan Macquarie then bound for Sydney. All the blustering, posturing and misery of the Rum Rebellion resulted in Bligh's exoneration and subsequent promotion, and Johnston being 'cashiered' from the military. Both he and Macarthur returned to Australia and to successful commercial lives. Bligh was promoted to rear admiral.

Castlereagh gave Macquarie a clear view of what he expected of the new governor, telling him, 'the Great Objects of attention are to improve the Morals of the Colonists, to encourage Marriage, to provide for Education, to prohibit the Use of Spirituous Liquors, to increase the Agriculture and Stock, so as to ensure the Certainty of a full supply to the Inhabitants under all Circumstances'.

Macquarie's first impression of his new bailiwick was mixed. In one account he noted it 'was in a perfect state of tranquility', but later wrote,

> I found the colony barely emerging from infantile imbecility, and suffering from various privations and disabilities; the country impenetrable beyond forty miles from Sydney; agriculture in a yet languishing state; commerce in its early dawn; revenue unknown; threatened with famine; distracted by faction; the public buildings in a state of dilapidation and mouldering to decay; the few roads and bridges formerly constructed rendered almost impassable; the population in general depressed by

poverty; no public credit, nor private confidence; the morals of the great mass of the population in the lowest state of debasement, and religious worship almost totally neglected. Such was the state of New South Wales when I took charge of its administration on 1st January, 1810.

One of his first acts was to annul all the appointments of the rebel government and their stopgaps; reappoint officers who'd been displaced; and shortly after, order the building of a hospital. Macquarie's proclamation announced,

whereas it has pleased His Majesty to express his high displeasure at the arrest and removal of William Bligh his late representative in this territory and its dependencies, from the exercise of the powers and authorities granted him in that behalf, and also to consider all appointments to situations and offices of public trust made by such persons as have assumed to themselves the executive authority since such arrest and removal, as illegal and invalid.

Macquarie also ordered the arrest of those pardoned by the rebels.

The Rocks was still the collection of tents and temporary dwellings that had grown around the waterfront shortly after Phillip's arrival in 1788. Macquarie thought it 'ruinous and unfit'. By the time he arrived the area was the hub of the colony's nightlife and skulduggery – full of liquor suppliers, thieves and prostitutes catering to both the local population and the sailors in town with their ships or taking a brief leave with food, accommodation, brothels and booze from the numerous taverns. It was home to the dock labourers and their families, many of who were former convicts who'd served their time and decided to stay on. Working on the docks gave them the opportunity to engage in crimes of opportunity like stealing liquor, tobacco, clothing or even barrels of salt pork from the warehouses, and then sell it through their network in the tangle of streets that was The Rocks.

NSW Chief Justice James Spigelman wrote in the *Sydney Morning Herald* of 26 December 2009 that The Rocks at the time of Macquarie's arrival was full of 'human flotsam'. But there was another side. Robert Campbell was building wharves and storehouses, and it was also a place where fashion was proving profitable. Sarah Bird, who ran the Three Jolly Settlers tavern in The Rocks, 'had a sideline in finery and I did a little trade in the passage here in a number of small articles such as sugar, tea, tobacco, snuff, thread, needles and everything that I could get anything by . . . I have sold my petticoats at two guineas each, and my long black coat at ten guineas, which shows that black silk sells well here,' (quoted in *The Coming of the Strangers: Life in Australia 1788 to 1822* by Baiba Berzins).

Macquarie's new hospital shows his pragmatic approach to problem solving. One of the major issues confronting him was the illegal trade in rum and its prominence as the preferred currency. Among his earliest orders was to dramatically reduce the number of licensed premises from around seventy-four to twenty, and crack down on the unlicensed operations around The Rocks. He had a fair idea of the needs of the thirsty workers though and, after representations by around fifty of the businesses that had been closed down, he ordered,

> that it would be a great accommodation to the labouring people, and to the lower classes of the inhabitants in general, to have plenty of good wholesome beer brewed for their drinking and permitted to be retailed to them at a moderate price; his Excellency the Governor in view to their convenience as well as to encourage the settlers to grow barley for this and other purposes, has been pleased to direct licenses to be granted to fifty persons at Sydney to vend and retail beer.

While dragging liquor sales back into a legal framework, he also applied an excise tax – a good way to start a revenue stream for the treasury and return to the use of formal currency.

However, in an intriguing twist, Sydney Hospital was built by an agreement not of cash but of rum. When Britain declined to fund the building, the cash-poor Macquarie cut a deal on 6 November 1810 with merchants Garnham Blaxcell, Alexander Riley and D'Arcy Wentworth to build the hospital in what is now Macquarie Street. Payment was a monopoly on the legal rum trade and over the next three years they imported 45,000 gallons (204,574 litres) with an excise of 3 shillings a gallon. No cash changed hands and the excise went into the construction. Though the building was criticised for some dodgy construction, it was the first successful government and private sector venture in Australia – but it wasn't quick and opened for business on 8 April 1816.

Macquarie's introduction of an excise tax on alcohol was a step to remedy the reliance on rum as a currency, and was hastened by the arrival of some real currency sent from Britain via the East India Company. Ten thousand pounds worth of silver Spanish coins, known in some parts of the world as 'pieces of eight', arrived in late November 1812. The centre was punched out, becoming a 15 pence coin, and the remainder, known locally as the 'holey dollar', was worth 5 shillings.

Macquarie's edicts on alcohol also achieved an unwanted outcome – they stimulated a black market trade later known as 'sly grog'. At its heart was liquor that slipped through the waterfront as cargo without excise being paid, and liquor stolen from the waterfront bond stores. The police weren't of much help, and Macquarie commented in 1811 that 'police of the town of Sydney were very defective to the preserving of peace and good order in this populous and extensive town'. To deal with this problem, Macquarie built on Governor Hunter's original division of the colony into specific policing areas, which required residents to number their properties. On 1 January 1811, he issued regulations splitting the colony into five police districts – a term that lingered until the late twentieth century – of seven constables each, and all under the command of the first Superintendent of Police, D'Arcy Wentworth.

Wentworth was given the power to 'punish all prisoners, freemen, rogues and vagabonds', while his constables had to 'stop every prisoner or other suspicious person being about the streets after the hour of nine o'clock at night'. Wentworth, as surgeon, magistrate, head copper, merchant and partner in hospital building was one of the busiest men in the colony.

Under his leadership, however, the waterfront boomed, with Macquarie proudly boasting,

> on my taking the command of the colony in the year 1810, the amount of port duties collected did not exceed £8000 per annum, and there were only £50 or £60 of a balance in the Treasurer's hand; but now duties are collected at Port Jackson to the amount of £28,000 to £30,000 per annum. In addition to this annual colonial revenue, there are port duties collected at Hobart Town, in Van Diemen's Land, to the amount of between £8,000 and £10,000 per annum.

Down around the dives, brothels and grog sellers of the waterfront, business boomed as well. Macquarie's attempt to literally straighten out the tangle of narrow streets and twisting lanes of The Rocks in line with the 1810 edict to widen the city's streets and plan the city's future around wide, straight roads was thwarted by the hills and coves of the old settlement with water on three sides. George Howe in the *Sydney Gazette* in 1803 quipped about The Rocks with its combination of tricky-to-negotiate streets and readily available alcohol that it would be a 'perfect place for a tumbling academy'.

Macquarie's attempts to straighten out the residents were similarly thwarted – and he didn't get much help from his soldiers, who, after church each Sunday would head, 'immediately to the place they call The Rocks where every species of debauchery and villainy is practised'. They joined sailors from trading vessels, and the sealers and whalers in port to sell their oils and skins.

By the early 1820s, The Rocks had around 1200 residents, and sprawled from Dawes Point in the east, Millers Point to the north, and Cockle Bay (now Darling Harbour) to the west. Convicts, emancipists, free settlers, opportunists and new migrants made their homes there. Macquarie was a liberal, and advocated opportunities for former convicts to prosper. Many of the convicts arriving in the colony were sent to labour in the new rural areas, and those who stayed in Sydney were mustered in the gaol yard and then broken up into work gangs. They were told to find lodging and to appear for work when the bell to announce the beginning of the day's work rang.

In 1819, Macquarie opened convict barracks built to house 800 men, and with his views on supporting the rehabilitation of convicts, they were able to find work for themselves on Saturdays after 1 pm. With the growth of trade, along with modern ships bringing in more cargo than ever, the demand for unskilled labour to do the heavy grunt work on the docks increased. If the convicts' allotted work was done ahead of time, they could find paying jobs to fill the rest of the day They joined free men who were picking casual work by the hour based on demand.

Along with the freemen working the waterfront, the convicts knew the employers needed them more than they needed the employers. Charles White wrote, 'many employers, to prevent the inconvenience, and perhaps ruin, which would follow the loss of the services of their assigned men, were obliged to wink at their crimes, and some agreed to pay them the same rate of wages and to allow them the same rations as their free servants'.

The growth on the waterfront, and the incentive to avoid Macquarie's excise, added motive to opportunity for those with criminal ideas. And in Sydney, crime thrived.

Though convicts were getting the same rates and rations as free men working the waterfront, and the chance of a supplementary income, their life was far from their own. Getting up, eating, working and sleeping were controlled by the ringing of a bell in their barracks, and they were under the control of a superintendent and his supervisors and overseers – usually trusted convicts. They had one hour of recreation between dinner and lights out in which they could play cards or marbles or dice games – gambling was illegal, but there wasn't money involved . . . that anyone would admit to; tell stories; make music on instruments they'd improvised. Good behaviour could be rewarded with a 'ticket of leave' which allowed them to work outside the convict system and to own land, or a pardon. Bad behaviour resulted in the lash, solitary confinement or transfer to a remote penal colony. As an example, in 1826 convict Thomas Haynes was charged with 'refusing bread offered to him in the Prisoner's Barracks' and 'exciting his fellow prisoners to do the same'. The *Sydney Gazette* of 11 February 1826 reported the Bench found the bread to be 'good and wholesome' and the troublesome Mr Haynes received fifty lashes as punishment.

6
THE NEW BROOM

Under Macquarie's governorship Sydney and Parramatta were finally looking like cities, and exploration both inland and at sea was changing the face and purpose of the colony. By 1813, it was close to self-sufficient, with a group of local leaders writing in a letter to London in June that year saying,

> the colony of New South Wales is in so flourishing a condition, that a memorial has been forwarded by the principal inhabitants, through the governor, to his Majesty's Ministers, praying, among other privileges, permission to distil from their surplus grain, and to export flour from thence to Great Britain; and pointing out that there is no farther necessity for any salt meat being sent thither, as the colony can furnish fresh beef, pork, and mutton at a cheaper rate. It appears also that the grower of fine wool in the colony consider that they are enabled to vie with Spain in the quality, if not the quantity of produce, which, however, is greatly increasing.

On Macquarie's watch, Hobart in then Van Diemen's Land had grown into a port city. Closer to Sydney, the Illawarra had been explored; Port Stephens on the NSW north coast was established and was a major supplier of timber for shipbuilding. Newcastle had moved on from being a place where the most dangerous convicts had been sequestered to the beginnings of a town with a commercial heart. In 1812, there were 100 convicts working on the side of the Hunter River, and by 1819 that had grown to 700.

Newcastle's focus was on the export of timber, coal, salt and lime to Sydney. In 1810, 800 tons of coal was sent, and by 1820 the figure reached 3915.

The early entrepreneurs of Sydney were also thriving under Macquarie's tenure, driving the development of the port along with them. One was Mary Reibey, Australia's first female commercial success story. She'd been arrested at the age of thirteen, while dressed as a boy and calling herself James Burrow, and sentenced to seven years transportation. Her real name was Mary Haydock, and on arrival in Sydney in 1792 she fell for the free settler Thomas Reibey, and the two married in 1794. They were partners in business as well, with Mary running the wholesale and retail trading during her husband's numerous voyages in search of goods.

Reibey looked after the operations, and her family of seven children, and watched her business grow from a small store she ran while her husband was away on sealing adventures in his sloop *The Raven,* to warehouse and residence by 1810. With the business expanding, Thomas pioneered the coal trade from Newcastle to Sydney, and opened up trade with the Pacific Islands, often leaving Sydney with a cargo of salt and goods to barter and returning with salt-cured pigs. Reibey was astute, and avoided the politics of the Rum Rebellion and William Bligh. After her husband's death in 1811, she assumed full control. She ruled with a firm hand, including doing her own debt collecting, which on one occasion saw her charged with assault.

Dymphna Cusack wrote of Reibey's success that

> their extensive waterfront adjoined the Government Wharf and faced the open area that in 1810 was named Macquarie

Place. All the traffic from the wharf ran past the house, and a motley crowd of Lascars [sailors usually from India], full-blooded Tahitians and Maoris, left stranded by unscrupulous ship-owners, jostled around the wharf waiting for ships. Foreign-looking sailors, carrying richly plumaged birds, which they hoped to exchange for something more useful, haunted the building. Within, the low substantial rooms crowded with incongruous and exotic stores, were redolent of sandalwood.

It was a trove of the exotic mixing with the practical, and Cusack gave a glimpse of the needs of the Sydneysider of the time when she wrote the warehouse contained,

Teas of sorts, sugar and sugar candy, rice and coffee, salt and salt petre, spices and pepper, bacon, pork and beef, hog's cheeks, lard, sausages, calicoes, nankeens [cloth], ready-made shirts, chemises, satins of sorts, black silks, silk handkerchiefs of sorts, velvet waistcoats . . .

and a detailed list of fabrics, furniture and kitchenware. Reibey's was a one-stop shop. She pioneered tempting the locals with 'sales', advertising in the *Sydney Gazette* in 1812 that she had a 'variety of articles recently imported' and was 'determined to sell at reasonable prices, assuring herself it is the best recommendation to public patronage and support'. These days she'd be selling Persian carpets in 'liquidation sales'. Margaret Catchpole, transported in 1801 for stealing a horse so she could meet her lover, and who became a housekeeper and cook for some of Sydney's well-to-do, wasn't convinced by the advertisement, and observed that 'reasonable' might have been overselling the retail opportunity. She said 'everything very deaar, butter fives shillens par lb'.

In 1817 Mary Reibey bought the brigantine *Governor Macquarie* for her son Tom, as part of her plan to set him up in Van Diemen's Land. Tom had his father's passion for the sea, and his mother's head for business, and when he settled in Hobart he advertised his first cargo as for sale at 'very reduced prices, for ready money'. With her son settled, she wound down her Sydney operations, selling all her properties, which by then included stores on the waterfront in George Street, the house and warehouse in Macquarie Place, seven farms on the Hawkesbury River, and a house and warehouse on Cockle Bay. In around twenty years of business, the former convict had amassed a fortune of around £20,000. She returned to England in 1820 for a year-long visit, and died in Sydney in 1855.

Robert Campbell had also done well under Macquarie, despite some years even rockier than his earlier times against the East India Company. Shortly after Macquarie arrived, Campbell and his family sailed to London to give evidence on Bligh's behalf at Johnston's court martial. Campbell wasn't keen on the trip, but wasn't given much choice by Bligh and the British hierarchy, but there was a small positive. While in London, his local agent, who owed him the vast sum of £30,000, went broke leaving Campbell with a major cash flow problem, but fortunately he was on the spot to salvage what he could. The Campbell family returned to Sydney in 1815 to find the business in dire financial straits, and so he liquidated Campbell & Company, and set about rebuilding his empire. In 1816, he was one of the key players in what would become the colony's first bank, the Bank of New South Wales (now Westpac), and in 1819 he was appointed Secretary of the Savings Bank which was set up for the 'Industrious poor of the Colony'. Macquarie also granted the public-spirited Campbell 607 hectares of farming land near Bathurst. In 1825 Campbell was given another grant of around 1619 hectares in what is now Canberra. He named the property 'Duntroon'.

By the end of Macquarie's tenure, Campbell's business was back on its feet, trading with the settlements in Newcastle and Van Diemen's Land. In 1825, he was again a shipowner and re-entering public life with his earlier vigour. He was appointed to the Legislative Council and petitioned the king to stop transportation and instead encourage free settlers. In Campbell's view, Sydney had long since passed its use-by date as a penal colony. One of the ironies of his return to fortune was that the dramatic success of the wool export trade – dominated by his former foe John Macarthur – drove his maritime and mercantile businesses.

By the end of the 1830s Robert Campbell was winding down his career. The catalyst for his withdrawal from public life was the death of his wife in 1833, after which he began spending more time at Duntroon, and significantly increasing the size of his holding. He died there on 15 April 1846, and was survived by six of his seven children.

John Macarthur's post Rum Rebellion career paralleled Campbell's. He headed to Britain for Johnston's court martial and while there he heard that Macquarie had been ordered to have him arrested for his role in the rebellion and taken before the courts in Sydney. Macarthur decided it was prudent to remain where he was, which did little for the performance of his Australian business interests. However, it proved to be a wise long-term strategy, and he used his time lobbying the government to have the possibility of arrest removed and to further his wool industry interests. He also travelled to Europe to study ways to improve wool production and grape growing and winemaking – another Australian industry of which he would be a founder but one that would take a little longer to mature into a major export business.

In December 1814, believing that Macquarie might be like King and interested in a spot of commercial gain, he wrote to his wife Elizabeth, directing her to talk with Mrs Macquarie about 'our Sheep and take occasion to lament that the Flocks should remain Stationary. If this excite attention, you might cautiously hint at an arrangement that was on the point of being made with Governor King before he was relieved, which would have secured a splendid fortune for both our Families as he possessed the power to give me any quantity of Land and any number of Servants that might have been necessary.' Macarthur had misjudged his mark, but did manage to clear his way for a return in 1817. Macquarie was disinterested in the discreet proposal and was also disinterested in granting more land, a situation that annoyed Macarthur who used his contacts in London to cast doubt on the governor's abilities.

By 1822, Macarthur's original Camden estates had increased to over 24,000 hectares, through grant and purchase. He followed this achievement up in 1824 when he realised his dream of a wool company – the Australian Agricultural Company – to control the industry and develop major farming enterprises. The company had a capital of £1 million, and was heavily supported by London investors and the British Government, who believed it would provide employment opportunities for convicts, thus reducing their cost in supporting them. To kick it along further, the company received a land grant of nearly one million acres (404,690 hectares) behind Port Stephens, along with rights to the use Newcastle Harbour for its exports. Macarthur added politics to his achievements when he was appointed, in July 1825, to the Legislative Council – a position he held until his increasingly erratic behaviour ended up with his removal in 1832, by the order of Governor Bourke, as he'd been 'pronounced a lunatic' and with 'little hope of his restoration'.

'Woolaway', writing in the *Sydney Morning Herald* on the centenary of Macarthur's death in April 1934, noted that in 1807, Australia exported 524 pounds (237 kilograms) of wool worth around £100, and that by 1933, 1,338,900 bales of wool worth £50,562,112 had been exported from NSW alone. Macarthur, 'Woolaway' asserted, had been the 'Father of the Colony'. Four years later Herbert Evatt's *Rum Rebellion* offered a different view with the foreword noting that, while Macarthur and the wool industry had been significant, 'not until many decades had passed [with] such things as railways, dry farming, plant experiments, refrigeration, fast steamships ... did Australian farming really get on its feet'. Evatt concluded his book by putting Macarthur and his colleagues in their place, writing, 'sooner or later, history will pronounce final judgement of William Bligh. It will be in his favour.'

Of Macquarie's legacy Marion Phillips, the Melbourne-born UK Labour MP, wrote in 1908 that his work 'to turn the criminal into a useful, self-respecting citizen populating the empty lands of a new country, and alone building up a new state, was a fine and generous plan'. However she also observed, 'for the most part the convict remained unreformed', but their children, the first generation of Europeans to be born in Australia were, 'creditable to the British stock from which they were descended. They bore no sign of a convict taint, no heritage of vice or weakness, and this strange method of colonisation which gave to the country a fast-increasing population, brought with it no penalty of physical or moral degeneration.'

Judge John Thomas Bigge's arrival in New South Wales on 26 September 1819 – primarily to look at the effectiveness of transportation, and more broadly on how the colony was operating – came as something of a surprise to Macquarie, who'd been expecting a response to his request to resign rather than an audit of his performance. To add further insult, Macquarie was ordered to comply with Bigge's requests.

Macquarie was noted for his humanity, progressive thinking and repatriating convicts back into society. Bigge was very different – a lawyer with experience working in the slave colonies of the Caribbean and a man with a hardline view on law, order and punishment. The *Australian Dictionary of Biography* noted that 'Bigge found more in common with the Macarthurs and resorted often to their company as, finding the governor increasingly irascible, he "nearly abandoned the hope of being able to influence him in any changes".' The two didn't get on.

Bigge's reports, tabled from 1822 onwards, while detailed, failed to acknowledge what Macquarie had achieved in turning a colony from the near anarchy of the Rum Rebellion into a functioning, prosperous and welcome addition to the United Kingdom. Macquarie said of Bigge's reports that they were 'false, vindictive and malicious'.

Lachlan Macquarie and his family boarded *Surry* on 12 February 1822, and three days later left Sydney, bound for London. It had taken three attempts at resignation for Macquarie to finally be able to leave and he had lingered for three months after the arrival of his replacement, Major General Sir Thomas Brisbane.

He left behind a colony very different from the virtual anarchy that confronted him on arrival years before.

Macquarie's departure from the colony was also vastly different from that of Bligh, with Sydneysiders giving him a rousing farewell, according to a report published in the *Sydney Gazette* of 15 February 1822, of 'a salute of 19 guns was fired from Dawes Battery. Launches, barges, cutters, pinnaces, and wherries, were seen crowded with those who appeared determined on catching a parting glimpse of the object of their profound veneration and fondest regard, who for some time stood up, uncovered, and kept bowing adieu as he passed. Never did Sydney Cove look so attractive and gay as upon this occasion; and the shores were lined with spectators innumerable.'

Under Macquarie's guidance, Australia had transitioned from a remote place to dump both physical and political problems, into the makings of a nation.

7
THE ADVENTURES OF BATMAN

When John Batman sailed into Port Phillip Bay in 1836, Major General Sir Richard Bourke was governor. White described Bourke's tenure as marked by 'vigour and firmness, zeal, liberality and humanity'. Bourke was under orders from Britain 'not to allow the population to become more scattered than it was', a comment directed at the proposed settlement of Port Phillip Bay. His response was a practical one and used the question and answer format now popular with Australia's politicians, 'how may Government turn to the best advantage a state of things which it cannot wholly interdict?' he asked, and then said, 'it may, I would suggest, be found practicable by means of the sale of lands in situations peculiarly advantageous, however distant from other locations, and by establishing townships and ports, and facilitating the intercourse between remote and more settled districts of this vast territory, to provide centres of civilization and government, and thus gradually extend the power of social order to the most distant parts of the wilderness'.

Batman wasn't the first of the colonists to head to Melbourne. On 31 January 1802, Lieutenant John Murray, commanding *Lady Nelson*, arrived off Port Phillip Bay – he'd sighted the entrance earlier that month, but finding it dangerous, moved on to survey the east coast of King Island first. After initially exploring the bay by launch, Murray sailed *Lady Nelson* in on 14 February and began a detailed exploration. Three weeks later, on 8 March, Murray claimed possession for Britain and named the bay Port King in honour of the governor and headed back to Sydney. King later changed the name to Phillip.

Matthew Flinders, commanding the *Investigator*, arrived in Port Phillip Bay on 27 April 1802, unaware that Murray had been there only weeks before. Like Murray, he was concerned about the danger of entering, but tantalised by the large body of water he could see in the distance. He wrote, 'a large extent of water presently became visible, and although the entrance seemed to be very narrow, and there were in it strong ripplings like breakers, I was induced to steer in at half-past one; the ship being close upon a wind and every man ready for tacking at a moment's warning'. One of the crew, a Seaman Smith, wrote in his journal that, 'thinking there was a good channel in a passage through, we got aground; but by good management we got off without damage. Here we caught a Shirk [shark] which measured 10 feet 9 inch in length; in girt very large.'

On 29 April, Flinders sailed *Investigator* around the bay, and concerned about the high possibility of running aground, returned to near the entrance, anchored and resumed his exploration by long boat. *Investigator* headed back to Sydney on 3 May. He reported that Port Phillip Bay was a 'useful but obscure port', and 'capable of receiving and sheltering a larger fleet of ships than ever yet went to sea'. He said the surrounding countryside 'has a pleasing and in many places a fertile appearance', and 'is in great measure a grassy country, and capable of supporting much cattle, though much better calculated for sheep'. Flinders didn't have a crystal ball, but he'd neatly predicted the rise of the wool industry that would play a major role in turning the 'obscure' port into a major player in the success of the nation's wool export trade.

In 1803, with Britain still spatting with the French, and worried they might try and get a foothold in Australia by claiming Westernport Bay, Governor King sent surveyor Charles Grimes onboard *Cumberland* to look for possible locations to set up fortifications. After encountering the French ship *Geographe* near King Island, and pointing out to her Captain Nicolas Baudin that a French settlement would be frowned on, Grimes headed to Port Phillip Bay, arriving there on 20 January. He wasn't initially enthusiastic after finding low swamp and country that was 'very barren', however explorations on 2, 3 and 4 February found the Maribyrnong and Yarra Rivers, plenty of fresh water and a fine site for a settlement where Melbourne now stands. In spite of that, Grimes wasn't enthusiastic about Port Phillip's future as a new penal colony and duly reported his findings to London.

Slow communications and bureaucracy meant Grimes' report arrived in London after David Collins, then lieutenant governor of the colony, had been ordered to establish a settlement at Sullivan Bay, now Sorrento. He arrived in October 1803, but lack of fresh water and local resources resulted in that plan being abandoned in February 1804 and trying Plan B – heading to Hobart and joining the fledgling town there. A little over three decades later, Port Phillip Bay was finally settled.

John Batman was a first generation European Australian, born in 1801 at Rosehill near Parramatta to William, who'd been transported in 1797 for receiving stolen goods, and his wife Mary, who'd paid her own fare and sailed on the same ship with their two children.

Batman started his working life as an apprentice blacksmith – a career cut short when his master was executed for burglary. Batman was 'sufficiently literate for any practical purpose, sociable, of fine physique; a promising bushman' according to his entry in the *Australian Dictionary of Biography*, and a man with a 'lively imagination, persistent vigour, logic, and bold sensibility'. He became a 'jack of all trades' after the abrupt end to his first career. In 1821, he headed to Van Diemen's Land along with his brother Henry, and became a successful grazier. In 1828, he married Eliza Thompson, a former convict.

By 1835, Batman was an influential member of the community in Van Diemen's Land and as Colonel Sir George Arthur wrote, 'one of the few who supposed they [the indigenous population] might be influenced by kindness'. All the available land on the island was put to grazing, but the convict population had grown to a point where demand was exceeding the supply of meat. There was only one viable solution – expansion. Batman had been lobbying for a land grant on the mainland since 1827 but a lack of policy from the government had slowed any action.

In May 1835 Batman sailed from Launceston onboard the schooner *Rebecca*, returning with a treaty for the sale of land by Wurundjeri tribal elders on Port Phillip Bay where Melbourne now stands. Despite Governor Bourke's proclamation on 26 August 1835 that any settlers would be trespassers, the city grew quickly. On 7 November, William Fawkner – another pastoralist from Van Diemen's Land – opened a hotel in a two-roomed hut in what is now the corner of Flinders Lane and William Street. Five months later, in April 1836, Batman returned with his wife and seven children and set up residence in his 'Mansion House', a mud building near today's Spencer Street and boasting chimneys made of brick he'd imported from Van Diemen's Land.

By June 1836 there were 177 residents, and around 26,500 sheep grazing near the rivers, and the foundations for Australia's obsession with real estate were about to be laid.

On 1 March 1837 Bourke visited Melbourne and succumbed to the inevitable by proclaiming the town, ordering a public holiday and authorising the sale of land. A month later he approved a development plan – the evolutionary spread of Sydney had taught the colonial masters a few lessons. The first plots of land were sold on 1 June, at one of Australia's first land auctions. Around 200 people gathered while Robert Hoddle auctioned the lots, achieving prices from £7 to £95. One requirement of the sale was the new owner had to build within twelve months – something that was conveniently overlooked in practice. One early buyer, Charles Ebden, sold three lots he'd bought for £136 for over £10,000 in 1839. By 1840, Melbourne was looking like a city, but unlike the city he founded, Batman didn't thrive – his health had declined rapidly since 1836 and he died on 6 May 1839.

The pastoralists and speculators weren't the only ones profiting from hard work and opportunity. Within the first months of Melbourne's settlement a flourishing market in stolen goods began. In the depths of the night, when the tides were favourable, food, alcohol (gin and beer were the preferred tipples of the Melbourne residents), tobacco and fabric were stolen from the ships moored near the sand banks of Port Phillip Bay, often with the complicity of the crew. The booty was loaded into boats that slipped away, carried by tide and careful oarsmanship toward the Yarra and then up the river to the new settlement. The thieves knew their way, using instinct, experience and the distant lights. Once landed, the stolen goods disappeared into a network of middlemen for distribution. It was tough work, but given the lack of any police or military presence, relatively simple, safe and highly profitable.

In a town short on supplies for a growing and affluent population, questions about where the goods came from weren't asked. The Melbourne waterfront thieves operated a slick business that Sydney's convict opportunists, taking their chances pillaging from the ships or warehouses, surrounded by police and the military, could only dream of. The Melbourne thieves' lot grew even easier when a jetty was built at Williamstown in 1839, and the first properly constructed wharves followed a few years later. There was no need to row out and board the ships – the product was simply piled on the wharves and ripe for plunder.

By the time Charles La Trobe arrived in 1839 as the newly appointed 'supervisor' of the Port Phillip Bay District, criminal networks were well established and running smoothly. To counter them, La Trobe set up the water police in 1841, and based them at Williamstown, with another unit later formed in Geelong. Elements of their mission, according to the *Manual of Police Regulations,* were to 'afford police protection and maintain order among the shipping in Hobson's Bay, Geelong Harbour and at the anchorage off Port Henry; to enforce the port regulations; to supervise the trans-shipment of power [gunpowder]' and among the various duties, 'to prevent the influx of criminals'. With the vast numbers soon arriving for the gold rush, the latter was more guesswork than police work as thousands of men poured from ships.

In a throwback to the Thames of the late 1700s, prisoners were kept on hulks – the *Lysander, President* and *Success* – with the police responsible for ensuring no one got within 150 metres of them. The Victorians also formed the world's first detective bureau in 1844, but the combination of water police and specialist sleuths didn't disrupt crime on the waterfront.

While Melbourne was going about its expansion in an orderly fashion, Sydney was still Sydney. Author James Maclehose, writing in 1838 in his book *Picture of Sydney,* said, 'although The Rocks were among the first parts of the township to be built on, this quarter has been little improved. Many wooden skillings and mean huts are still standing, inhabited by the poorer parts of the community. The road and footpaths are in such bad repair and so filthy, that no respectable person will pass through them if avoidable.' This was where Sydney's waterside workers lived with their families and was the first Australian home to many free settlers stumbling off ships after long, uncomfortable and often hazardous voyages.

Woolloomooloo, to the city's east and the home to John Palmer in the early days of the colony, was slowly expanding into a port area to take advantage of its deep bay. On the hills above, the governor had encouraged the affluent to build in 'a high status area which would serve as both example and chastisement to the debased populace of Sydney town'. In the latter part of the twentieth century, those hills were better known as 'Kings Cross' and home to the 'dirty half mile' and a drawcard for crooks, cops and those in pursuit of a good time.

To the west, Balmain was being settled. William Balmain, the First Fleet surgeon, had been given the land grant in 1800, and a year later sold it to fellow surgeon John Gilchrist for 5 shillings. The land remained unused, except for kangaroo trappers who took advantage of its peninsula shape to drive kangaroos from the nearby plains and corner them at the point. It wasn't until 1825 that Gilchrist began subdividing some of the land, and shipbuilding began. The boost for the area came in 1840, when a ferry service to Millers Point began – making the peninsula, at least in its early years, a fashionable alternative to the heights of Woolloomooloo.

That same year, British criminals could either breathe a sigh of relief if they weren't keen on long sea voyages, or resign themselves to a miserable existence in grimy prisons, as transportation to the colony of New South Wales came to an end. They weren't missing much according to Robert Therry, a lawyer who became a judge in Sydney in the 1830s. He observed that, for convicts, not much had changed since the first days of the colony and wrote of seeing 'out of the prisoner's barracks a party consisting of four men who bore on their shoulder a miserable convict writhing in an agony of pain. I was told that it was "only a prisoner who had been flogged and who was on his way to hospital." It often took the sufferer a week to ten days after one of these lacerations before he was sufficiently recovered to resume his labour, and I soon learned that what I had seen was at that period, an ordinary occurrence.' Therry was equally appalled that when at a police station 'a convict was sentenced to fifty lashes for not taking off his hat to a magistrate as he met him on the road'.

But those days were fortunately nearing their end and, within a few years, one single event would bring with it great change to the face of Australia, its people, businesses and the island's gateways since the arrival of European settlers in 1788 – the gold rush.

8
BOOM TIMES

William Clarke was a vicar with a sideline in geology. He became a fellow of the Geographical Society of London in 1826, travelled in Europe, and penned learned papers on the emerging science of geology. In May 1839, along with his wife and four children, he arrived in Australia to take up the post of chaplain at St Peter's, Campbelltown. That lasted a week and ended when he was appointed headmaster at The King's School in Parramatta. His poor health didn't stop him venturing out into the bush to collect fossils and rocks and, in 1841, near Hartley in the Blue Mountains, he found gold. Further adventures to the Bathurst district uncovered more.

In 1844, the excited Mr Clarke, correctly thinking that Australia was on the cusp of its first minerals boom, showed the Governor Sir George Gipps his finds. Gipps wasn't interested and told him, 'put it away Mr Clarke or we shall all have our throats cut'.

Clarke maintained his enthusiasm for gold, but did so privately, and nothing much happened until 1851 when Edward Hargraves found gold at Ophir, near Bathurst in 1851. Unlike Clarke, he didn't keep quiet.

Hargraves had gone to sea at fourteen and two years later, in 1832, arrived in Sydney. He worked on the land near Bathurst and Wollongong, collected tortoise shells in the Torres Strait, and as an agent for the General Steam Navigation Company that operated the latest in maritime technology, the steamship.

Hargraves, like thousands of others from around the globe, was drawn by the prospect of fame and fast fortune to be had in the California Gold Rush. He left Sydney in July 1849 and returned in January 1851. He hadn't struck it rich, but he'd learned the techniques of gold panning, the best places to look, and he had a cunning plan – to start his own gold rush.

On 12 February 1851, he and colleague John Lister found specks of gold near Guyong, about halfway between today's Orange and Bathurst. With the help of locals William, James and Henry Tom, the search ratcheted up. Then Hargraves did something some mining entrepreneurs allegedly did in the following century and a half – he lied about the size and potential of his discovery. In March he returned to Sydney and told the Colonial Secretary, Sir Edward Thomson, of his success – and in a bold PR move, wrote to the *Sydney Morning Herald* to tell about the rich pickings.

Hargraves was given a ten thousand pound reward by the NSW government for his find, and appointed a commissioner of crown land. The Australian gold rush had started, and by May, 300 hopefuls were prospecting around Ophir. The *Bathurst Free Press* reported, 'a complete mental madness appears to have seized almost every member of the community. There has been a universal rush to the diggings.' The paper also accurately speculated the rush would bring with it a 'complete social revolution'. In 1851, the NSW population was around 198,000, and by late July, 6000 of those had moved to the goldfields.

The Toms didn't strike it rich, and it finally dawned on them they'd been 'handled' by Hargraves. They complained to the government and were awarded £1000 each by the Legislative Council in 1853.

On 1 July 1851, barely two months after the gold rush had begun, the government passed legislation to separate Victoria from New South Wales. For the rapidly developing new city of Melbourne, then with nearly 80,000 citizens and around six million sheep grazing on more than 1200 stations, the new state was the dominant force in wool export. Geelong, closer to the wool production areas of the Western Districts, had started as a small settlement shortly after the establishment of Melbourne, and by the time Hargraves had discovered gold it had become Victoria's second city, a manufacturing centre, and a busy port with a focus on wool exports.

But there was a problem. When news of the gold finds hit Melbourne, a merchant called William Hall recalled, 'I cannot describe the effect it had upon the sober, plodding and industrious people of Melbourne. Our labourers left us by shiploads for the fields of Ophir and Sofala, and it became difficult to carry on trade, labour became so scarce and valuable.' Victoria was off to a very shaky start – but not for long.

To deal with the issue, Lieutenant Governor Charles La Trobe, on 9 June 1851, offered a reward of £200 to anyone finding a viable gold deposit within 200 miles of Melbourne. It wasn't the sort of cash that New South Wales had given Hargraves, but still tempting. By late July gold had been found in Warrandyte, Clunes and a Yarra tributary called Anderson's Creek. In August, large fields were found around Ballarat. As the year moved by, there was find after find, but the impact on the population didn't have the effect La Trobe had expected when he announced his reward. William Hall, commenting this time on the local gold rush said, 'the excitement it created in Melbourne was so intense, so all absorbing, that men seemed bereft of their senses, magistrates and constables, parsons and priests, merchants and clerks, policemen and paupers, all hastened to the Golden Point [near Ballarat]'.

On 10 October La Trobe wrote to Earl Grey, the Secretary of State for War and the Colonies, saying, not only have the idlers to be found in every community, and day labourers in town and the adjacent country, shopmen, artisans, and mechanics of every description, thrown up their employment, and in most cases, leaving their employers and their wives and families to take care of themselves, run off to the workings – but responsible tradesmen, farmers, clerks of every grade, and not a few of the superior classes have followed. Cottages are deserted, houses to let, business is at a standstill, and even schools are closed. In some of the suburbs, not a man is left and the women are known for self-protection to forget neighbours jars, and to group together to keep house. The ships in the harbour are, in a great measure, deserted. Fortunate the family, whatever its position, which retains its servants at any sacrifice. Drained of its labouring population, the price of provisions in the towns is naturally on the increase.

For the criminal fraternity who'd been developing their thieving and distribution networks along the waterfront since Batman's arrival, it was a golden time as well. Demand and supply was dramatically increasing, the focus was on gold and little else, and as Hall noted, the constables had been seduced by gold, not career prospects. Along with the basics of life on the field, miners with pockets full of cash from their success had other needs. Alcohol and prostitution were in demand and soon to arrive through the nation's ports was the first recreational drug of choice – opium – a habit brought by the Chinese prospectors.

News of the New South Wales strike hit London on 2 September 1851, when *The Times* reported finds that may 'put California to shame'. The story was picked up around the nation, in Europe, China and North America. News of even bigger strikes in Victoria followed. With the coming of yet another bleak northern hemisphere winter and the promise of a fortune in Australia, gold lust took a firm grip. With the action switching from the smaller NSW goldfields to the Victorian fields where nearly each week brought news of another lucrative strike, the Port of Melbourne became busier than Sydney, dealing with boatloads of would-be miners, their equipment and the food and clothing needed to support them. Multiculturalism had arrived in Australia but it was off to a rocky start.

Thomas Park, among the many to leave London to find a fortune, arrived in 1852, and commented that while en route, people from the 'Celestial Empire' as he called it, joined their ship, and 'loud were the complaints about having these Chinamen forced upon us. We absolutely refused to allow them to join us in the saloon.' The *Bathurst Free Press* described the Chinese prospectors as 'a race with whom we have little more in common than with a race of baboons or a tribe of orangutans'.

In September 1853, twenty ships carrying 6000 passengers were heading to Australia from Britain's Merseyside ports alone. The pace continued in October with 3000 people arriving each week, and in 1853, five ships were leaving Britain weekly.

In China, businessmen profited from onerous loans to men to fund their way to Australia – as Eric Rolls noted in *Sojourners* in 1992, the men bound for the goldfields 'put up their land as security; in some cases they mortgaged their very families' – it was the beginning of a trade in humans for cheap labour that the Triads would later use to great profit. By 1855 over thirty ships from China had arrived in Melbourne, with 6000 Chinese headed for the goldfields. Australia replaced California as the destination of choice, and Victoria as the focus. Within three years, the population of Melbourne, then barely fifteen years old, was nearly 284,000, surpassing Sydney's 242,000; six years later, in 1860, Melbourne had surged past the half million mark. It wasn't until 1891, with the gold rush long past, that Sydney returned to the top spot.

Along with the prospectors, gold brought with it a sharp rise in imports, carried in steamships and elegant clippers that were a revolution in transport. The paddle-wheeled steamers that

Hargraves had dabbled in prior to heading to California became outmoded when SS *Great Britain* was launched in 1843. The ship was designed by the engineering genius of the age, Isambard Kingdom Brunel, and seized the dual titles of first ocean-going ship to be driven by a screw (propeller), and the largest ship ever built. *Great Britain* was built to carry passengers, and was the first of the great ocean liners, with cabins for 750 people. When the ship arrived in Port Phillip in 1852, and moored in Hobson's Bay near Williamstown, she caused a stir among the population who weren't focused on gold. Four thousand people paid a shilling each to board and inspect the marvel of the age. Her average trip took 120 days, and in a career of nearly thirty years on the Australian run, carried over 15,000 immigrants and the first English cricket team to tour Australia.

The American entry into the maritime revolution was the clipper. With the demand for passage to Australia, British shipowners began by diverting ships from the Indian run, but when demand still exceeded berths, they began chartering clippers from America.

Unlike *Great Britain,* clipper ships were sail only, but of a contemporary design – replacing the slow, small and difficult to handle blunt-nosed ships that had been the staple of world shipping for centuries. The first clippers were built around Baltimore in the 1830s and were distinctive for their sleek lines, extremely tall masts, vast amount of sail, and speed. They carried cargo around Chesapeake Bay, and during the American Revolutionary War were famous for their speed and ability to break through the British blockade of Baltimore. Many of the largest were used on the China tea trade, with a sideline in opium.

Their size, speed and sailing ability meant the clippers could reduce the time to Australia and use a faster course than the older Admiralty route. It became known as the Great Circle Route – taking the ships well south of the Cape of Good Hope and deeper into the Great Southern Ocean where the westerly winds were stronger, but hazards of snow, huge waves and ice were common. The route also meant the clippers could do the trip without a stop. They reduced the time from Britain to around seventy days. *Marco Polo* set the record in 1852, when she sailed from Liverpool to Melbourne in sixty-eight days. Nine hundred and ninety passengers were crammed on board and the price of ticket was around £10, and it wasn't a comfortable trip.

The fast new ships did face one problem when arriving in Australia – their crews succumbing to gold fever. At one point, there were fifty ships lying in Port Phillip Bay without sufficient crew to take them to sea.

Passengers and shippers found themselves the victims of waterfront blackmail. Shipping goods from Britain to Australia was around £3 per ton, and moving them from the moored ship up the Yarra to the city, or to wharves being built on the side of the bay, was 30 shillings a ton, and cartage from the wharves into the city, a further sum. William Howitt, a prospector who arrived in 1852 said the cost of moving his possessions from ship to his temporary home in Melbourne was 'actually more than bringing them the previous 13,000 miles including the cost of conveying them from your house to the London Docks'.

For the dock owners, the gold rush was on the waters of Port Phillip Bay. Business was extraordinary. The port and river areas were clogged with ships and lighters. By Sunday 3 October 1853, 341 ships of varying sizes arrived from all points of the globe, carrying wheat and flour from South America, French wine, US whiskey, Scotch whisky, Irish butter, linens and cloth from Britain, toys from Germany, and inevitably white spirits (rum) from Bengal. Such was the extraordinary demand and supply some products like shoes were actually cheaper to buy in Melbourne than in stores close to where they were made in Britain.

Australia sent back gold. *The Times* of 24 November 1852 reported three ships laden with gold from the Victorian fields had arrived in London – some of it headed to the Royal Mint to be made into sovereigns and returned to Australia.

But amid the oceans of lucrative enterprises there were problems. The dock owners had focused on profit rather than practicality, and their meagre investment in infrastructure quickly became apparent. Unlike Robert Campbell and Mary Reibey, who invested in warehousing and anticipated the growth of their businesses, the Melbourne entrepreneurs hadn't thought that far ahead. Around the docklands were piles of goods sitting in the sun or the rain. To fill the void, one clever Methodist congregation offered part of their hall for storage of more valuable products.

One of the stranger imports sitting on the docks, and one that added to the hefty burden of the dock workers, was tombstones from English stonemasons who expected a booming business, based on experiences from the Californian goldfields. Their product ranged from the plain to the ornate, and most came pre-engraved so all the local artisans had to do was fill in the basics like the name of the recently deceased and the where and when. The miners in Australia were a little better behaved than in America, and stones remained on the wharves.

William Howitt wrote in 1854 'the city is crowded with all kinds of goods to repletion; the shelves of the shops are groaning and you may see piles of goods, bales and packages standing in back streets, before warehouses which are unable to take any more, and are merely protected by a tarpaulin, and sometimes not even that'.

The dock owners and their colleagues had just presented the waterfront workers with a golden opportunity. The Melbourne–Sydney rivalry has been a set piece in Australia for well over a century, however one area that the Victorians have never vied for ascendancy is in crime Yet the gold rush period in Melbourne made the Sydney criminals look like amateurs. All you had to do was stroll to the waterfront and take your pick. There was no security, and the local police force was small, ineffective and equally larcenous.

The waterfront thieves could steal to order, move the goods into the networks of trusted friends and family, and through the back door into homes or retailers. Criminals from Sydney and Van Diemen's Land headed to Melbourne to join in – like the gold rush, there were opportunities for all.

The blind eye of the law, and the opportunity for profit meant the Melbourne waterfront was also a hub for the saddest of cargo – humans. Prostitution was part of life on the goldfields, and 'Madams' could make a very comfortable living without the need for the muddy business of prospecting – but they required a supply of young women desperate enough to enter the trade or who had been press-ganged into it. Unscrupulous officers on ships would provide the names of young women who'd sailed with them to waterfront recruiters who lurked on the docks. Innocents would soon find the promise of a comfortable life was in fact long working days in the world's oldest profession. Fear, violence and isolation kept the women in place. *The Age* of 3 February 1857 described it as 'a crying evil of most hideous character'. Sadly for the women conned into the sex trade, *The Age* article didn't stir the government into action over what these days is called human trafficking. The women and their plight were quickly forgotten and the police didn't lift a finger to stop the trade.

9
SOLIDARITY FOREVER

The gold rush changed the world's view of Australia. The writer Marjorie Barnard said in her 1962 *A History of Australia* we could 'hardly fail to impress the world. Wool had offered fortunes to the few, gold to the many' and that 'nothing would could be quite the same again'. In Britain, with transportation now consigned to history, the colony's growing population presented the British Government with another opportunity.

Until then, Australia was seen as the poor relation to New Zealand for those planning on starting a new life on the other side of the planet. Sydney and Van Diemen's Land had the stigma of convict origins and the reputation of the colonies for wild and roguish behaviour didn't sit well with dour churchgoing Scottish and English aspiring settlers. One Scot who'd made the journey wrote a letter to the *Aberdeen Herald* on 20 September 1845 warning those contemplating a similar trip that business failures had become 'so numerous, pass unnoticed' and 'robbery, violence and indolence stalk through the land'. He finished by saying that he could only 'earn a miserable subsistence in this degraded colony'. Opportunity, however, triumphed over bad public relations and moral qualms, with the Scots accounting for around 15% of all the British immigrants.

The British Government also had a problem with the poor – just like the convicts of half a century before, they were becoming an embarrassment. Australia was surging ahead, the gold rush had depleted the stock of people prepared to work instead of prospect, and an elegant solution presented itself – a sort of voluntary transportation that was a forerunner of the assisted migration of the 'ten pound poms' who arrived during the boom of the 1960s. With financial assistance from the government, over 85,000 of Britain's poor arrived in Australia in the decade from 1851 and, like the Chinese, they weren't welcomed with open arms.

Like the early days of transportation, careful planning wasn't a feature of the enterprise, and so the swelling ranks of migrants were often unskilled, and even the most rudimentary of housing was in short supply. But it wasn't Britain's problem anymore. Melbourne, with its lustre of gold, was usually the first port of call on the Australian mainland and took the bulk of the new settlers. They joined the increasing number of disillusioned prospectors returning to the city with their pockets empty, and their hopes of a fortune gone. The reality of weeks of hard labour in mud and living under canvas in shanty towns with little in the way of comfort had struck home, and Melbourne at least offered the chance of an income, reasonable working conditions and somewhere dry to sleep if you were lucky.

The industrial revolution in Britain brought with it trade unions, and by the time of assisted passage to Australia, there were around 100,000 union members in Britain. Until the gold rush, industrial organisations in Australia were more like associations of skilled workers, like the Shipwrights Society of Sydney formed in 1829. These associations were trying to keep a degree of exclusivity to their work, which meant healthier profits and less competition.

An early attempt at a waterside union in Sydney in 1837, with workers collectively demanding an increase in daily pay from 3 to 4 shillings, failed and unionism went back to being part of a wish list, well behind food and shelter.

The first Australian trade union was a branch of the British Amalgamated Society of Engineers, formed on the voyage from Britain by twenty-seven men onboard *Frances Walker* in 1852. They'd been locked out of work in the factories and, rather than starve, decided to try their luck in Australia. They brought with them news of labour struggles, and the hopes of what a union could do to improve the life of the workingman. Because of the members' expertise with fitting, turning and the maintenance of steam-powered engines, they soon became an essential part of the Australian waterfront. Bradley Bowden in *Labour History May 2011* said of the society that by the 1880s it was powerful and 'monopolised the supply of fitters and turners. Without a coterie of ASE men, and a sprinkling of members from its specialised rivals such as the Boilermakers Society, more complex undertakings such as locomotive and ship repair were impossible.'

The arriving UK unionists found a bustling waterfront; wharf labouring was a highly desirable and well-paid job. With Melbourne's ports crowded with ships arriving, and population numbers soaring, shipowners found themselves desperately in need of labour and were prepared to pay for it. In 1852, labourers were working an eight-hour day in two four-hour shifts, and paid 30 shillings per day – but the good times didn't last.

The destitute and disillusioned were sleeping rough around the dockland, grabbing shelter for the night wherever they could and vying for labouring jobs to keep them alive. Dock work had always been on a day-to-day basis depending on ship arrival and departures, with the destitute vying for work along with the experienced hands. Brawls were common as men fought for a job at low rates and long hours. The shipowners sensed a chance to reduce their costs, and men who would jump at any chance, even with lousy pay and conditions, were in their sights.

For the stevedores of Port Phillip Bay, the modernisation of shipping added to the problem of oversupply of labour. On a ship driven by sails full of breeze, assuring the load is properly placed and secured is a skilled task and essential to prevent the ship capsizing in heavy seas and winds, particularly those on the Great Southern route. The arrival of steamships, however, designed with easier cargo access and with better stability and cranes to make loading and unloading faster, reduced the need for these skills. When combined with the plethora of willing workers, the affluent days of the early stevedores were on the wane shortly after they'd started.

In 1857, Australia had one of its first major dockland strikes. Around 1853, the stonemasons had won an eight-hour day from their employers in Sydney, and they'd repeated their success in Melbourne in 1856, with a march of around 700 men through the streets. The 1857 dock strike was prompted by the stonemasons' success, but it wasn't 'union' organised action. Instead it was the collective decision of around 100 men to walk off the job to make the point to the shipowners that they needed shorter working hours and better pay. It was a reasonable plan, but failed to factor in the legion of recent arrivals such as Britain's assisted poor or failed prospectors, who were happy to fill the void for whatever money they could get. Shipowners one, stevedores nil.

According to *The Age* the owners had been allowed to 'run wild' and were 'amenable to no one, not even an optional surveillance, but may risk the lives of seamen, and the property of the community, precisely as he pleases'. The waterside workers didn't rate a mention – they were so far below the public's radar they didn't matter. Organised waterfront unions were the fodder of talk in pubs but were nearly two decades away.

Sydney waterside workers were also not having much luck. The Rocks was still their home – crowded, filthy, and ramshackle. The gold rush brought with it large numbers of Chinese immigrants who used The Rocks as either a stopover en route to the fields around Bathurst and Young, or a place to contemplate their future after failing as prospectors. A by-product of the migration was the arrival of smallpox, which, in the abysmal conditions of The Rocks, spread with deadly ease.

Into this scene walked a man who would be pivotal in the development of maritime Australia.

Thomas Sutcliff Mort was born on 23 December 1816 in Bolton near Manchester. The town was a major textile manufacturer during the industrial revolution and Mort grew up in an aspiring middle-class family, but the family cash flow, owing to his father's less than successful business dealings, didn't meet their aspirations. At the end of his schooling Mort went straight to work in a dead-end job as a clerk, rather than university or a post in the family business. Mort was restless, and when an opportunity arose for a job in Sydney in the trading firm of Aspinall Browne & Co, he seized it. He arrived in Sydney in February 1838, followed by his younger brothers Henry and James, motivated to restore the family fortunes and reputation.

Wool was still king, and Mort saw an opportunity. In 1843 he revolutionised the way it was sold by bringing a structure to the process. Instead of the unruly auctions where wool had been one of many commodities on offer, he started regular, specialised auctions where he brought together the best producers and buyers. Building on his success, Mort moved into rural auctions, trade financing, and acted as a wool broker between the primary producers and the London market – a blueprint for the wool broking firms that prospered in the twentieth century. His older brother William handled the London end of the business.

In addition to auctioneering and brokering, Mort expanded his business interests into the sugar industry around Brisbane's Moreton Bay, which was poised to grow significantly, railways, mining and media – financing Henry Parkes' *Empire* broadsheet newspaper, first published in December 1850 – and later pioneered sending refrigerated cargoes of meat to Britain. However, one of his most memorable ventures was his dockyard that opened in Balmain on 1 January 1855.

Rupert Murdoch once said that the key to success was to 'find the gap' in the market – a talent Mort possessed in large measure.

In the early 1850s the large steamships heading to Australia with immigrants, cargo and the all-important mail from Britain needed somewhere at the end of their long journey for repairs, as did the colliers bringing coal from Newcastle to feed the energy needs of both Sydney and Melbourne. At that time, there were no docks anywhere in the Southern Hemisphere capable of undertaking major work – the docks were suited to dealing with smaller timber vessels and their comparatively lightweight fittings and not the hefty new steam-powered iron ships and complex machinery.

The 1853 arrival of SS *Chuson,* the first mail steamer to arrive from Britain, showed the gap to Mort and his soon-to-be business partner Captain Thomas Rowntree, a master mariner and shipbuilder. They bought land on the northern side of the Balmain waterfront at Waterview Bay. The location was ideal – offering shelter from Sydney's savage southerly and westerly winds, and deep water up to the shoreline.

Mort's Dock, then called the Waterview Dry Dock Company, opened a year before the government built Fitzroy Dry Dock on nearby Cockatoo Island, and was the only dock of its type for thousands of miles. The closest other dock was Bombay. The first customer was SS *Hunter,* a mail steamer on the coastal run from Newcastle, in March 1855. Rowntree ran the operation and by 1861 found himself in conflict with the government who'd breached their undertaking not to take on private work at Cockatoo Island Dock. He decided it was all too hard and left the company. The dock was renamed Mort's Dock in 1863, and after a few other operators hadn't made a success of it, Mort took over in 1866, expanding from shipbuilding and repair into general engineering, building railway locomotives, and making steel pipe for the water supply. His intervention was timely and the business prospered.

On the early steamers that were the core of the dock's business, the work was hard, dirty and dangerous – there was no workers' compensation, no occupational health and safety, and serious injury was common. The men worked with hot metal and sharp cutting tools. They scrubbed the steel hulls clean, clambered up cranes and masts, painted, and the worst job of all – cleaned the coal-fired boilers. Lew Hillier in *Meet the Ship Painters and Dockers* described the lot of those unlucky enough to get that latter task, writing, 'when men had worked inside boilers covered in carbon black and oil from the oil tanks, no matter how much they scrubbed their bodies and soaked themselves for days after, the outlines of their bodies would remain on the bedsheets as the residue of these substances came out of the pores of their skin'.

The community supported injured men. Fred Whitton had been a worker at Mort's Dock and was a major fundraiser for those hurt in the workplace, organising 'moonlight or weekend excursions or perhaps a band recital or a "smoke concert" to raise some little assistance for the injured worker'. Fred was later seriously injured and the fundraising put together enough cash for him to buy a tobacconist and stationery store in Mort Street, Balmain, which became a gathering place for men who'd later be the core of the Balmain Labourers Union.

Balmain had been a suburb for the well-to-do, but with the arrival of the dock, and associated engineering works and wharves, the population demographic changed. A large number of skilled and unskilled labourers flooded into the area and the affluent started looking elsewhere. Small, often poorly built workers' cottages started springing up on the Balmain Peninsula. They were generally attached row houses, reminiscent of the housing that had sprung up in the industrial cities of Britain – narrow so more could be stacked along the street. Luxury was a house with a front door opening onto a hallway running down one side. Two bedrooms if you were lucky – one for the parents and one for the children, a small living room with kitchen at the rear.

Laundry, rudimentary bathing and a toilet – often just a hole in the ground – were in a lean-to attached to the back. Sophistication for the lucky few was a 'pan' toilet with a removable receptacle collected by the 'night soil carters' who used the narrow lanes joining some of the properties to collect the full pans and deliver the empty. Thieves found the lanes ideal to sneak into houses and burgle them, but in places like Balmain, the growing unity of the community meant you never stole locally.

The emphasis on speed and quantity rather than the quality of construction meant the area had the makings of a slum, which happened within a few decades. Walter Bunning, an architect and town planner, wrote in 1947 in a foreword to a symposium on 'Housing Problems in Australia' that these properties were, 'cheap, mean houses built all round and in between the factories. With no legislative restrictions to set even modest standards of space and light, or even the humanitarian considerations of health and privacy, row upon row of workers' dwellings were jammed into every street.' Women and children stuck to their homes; and husbands, when not working, could be found at the small pubs that had sprung up on corners close to the dock, handily located to catch the men as they finished their shifts. The development of Balmain was a reversal of its earlier gentrification – another century would pass before it spruced up to become a desirable inner city suburb again.

Rowntree and the dock's general manager James Franki lived in Balmain, but in mansions 'as distant from their industry as possible and clear of the over-crowding clusters of workmen's cottages' as unionist and historian Izzy Wyner wrote in *With Banner Unfurled* in 1983. Mort didn't succumb to the local temptations and proximity to the office – he preferred the eastern suburbs and bought property in Darling Point in 1846, calling it 'Greenoaks'. The substantial pile built on the site was in the fashionable Gothic style and designed by Mort's friend, the architect Edmund Blacket. It included a gallery open to the public which displayed decorative arts Mort had collected on his visits to Britain, and lavish gardens – Mort was both a fan of the arts and a keen gardener. These days, the house is called 'Bishop's Court' and is home to the Sydney Anglican Archbishop. Mort was also an avid supporter of the church and had Blacket build St Marks on land beside his home.

Under Mort's guidance, the dry dock and engineering works in Balmain became the largest privately owned business in the colony and, with the size of the work force, ripe for the formation of a union.

The waterfront workers had been behind the pace in the spread of the union movement and it wasn't until September 1872 that they took the first serious step past muttering in the workplace or griping over a beer with their mates in the local pubs. They were driven by a need to organise to improve their wages, reduce their working hours and make their work places safer. Melbourne had been the first with its Trades Hall Committee forming in 1856, followed by the Labour Council of Sydney in 1871, which Raymond Markey described *In Case of Oppression* (2009) as 'a small coterie of craft unions with tiny memberships'. Workers in rural areas, like shearers, followed much later. Unionism was off to a slow start. The first meeting to form what would be known as the 'Sydney Wharf Labourers Union' happened at the Orient Hotel in The Rocks on Tuesday 17 September.

The meeting was prompted by an unsuccessful strike where men who worked on a casual or weekly hire basis – and at the whim of the tides, weather and shipowners – demanded a pay increase to 10 shillings for a ten-hour day (the average was eight shillings) with a rate of 1 shilling 6 pence per hour for work at night. A collective and consolidated approach was needed – the stonemasons' success and the union movement spreading throughout Britain, where demands for both money and working conditions were the focus, provided the blueprint. One unnamed union member quoted by Margo Beasley in her book *Wharfies* wrote, they had 'set out on the long road of self-sacrificing struggle of uniting all of the waterfront cargo workers into a single independent body strong enough to enforce the preference for the work, ship and shore'. The union would become the Waterside Workers Federation (WWF).

The *Sydney Morning Herald* reported on 18 September 1872 that around 400 to 500 men gathered to elect a committee to 'frame the rules. The utmost order and decorum prevailed and from the enthusiasm manifested, there is no doubt the society will become successful.' The paper also noted 'the object of the society is to benefit the conditions of the labourer, socially, morally and politically'.

It was a similar story around Australia. In Adelaide, the waterfront workers, described in a recruiting poster as men who 'must be powerful, steady and of sober habits', formed the Port Adelaide Working Men's Association in 1872, and were described by one journalist as 'a set of honest, hardworking men'. Their purpose was to raise funds to support members in financial trouble or with illness and injury, and fight for 'a fair day's wage for a fair day's work'. Up in Brisbane, the eight-hour day was becoming common in the workplace, but on the city's small docks, the government, wharf and shipowners were resisting the change. Dock workers went on strike, demanding similar treatment to other workers, and while they got their wish, they had to reduce their wages – it was a victory but at high cost.

Melbourne dock workers were also on strike in 1872 and were as unsuccessful as their Sydney counterparts. Melbourne's regular workers tried to prevent the use of 'outsiders', which led to the 1874 formation of a co-operative society, with membership costing £1 each, and targeted to make sure that first preference for work was given to members; men's hours were formalised into rosters and they were led by 'work leaders' who were also co-op members. It was the beginning of the 'closed shop' that would guarantee dock workers' rights, improve their lives, forge tight-knit local communities, plague the nation with frequent strikes, and provide the breeding ground for criminals from petty thieves to leaders of crime syndicates.

The target of one of the first major waterfront industrial disputes was Thomas Mort. He'd been savvy to the changing industrial landscape and in 1870 taken the then unusual step of giving his workers an equity in their workplace by offering shares in the company – some took him up on the offer, which meant the management was shared by Mort, his executives and 'shareholder' representatives. It was a timely move – the Trades and Labour Council was formed in May 1871, gathering not only the fledgling unions and their supporters, but looking to the political muscle a unified workers' bloc could flex. One key member, Francis Dixon said that it was, 'expedient and highly desirable that labour should be directly represented in Parliament'.

The political climate was warming up and the goodwill created by Mort's arrangement was short-lived. In late 1873, unionists served him with a log of claims, demanding an eight-hour workday along with a pay increase of around 16%. The claim was rejected and 1000 workers went on strike.

Mort realised early in the strike that the workers were resolute, so rather than prolong the misery, he capitulated. The workers had a major victory.

Mort was looking toward retirement, and began preparations to take his company public, and in 1875 Mort's Dock and Engineering Company was incorporated. He died on his farm Bodalla on the New South Wales south coast on 9 May 1878. The industrial disputes of his last years were put aside, and his former workers commissioned a sculpture of him by American-born Pierce Connolly. It was unveiled in Macquarie Place in 1888 at a ceremony attended by hundreds of Mort's former employees who'd given up a day's pay to be there as a mark of their esteem.

These moments of goodwill between employer and employee were a honeymoon. The times were about to drastically change with the arrival of a powerful union movement and a major political party – both conceived, born and nurtured on the waterfronts of Sydney and Melbourne.

One of the leaders of the strike was Jacob Garrard, a keen follower of Dixon and a man on the verge of a career in the union movement and politics.

Garrard was born in England in 1846, and at the age of thirteen, migrated with his family to New Zealand, where he'd worked on coastal ships and apprenticed as an engineer. He arrived in Sydney in 1867, bringing with him some firm views on the rights of the workingman, including the introduction of the forty-eight hour working week already in place in New Zealand. He moved into Balmain, living in one of the simple houses, and began working for Mort. He was also a member of the Amalgamated Society of Engineers.

Garrard's work on the successful Mort strike boosted his career, and in 1880 he became the member for Balmain in parliament – then an unpaid position – while keeping up his day job as an engineer now on the Pyrmont docks. He rowed from Balmain to Pyrmont for work, and at 4 pm he'd row home, change, then head to Parliament House in Macquarie Street, sometimes for an all-night sitting – 'a dog's life', he recalled in an interview marking his eightieth birthday published in the *Sydney Morning Herald* on 3 June 1926. He rose quickly in the ranks and in 1885–86 was Minister for Public Works and Railways in the government of Sir John Robertson, and later became Minister for Education and Minister for Labour and Industry. He lost his seat in 1898 and became President of the Water Board – at one point one of the major clients for Mort's engineering workshops. In the interview, Garrard made it clear he was no fan of the approach of the labour movement of which he'd been a founder. He said, 'in the old days some of the employers were tyrants. I have worked under the type. But some workmen, when they come into power, are the biggest tyrants of all.'

10
STRIKE!

Mort's Dock and its related infrastructure, along with Sydney's natural charm as a harbour, saw Port Jackson return to prominence as the nation's premier port during the 1880s. The gold rush had put the nation on the global map and brought with it strong investment both locally and from offshore, and wool was still the leading export. Australians were enjoying one of the world's highest per capita incomes, but it wasn't evenly shared. Around dockland areas like Williamstown, Balmain and The Rocks, men were still working long and often dangerous days, and the adjacent suburbs where they lived with their families were deteriorating.

The news of their fellow dock workers in Britain was worse and gave a glimpse of what might happen if they failed to organise themselves into bodies to fight for basic rights. The British Parliament heard evidence from Colonel Birt, the General Manager of London's Millwall docks, who said, 'the poor fellows are miserably clad, scarcely with a boot on their foot, in a most miserable state. These are men who come to work in our docks who come on without having a bit of food in their stomachs, perhaps since the previous day.' Ben Tillett, the British trade unionist and later politician, described the scene of men vying for jobs as 'a crowd of men, who, in their eagerness to obtain employment, trample each other under foot, and like beasts they fight each other for the chance of a day's work'. Their families lived in slums clinging to the fringe of the docklands, and disease and petty crime were rife. The Australian docks were relatively civilised by comparison.

Spurred on by the news from Britain, and the divide between the workers' lot and that of the affluent, the union movement was growing. Taking a lead from Sydney, the Victorians formed the Wharf Labourers Union of Victoria in 1880 and the Melbourne Coal Lumpers Union – for the men with the filthy task of unloading coal – in 1881, but neither lasted.

The Port Phillip Labourers' Eight Hours Association was formed in 1882, and later had a name change to the Port Phillip Stevedores' Association – according to waterfront union historian Margo Beasley the name change was to include the word 'stevedore' to emphasise the superior skills of the stevedore above those of the unskilled labourer also competing for work on the docks. Like their kindred spirits in Sydney, the members came from the clustered community surrounding Hobson's Bay (Williamstown). The union was early to recognise that crime was part of waterfront life, and one of its rules was 'any member of the Association found guilty of broaching cargo or pillaging, upon proper representation from the employers of conviction by a court of justice, shall be summarily dealt with by the General Committee'. It wasn't, as history has proven, an effective deterrent nor did the acknowledgement of the issue last. The union was joined in 1885 by the Melbourne Wharf Labourers' Union, formed after a walkout by dock workers. Muriel Heagney, a trade unionist and feminist, wrote of their strike that it was 'a spontaneous but ill-considered gesture. The men had no leaders and no definite policy. All they had was a common grievance.' Both unions opened branches in the nearby wool port of Geelong.

In 1883, one of the most significant players in Australian union and crime history was formed. The Balmain Workers Union, which became infamous as the Federated Painters and Dockers, represented the men who did the dirty, hard and dangerous work at places like Mort's Dock. These were the men who lived with their families in the decaying houses of Balmain. Their associates on the wharves – who loaded and unloaded ships – formalised their union on 10 January that year, registering themselves under the Trade Union Act. Over the next few years, strikes for better pay and conditions were common but equally as common was their failure – most were broken by 'scab' labour. With regular failures, it was obvious the unions needed some political clout to make their cases.

News of the Great London Dock Strike in 1889 provided further stimulus for the unions. Work on London's docks was seasonal – sugar came from the West Indies; the cornerstone of British life, tea, came in from the Far East; timber mainly from the great forests of northern Europe; and wool from Australia and New Zealand. In the time before modern communication, the weather and port delays meant that the arrival of the ships could be sporadic, with days when nothing would arrive, to dribs and drabs or a fleet. Notice of arrivals was often when the ship was sighted either sailing or steaming into the Thames. Like in Australian ports, most work was on an 'on call' basis rather than full-time employment. You didn't work, you didn't get paid. There were two calls on the docks each day, either for a full or part day of work, and employers were keen to limit the amount of hours they had to pay for. Those not selected for the first call returned later for the second call in the hope of grabbing a few hours. Of the system, Ben Tillett said, 'a foreman or contractor walks up and down with the air of a dealer in a cattlemarket'.

In the year before, the growing militancy of the British workforce saw women – the match girls – striking at the Bryant and May match factory. Their days were up to fourteen hours long, and they worked with white phosphorous, which was highly volatile and risky for the health. Around 1400 women at the factory went on strike in July 1888, and two weeks later management capitulated to the demands for better pay, safer conditions and a process to resolve disputes. In the first half of 1889, a strike by gas workers achieved shorter hours and improved pay.

On 14 August 1889, Tillett led workers from London's West India Dock on a strike. The catalyst was the unloading of *Lady Armstrong*. The usual practice had been that if the unloading was done quickly, a bonus, or 'plus' payment was given to the men. However, the market was in one of the occasional slump periods and competition for business on the docks was extreme, so the management had engaged in price-cutting. One of the early cuts to compensate for their reduced revenue was to the amount of the 'plus' payment; the incentive to work fast became an incentive to strike. Under Tillett, the dock workers demanded an increase to 6 pence per hour, an increase in overtime pay to 8 pence per hour, an abolition of the 'plus' system and a guarantee that, if picked to work, they were entitled to four hours pay.

Picket lines were set up at the dock yard gates, the men marched through the City of London in an orderly protest and a manifesto was published, announcing 'we now appeal to members of all trade unions for joint action with us, and especially those whose work is in connection with shipping – engineers and fitters, boiler makers, ships' carpenters, etc. and also the coal heavers, ballast men and lighter men. We also appeal to the public at large for contributions and support on behalf of the dock labourers.' Non-union labour, known as 'blacklegs', were persuaded to join the strikers, so the usual strike-breaking methods were denied to the dock owners.

The dock management took a strong line, keen to protect their revenue and the shareholders' dividends. Sydney Holland, director of the dock, gave an interview on 16 August, saying, what the cost would be of granting the demands of the men, I cannot exactly say, but it would be at least £100,000 and that would mean we should have to raise our rates. We cannot afford an advance in wages, for it would either destroy any possibility of dividend to the shareholders of the joint companies or tend to drive shipping from the port. When the pinch comes, as come it must, the hopes of the strikers will receive a severe shock and I shall be surprised if there is any backbone left.

He'd failed to understand the resolve of his opposition and the severe shock would be his.

Tillett was a canny political operator and knew that for victory he needed both strength and solidarity. By 27 August he had achieved just that – his men were joined by members of the Amalgamated Stevedores' Union along with other waterfront trades and factory workers from the East End. Around 130,000 men were now on strike and the port had come to a standstill. The unions handed out around 25,000 meal tickets each day to keep families fed.

The *Evening News and Post* reported on 26 August that 'dockmen, lightermen, bargemen, cement workers, carmen, ironworkers and even factory girls are coming out. If it goes on a few days longer, all London will be on holiday. The great machine by which five millions of people are fed and clothed will come to a dead stop, and what is to be the end of it all? The proverbial small spark has kindled a great fire which threatens to envelop the whole metropolis.'

With neither side prepared to budge, the strike was running longer than planned. By early September, funds were running out and families were staring down the barrel at starvation. Harry Champion, treasurer of the strike committee recalled, 'things looked very black indeed – for though the collections made in workshops and in the streets, supplemented by contributions from the older trade unions and from private individuals, had reached a considerable sum, they were totally inadequate to provide even a shilling a day for a tenth of the families who were without means of subsistence'.

Enter the recently organised Australian waterfront unions. In those desperate first days of London's September, when capitulation simply to feed families was considered, £150 from the Brisbane Wharf Labourers Union arrived along with the promise of much more to come. The *Pall Mall Gazette* of 5 September reported action in Australia,

> meetings at which resolutions of sympathy with the strikers are passed are being held nightly throughout Victoria, and a similar movement is on foot in Sydney, Brisbane, Adelaide and Hobart. A large and important meeting of citizens was held here yesterday at which resolutions were adopted expressing sympathy with the London dock workers on strike, and promising to support them to obtain their demands. The Chairmen announced that over £500 had been collected from all classes of the inhabitants, including Cabinet Ministers, and nearly all the members of the Queensland Parliament.

Australia would be there – at least in spirit. The Australian supporters raised around £30,000, putting life back into the strike by guaranteeing families could eat – the largest single donation was £500 from the Sydney Wharf Labourers Union.

Faced with a strike that was crippling his city, Lord Mayor Sir Henry Isaacs convened the Mansion House Committee to broker a peace – Ben Tillett was advocate for the workers, and John Burn for the dock owners. On 16 September the strikers returned to work with nearly all their claims met. Burns said of the outcome,

> labour of the humbler kind has shown its capacity to organise itself; its solidarity; its ability. The labourer has learned that combination can lead him to anything and everything. He has

tasted success as the immediate fruit of combination, and he knows that the harvest he has just reaped is not the utmost he can look to gain. Conquering himself, he has learned that he can conquer the world of capital whose generals have been the most ruthless of his oppressors.

A by-product was the surge in union membership in Britain from 750,000 in 1888 to 1.5 million by 1892.

Closer to home, the industrial climate was also on the boil. In early July 1890, the Amalgamated Shearers Union placed a boycott on the use of non-union labour in shearing sheds, and the following month, the Mercantile Marine Officers notified its members that negotiations with the Steamship Owners of Victoria over a log of claims with regard to pay and conditions had broken down after six years. One significant link between the two was William Guthrie Spence, the head of the shearers' union.

Spence was a Scot from the Orkney Islands. Born in 1846, he arrived with his parents in Geelong in 1852 as part of a tide hoping to make their fortune in gold. Though only a small child at the time, he recalled being at Eureka Stockade in 1854, and said that life on the goldfields 'made such a deep impression on my youthful mind that nothing but the grave will efface it'. He went on to pivotal positions in the mining unions, and as a natural negotiator, and as the *Australian Dictionary of Biography* noted, 'genial and imperturbable', spearheaded their industrial campaigns.

Spence wasn't a rousing public speaker, but he was a fine listener, personable and once quipped he'd 'never missed a conference'. In 1886, he was poached to lead the new shearers' union, which, with the itinerant life of shearers, moving from shed to shed around the bush, had been difficult to organise. The *Shearer's Record* reported in April 1889 that Spence 'was received with open arms, and in very few incidences indeed did he meet with refusal to join the new union. The fact of Mr Spence being connected with it gave the shearers confidence in the outcome as several of them had heard of the good work he had done in furthering the cause of trade unionism, and as leading executive officer of the Amalgamated Miners' Association.'

By 1890 he'd unionised around 85% of Australia's shearing sheds. Spence said of his meetings around the country that he 'was not, as generally understood, a professional agitator, but as a sanitary inspector come to stir up stagnant pools'.

Spence succeeded with his stirring – aided by letting the pastoralists know that he and his union would work with other unions to prevent non-union sheared wool being exported. It was originally intended as a bluff, but one that the pastoralists called, sending non-union wool to Sydney for export. However, the pastoralists were better at wool production than commercial intelligence gathering and the wool arrived for export at a time when the Mercantile Marine Officers Association, who represented the ships' officers, were poised to strike.

On 15 August 1890, the mercantile officers began their strike – precipitated by the shipowners refusing to let them affiliate with the Melbourne Trades Hall Council. Officers walked off ships berthed around the nation's ports, and as ships arrived, their officers joined the strike. Within days, trade between Victoria and Tasmania stopped. On 19 August, the Sydney wharf labourers joined the strike.

By that time, the Sydney Wharf Labourers Union had over 2000 members and was the largest urban union in the country. Margo Beasley said in *Wharfies* that the strength of the union was a 'great tribute to its largely unskilled and illiterate membership'. The union paid their men £1 a day in strike pay. Coal lumpers, seaman and other unions followed, resulting in gas and coal shortages that grabbed the attention of the broader population.

Brisbane workers joined the strike as well, followed by strikes up the Queensland coast. By September, 50,000 were on strike and the country, reliant on exports for profitability, was grinding to a standstill. One positive was that London dock workers remembered their Australian colleagues, and sent around £20,000 to provide support to the strikers.

The strike resulted in massive public meetings. In Melbourne, then a city of 400,000, a crowd estimated to be almost a quarter of the population gathered in Flinders Park to talk about arbitration and workers' rights. The gathering was well behaved, but police and military were prepared for any eventuation. The day before, Colonel Tom Price, then the commanding officer of the Victorian Mounted Rifles, told his men who were to be at Flinders Park to support the police in maintaining order, 'I do not think your aid will be required, but if it is, let there be no half measures with what you do. If the order is given to fire, don't let me see one rifle pointed up in the air. Fire low and lay them out.'

In Sydney, the meetings were on a much smaller scale, with the largest in George Street North in The Rocks where around 7000 gathered. The *Sydney Morning Herald* reported on 8 September the street was 'filled by a seething mass of humanity. It seemed as though all Sydney were out to participate in or gaze upon the spectacle of labour defying capital.'

The 'capital' responded by transporting bales of wool through the city to the wharves at Circular Quay. On 24 September, around 35,000 shearers and shed hands joined the strike. The months of hardship and high passion came to an end in November as the maritime strike crumbled. On 5 November, the Sydney Wharf Labourers Union directed their members to return to work. One said his union was 'smashed'. It was a pragmatic decision as many of their membership had joined the 'scabs' working on the docks to keep their families fed. Melbourne wharf labourers returned to work on 10 November, joining the non-union labourers that had been working the docks during the strike to keep basic services operating. Geoffrey Moorhouse, in his 1999 book *Sydney: Story of a City*, wrote that 'a week after the strike's end, a meeting of the SWLU was a stark contrast to the union's pre-strike circumstances. Where formerly it had nearly 2000 financial members anticipating full employment at increased rates for reduced hours, its membership was now splintered with at least 800 former members debarred from the union because they had worked with non-union labour. The unions five guinea membership fee quickly slipped to a paltry one shilling.'

The maritime officers who'd caused the dispute went back to work in late November – on the terms dictated by their employers, including no affiliation with the Trades Hall, and leaving an embittered union movement in a state of disarray. The shipowners and stevedoring firms now had the upper hand and used it. Lucy Turnbull, writing in *Sydney: Biography of a City,* aptly described the system of selecting waterfront workers for a day's work as 'sometime arbitrary and capricious'.

Author Laurence Fitzhardinge wrote in *W M Hughes and the Waterside Workers* 'members of the union [SWLU] were blacklisted and its organisers hunted off the wharves. In some cases "company unions" were formed, to which the men had to contribute one and half pence out of every shilling earned in order to get employment. Unskilled labour in the nineties was superabundant and the men dared not resist. Wages were very low, work was irregular.'

Stories of harsh treatment were common – one man said that he'd been put off work while swimming in the harbour to push wool bales from a capsized barge. Complaints were dealt with by blacklisting. Payback was decades away.

Unsurprisingly, the SWLU membership continued to drop until 1896 when only 100 remained and the executive made the decision to forget the old wounds and open membership to those they'd kicked out six years before.

Two months after the end of the maritime strike, shearers at the Logan Downs Station in Queensland were asked to sign a contract designed to break the union's power, and rolling strikes broke out around Queensland's woolsheds. Unlike the maritime dispute, it was violent with riots, assaults, and the arrest of unionists by armed soldiers. The strike lasted until July with the shearers defeated by poverty and the prospect of a cold and hungry winter. Spence was swift to try to deflect the blame elsewhere, saying 'backed by a corrupt and capitalistic press, and by governments of the colonies, the employers have won a temporary victory in a strike which they boast of having fomented', and warned that 'at no distant date the tables will assuredly be turned and justice and truth will prevail'.

Failure by Spence to achieve his ends, or accurately predict the near future, wasn't an impediment to a political career – he was elected to the NSW Legislative Assembly as the member for Cobar from 1898 to 1901, and after Federation, the Member for Darling from 1901 to 1917. His parliamentary career ended when he sided with W. M. 'Billy' Hughes with his support for conscription for World War I.

With two major losses on the run for the unionists, the NSW Labour Defence Council observed, 'the time has come when trade unionists must use the parliamentary machine that in the past has used them'.

The parliamentary machine kicked into gear – not in stylish buildings designed by Francis Greenway in Macquarie Street, but in a corner pub in one of the poorest suburbs in Sydney: Balmain.

11
THE CONTENDERS

Balmain was the perfect fit for the foundation of a political party to represent the workers. By 1891 it was home to a second generation of the labourers and skilled tradesmen working the waterfront industries from Balmain, the government docks on Cockatoo Island through to Sydney Cove, and the factories that covered this populous and now industrialised part of inner western Sydney. A close-knit community had been forged through hard work, uncertainty, poverty and the recent failure of their unions. They also had a common purpose to improve their lot. Balmain, with NSW elections looming, was both the right place and the right time to stop complaining into the head of well-poured beer, and get serious about politics and power.

The *Sydney Morning Herald* on Saturday 4 April 1891 carried an advertisement placed by the Trades and Labour Council, for 'meetings to inaugurate' branches of the Labour Electoral League of New South Wales. That night, a meeting was held at the Labour Hall in Darling Street, Balmain, (now part of the Unity Hall Hotel) and the *Herald* reported,

> A public meeting was held in the Labour Hall, Darling-street, Balmain, on Saturday evening, for the purpose of forming the

first branch of the Labour Electoral League of New South Wales. The meeting which was organised by the Balmain Labourers' Union, was a great success. Amongst those who occupied seats on the platform were several members of the Trades and Labour Council. The various speakers dealt at length upon the principal planks contained in the labour platform recently adopted by the council and published in these columns, and very strongly urged the necessity of unity and of a solid labour vote at the next general election. It was pointed out that the workers should sink all prejudices in reference to the fiscal policy, and should not allow personal feeling in any way to influence them but to support in a body the candidate chosen by a majority of votes by the representatives of the unionists.

The article said the speakers told the meeting that if the workers would stand shoulder to shoulder and allow no split in their ranks, they would have a majority of representatives in the next Parliament, and would be able to claim their rights, which were now encroached upon in a most dastardly manner by the capitalists.

The report noted the speeches were 'frequently applauded by the enthusiastic meeting' and 'a large number ... handed in their names as intending members.'

During the shearers' strike and its immediate aftermath, the Queenslanders had been busily organising themselves into a political party, but the meeting at Balmain was the first cohesive move to what was to become the Australian Labor Party. Among the speakers that first night were William Holman, recently arrived from London and later to be the second Labor Premier of New South Wales, and William Morris Hughes, a not so recent arrival from London and destined for even greater things. The two could not have been more different. Holman, then barely twenty-one years old, tall, pale, with flowing curly hair, privately educated and lacking in humour, was in contrast to the sun-burned, short and slightly built Hughes who had an affinity for the workingman and a robust sense of humour. Hughes would soon outshine Holman.

Hughes was born in Pimlico on 25 September 1862 to Welsh parents, William and Jane. His father was a carpenter at the nearby House of Lords and a deacon of the Particular Baptist Church. Hughes was only seven when his mother died, and he went to live with his father's sister in Llandudno, in the northern end of Wales. In 1874 he returned to London, rejoined his father and started his working life as a student teacher.

Shortly after midday on 6 December 1884, William Morris 'Billy' Hughes, an 'assisted migrant' and one of 408 steerage passengers on board SS *Duke of Westminster*, stepped down the gangplank and onto Australian soil in Brisbane. Frank C. Browne, in *They Called Him Billy*, wrote that Hughes had been staring out the porthole as the ship made its way up the brown stretch of the Brisbane River toward the city, and beside him was a 'remittance man'. 'What a place', the remittance man groaned, 'not even a house in sight, much less a pub. Of course, no civilized man could stay here. I'm off as soon as I can rake up the fare. What about you?' According to Browne, the diminutive Hughes, then just twenty-two years old, around 155 centimetres tall and around fifty-five kilograms, said, 'Well, I'm going to stay, this is a young country – I'm a young man. If I can't do well here by the blithering blazes I don't deserve to survive.'

For a man who would play a pivotal role in Australia's history Hughes' maritime experience was limited. Stepping ashore in Australia, he was unsure of what to expect – Britain's knowledge of its colony was limited to notions of gold rushes and rogues, or another India replete with staff to cater to your every whim, or a new country without class prejudice. Hughes, believing his London teaching experience would open doors, approached the Queensland Department of Education and was offered a post at Thargomindah, a fly speck on the map about 1100 kilometres west of Brisbane. He did a quick calculation and decided the salary of £72 per year, after the deduction of living expenses, would leave him with £7 to spend. He declined the offer and, after three unsuccessful weeks job hunting, was penniless and sleeping in the Botanical Gardens.

His first stroke of fortune was an offer from a German who owned a pineapple plantation. With no other choice, Hughes accepted the offer of 10 shillings a week and a fourteen-hour day. The German threw in accommodation in a lean-to that provided little else than shelter from the rain. Hughes got to meet Australia's unique fauna close-up, and as Browne noted, acquired an 'undying dislike for exotic fruit'. In hindsight, the teaching job was looking good.

Hughes didn't last long in the pineapple business, and soon drifted to Western Queensland taking itinerant jobs, like a tally clerk at a railway shed, a grape picker, sleeper cutter and general hand around cattle stations. So miserable was his existence that volunteering for the Queensland Defence Force was an improvement. The force had been raised because of a perceived threat from the Russians after the 'Battle for Kushka' in which they seized Afghan territory – offending the British and causing a chill in diplomatic relations.

Fortunately the Russians decided against attacking a country most of them hadn't heard of let alone knew how to get to, and so Hughes returned to civilian life after an unspectacular military career guarding a coal hulk on Thursday Island. He became a drover, a cook and steward under sail on an island trader, and seaman on a coastal steamer. His wandering life ended when he arrived in Sydney around 1886.

Work was hard to find, wages were low, unemployment was becoming an issue, but theatre was popular and he landed a spot as a supernumerary – an extra – in a production of Shakespeare's *Henry V* at 12 shillings and 6 pence a week for seven performances. The show was a hit and Hughes carried spears with great élan for 150 nights. He also worked as an oven maker's assistant, and found some social stability living in a boarding house in Moore Park. It was here that Hughes either married, or became the common law husband – historians seldom agree on this point – of Elizabeth Cutts, the daughter of his landlady. The two moved to a rundown weatherboard shop at 16 Beattie Street Balmain in 1890, described by Browne as 'a Sydney industrial suburb, then chiefly populated by dockers, coal lumpers, and wharf labourers – and went into business as a knife grinder, second hand book seller, and general odd job man'. Hughes also had a profitable sideline in umbrella repairs, while his wife took in washing to supplement the meagre returns from the shop. But as Browne pointed out 'business was less than prosperous' in a suburb where money was scarce.

Hughes became a regular Sunday visitor to the Domain, listening to orators standing on their boxes and offering a variety of opinions from the lucid to the absurd, and met William Holman. While his shop wasn't a hub of commerce, it soon became a hub of politics with Hughes and Holman holding court. One of the regular attendees noted, 'we grew to recognise the symptoms of impending oratory in Billy. Invariably he began to fidget, chew nervously and tense himself. Then he would toss his work aside, spring to his feet and launch his attack.' Though not part of the 1890 strike, Hughes was witness to the impact on his local community, and he wasn't a fan of the methodology. He later wrote in his 1910 book *The Case for Labor*

> the enrolment of all workers in one great organization for the purpose of cessation of work is impracticable – the idea of a general strike an idle and fantastic dream. To advise 85 per cent of the people, with their minds made up, in a country where the wishes of the majority, constitutionally expressed can go to any lengths to cease work, instead of voting for men pledged to get them what they wanted would be the advice of

fools or madmen. They can give effect to their desires through the ballot box. To vote is much easier to strike.

Hughes, however, would later be a founder of a union that was very fond of striking to make their point.

Hughes and Holman were at the Labour Hall that night in April, with Holman as the principal speaker. Browne wrote of the formation of the Labour Electoral League in Balmain that 'it scarcely rippled the water. To associate with a losing side in the recent strike was to court disaster, in the minds of most wage earners in that employer-dominated year.' However, while members were short on the ground, the electoral league did manage to spread, and by June, when Premier Henry Parkes called an election, they were represented in forty-five out of 137 electorates. Hughes didn't contest any of the seats, and as Browne wrote, 'his desperate poverty was the controlling factor in his apparent lack of political ambition. He was asked to contest a country seat but lacked even the train fare to his proposed constituency.' Going into the election, the party's total funds were about £100 – with most of it used for the candidate's deposits to contest each of the forty-five seats. Jim McIlroy wrote in *The Origins of the ALP – A Marxist Analysis* (2004) that one unnamed candidate commented post-election, 'we were a band of unhappy amateurs, made up somewhat as follows: several miners, three or four printers, a boilermaker, three sailors, a plasterer, a journalist, a draper, a suburban mayor, two engineers, a carrier, a few shearers a tailor, and – with bated breath – a mine owner, a squatter and an MD'.

Today's regular complaints about media bias are nothing new and in the lead-up to the June 1891 election, Hughes and his colleagues were the targets. George Dibbs, the Protectionist politician, disparaged the newcomers as, 'this gang of sweat rag politicians, this aggregation of anarchists, hooligans and revolutionaries, who have neither followers, funds nor even loyalty'.

The *Sydney Morning Herald* gave voters a rev-up on the eve of the poll, warning, without a shred of irony, that a vote for the new party would lead to 'a system of representation of class interests, the ultimate effect of which would be to degrade parliament into a nominee chamber of the Trades and Labor Council'.

The election was held on 17 June 1891 and the result surprised everyone. The Labour Electoral League won thirty-six out of the forty-five seats it had contested. Parkes was reduced to forty-nine seats and Dibbs had fifty-one. To add to the confusion, there were five independents. Of the remarkable victory for the league, Browne added a splash of colour, writing the political establishment was 'appalled by the Frankenstein which now panted on its doorstep'. It was even more appalled by the realisation that many middle-class people must have voted for the Labour ticket. Alfred Deakin observed the growing strength of labour in politics 'is more significant and more cosmic than the crusades'. The *Sydney Morning Herald* was quick to sense a major shift in politics, and within days changed its position from critical to conciliatory, telling the new parliamentarians they were now in 'a position of power, of responsibility for which they could have fully prepared'.

The *Herald* was on the money, but the lack of preparedness was soon manifest not by problems with power and responsibility, but with internal dissent. Hughes had analysed the results and, rather than rejoicing, had come to the conclusion that his league was 'very shaky', with some of the new members committed to getting themselves into parliament by any means, rather than to the beliefs of their party. At the first meeting of the new elected members, George Black, described by Browne as a 'brilliant journalist and self-styled schoolmaster of the Labour Party' spoke passionately of the need for solidarity to make the most of their political power. George, however, wasn't as adept as Hughes at reading the intentions of his colleagues – eight declared they'd made commitments to their constituents that they would vote with Gibbs and his Protectionists, and one then declared himself to be an independent. But that wasn't all. The new party had one other major problem – no leader. As Browne observed 'because they were unschooled in Parliamentary procedure and tactics, they had not realized the necessity of electing one of their number to this office'.

The lack of political skill was a gift for the more experienced politicians. Parkes, now premier in a minority government, promised a long list of concessions in return for Labour support. Dibbs, in hearing that eight members had promised their constituencies they would support his policies, called an issue before the house, forced a vote, and had the great pleasure of watching the eight forced to cross the floor to vote with his party. The success of the election was rapidly turning into the reality of a political disaster.

In the early days of the new parliament, George Black, as member for West Sydney, stepped up as the de facto leader, and promised that his party 'have not come into this House then, to make or unmake ministries, we have not come into this House to make or unmake social conditions. We intend to deal with the living present' but despite his rousing speech and prominence, he found himself leading a faction that espoused solidarity with colleagues, but declined to commit formally to that solidarity. Facing him were Holman and Hughes – leading the Solidarity Group – who were committed to control of the rank and file members and, as Brown put it, 'this group visualized the Movement as master, the Parliament as servant'. In the centre were those who favoured support for Protectionists. The Solidarity Group was driven hard by Hughes and Holman to become the dominant group – Black, never a fan of Holman, referred to him as 'Hamlet'.

Straddling the factional problems was caucus – devised initially to deal with what the newspaper *The Worker* described in August 1891, as the 'loose methods of selecting parliamentary representatives'. Caucus was a victory for Hughes and Holman and brought discipline to the party, requiring all members to agree to a majority decision – particularly handy if your faction had the numbers. To shore up those numbers, Hughes went back to travelling around the bush, but this time as an organiser for the shearers' union. Money was still in short supply and Hughes' usual method of travel was an old two-wheeler bike, but the time slugging from town to town was well spent as he formed new Labour Leagues, and gathered votes for his faction.

In November 1893, the conference of the Labour Electoral Leagues carried a resolution that 'any man engaged in creating dissensions within their ranks must be regarded as an enemy of Labour and a traitor to its cause'. Hughes and Holman had won the factional battle and laid one of the cornerstones of the modern Australian Labor Party.

The political party with its heart in the Sydney waterfront spread quickly. In 1892, Queensland elected four Labour members – all representing rural seats, and the following year it won sixteen. In South Australia, Labour won two Legislative Council seats in the 1891 election, and two years later added ten Legislative Assembly members.

There were, however, problems gathering on the horizon.

12
ENTER THE PUSH

Years of prosperity came to an abrupt end in Australia when 'The Panic of 1893', as it was known in the US, set off a chain of events around the globe.

It brought an end to the 'Gilded Age' – the name given to the period by Mark Twain and Charles Warner in their 1873 publication *The Gilded Age – A tale of today* – of US economic growth, industrial expansion, innovation and massive immigration spurred by the prospect of opportunity and wealth. One cause of the panic was a run on US Gold Reserves after investments in Argentina went down the tubes because of a coup and crop failures. One of the merchant banks who'd been pushing investments hard was an associate of the UK's Barings Bank, who defaulted on a £21 million debt for which the Argentine crops had been collateral. The Bank of England saved Barings by borrowing from banks in Europe.

In the US, the panic saw the financial crash of railroads, and ordinary citizens racing to their banks to remove their savings. Around 500 banks closed, 15,000 businesses failed, and unemployment soared. In the state of Michigan, unemployment during the panic reached 43%. In the south, the panic arrived at precisely the worst time, after a few years of failed cotton crops in the already depressed region. President Grover Cleveland, recently re-elected for his second term, had to borrow $65 million from Wall Street's JP Morgan and the Rothschild banking family in the United Kingdom to prop up his nation's gold reserves.

Down in the bottom half of the world, the timing was also dismal. The recent maritime and shearers' strike had hit the country at its two most vulnerable points – the major export and where those exports made their way to market. By 1891, sixteen small banks and co-operative banks had gone broke, along with a slew of companies.

With the destabilisation of the world markets, Australia's problems deepened – particularly in the commercial powerhouse of Melbourne. The nation had relied heavily on offshore investment capital during the 1880s, and the balance of payments weren't keeping up. In Victoria, there had been a building boom of speculative properties that outstripped the demand – and these had been funded by building societies without the assets to cover their investment in the case of a financial hiccup, resulting in collapses starting with the Premier Permanent Building Association in December 1889. Overseas investors, particularly in the United Kingdom, became nervous about their investments in places like Australia, and when the Barings mess came along, their nerves turned to action and they pulled the pin on further involvement.

The Age of 22 June 1892 reported the financial downturn was biting hard with a 'generally deplorable state of affairs in working class suburbs', and many were 'sleeping rough'. At that time, those working-class suburbs were home to most of Victoria's waterfront workers. Families were tightly packed into small and poorly built houses owned by landlords usually with little interest in maintenance. Poor sanitation and a diet that started with bread and dripping in lean weeks, made it a tough existence. Henry Parkes later estimated there were 30,000 unemployed in

Melbourne at a time when the colony's population was around 1.1 million.

The Federal Bank of Australia collapsed in January 1893 and was followed by the Commercial Bank of Australia in March. By mid May around eleven banks had collapsed. On 1 May 1893, the *Argus* reported on the Victorian Government's decision to close the banks for a five day 'holiday': 'Financial Crisis – Grave Act of State – Time for Calm Consideration' was the headline. The government believed the holiday would also give the banks time to consider amalgamation, give the various colonial governments an opportunity to discuss the problem to come up with Australia-wide rather than parochial solutions, and as the *Argus* noted, 'force the public to reflect on the folly of rushing a bank'. Some of the banks reacted by instructing their London bankers, where their gold reserves were held, to send gold back to them. The Bank of Australia and the Union Bank called for £500,000 worth, and the Commercial Banking Company of Sydney called for £250,000.

The worldwide crisis meant the demand for Australia's exports of wool, wheat and products from the developing mining sector dropped, along with the imports – bringing with it a decline in work on the docks and, as Margo Beasley wrote in *Wharfies,* 'the Melbourne Wharf Labourers and the Port Phillip Stevedores were also nearly battered out of existence by the strikes [maritime strike] and the depression'. The only part of Australia's waterfront unscathed by the crisis was Western Australia where a gold rush, the expansion of the city and development of mining opportunities kept the cash flowing. The official history of the Port of Fremantle noted the gold rush 'provided both the funds and the impetus for the development of new port facilities' which included 'quays and warehouses'.

Within a year, the nation was recovering. The recovery began in 1897, in part due to confidence brought on by the Klondike Gold Rush in Canada and Alaska.

One positive to come out of the economic downturn, the failed strikes and the unhealthy state of the union movement was that the people in waterfront communities grew closer and more reliant on each other's support.

As Melbourne and Sydney spread deeper into countryside areas, the waterfront communities remained in the same suburbs – it was their livelihood and strength, and these were also rather handy for the development of the criminal infrastructure that dominated the Australian scene for the next century.

While 'bushrangers' were crime gangs that quickly became part of Australia's folklore because of their exploits and a whiff of Robin Hood, it was the 'pushes' that brought crime gangs to prominence in Sydney.

Pushes were gangs of young men who were organised, professional, ruthless and territorial. Like some of today's gangs, religion and ethnicity played a major part in the formation of each push, but inevitably power and profit beat principle every time, and like today they were usually disenfranchised and unskilled. The gang gave them structure and kindred spirits, and started them with petty crimes like mugging drunks for their wallet or watch – it proved their loyalty and also gave gang leaders a crime to hold over them if their enthusiasm for membership wavered.

The pushes began on Sydney's waterfront in the early 1870s, with gangs like the Rocks Push, the Millers Point Push, the Argyle Cut Push and the Glebe Push and later spread to poor industrialised inner city suburbs like Waterloo. As their notoriety increased thanks to newspaper coverage of their exploits, so did membership and competitors – the same way today's outlaw biker clubs numbers grow with every lurid headline.

By the 1890s, the pushes were a powerful force in the underworld. They made their money from stealing – targeting warehouses and shops around the docklands – and opportunistic thefts like mugging the drunk or the easily overwhelmed, or using their girlfriends as decoys to lure cashed-up sailors into a dark place where the boys were lying in wait. They also dabbled in debt collecting, violence for hire, and prostitution. 'Larrikinism' was a term often used when talking about the pushes, and their rise in the poorest suburbs was put down to a variety of social factors – poverty, class, a feeling of separation from the broader community and so on. But, as with any criminal enterprise, opportunity for fast and easy cash was also a factor.

One push had its own poet, and in 1893 the unpleasantly titled 'Kicking Their Livers Out' appeared. Anon was the wordsmith, and the title a reference to their preferred method of attack; kicking stopped the assailant's hands being damaged. The poem spoke of what to do when arrested:

> *Don't attempt the least resistance or he'll get you in a fix,*
> *He'll grab you by the collar and the bosom of your breeks,*
> *And upset you in the manner of the ancient wrestling Greeks*
> *He will use both boots and knuckles, he will bark your bleeding shins,*
> *While you've simply got to wear it with your meekest of grins,*
> *For he'll charge you with offences of the most atrocious kind,*
> *And he'll swear you tore his tunic though you're paralyzed and blind,*

The leader of the Rocks Push in its early days was Larry Foley. He was a gifted boxer, born near Bathurst in 1849 to a schoolteacher father and mother 'in service' to a local family. Foley's parents were keen for him to enter the priesthood, but Larry had different ideas, and by the age of eighteen he was living in The Rocks, working as a builder's labourer, and part of a gang of Catholic boys trying to cut out a slice of Sydney as their criminal turf.

Foley took boxing lessons from John 'Black' Perry, and in March 1871 fought Sandy Ross, a Protestant then heading Rocks

Push, for leadership of the gang. The fight took place on neutral turf near the George's River in southern Sydney. Ross entered the battle older, more experienced in the art of the street fight, heavier and taller. What he didn't know was that his adversary had training, skill and stamina. Seventy-one rounds into the battle, and the police intervened. Foley was the winner and became leader with Ross his deputy.

Fortunately for Foley, leadership of Sydney's largest and most well-known push brought with it an opportunity to escape life on the waterfront. He added to his income from crime and labouring work by entering, and winning, the bare-knuckle fights that were popular with both rich and poor sportsmen. His talent was spotted by George Hill, a Sydney council alderman, sports fan and 'gentleman of fancy' (a man about town) who lured Foley away from the gangs and into a boxing career. Foley was never defeated. He became Australian bare-knuckle champion in 1879, beating Abe Hicken in sixteen rounds and winning £600.

Foley gave up crime and used his building knowledge to establish a successful demolition company, and that hallmark of success for many Australian men – buying a pub, in his case the White Horse in George Street, Sydney. The term 'happy as Larry' is attributed to Foley's charm and rise to national popularity. The *Arrow* of 14 July 1917 reported his death and noted, 'he had an unusual amount of natural ability, and a punch in his speech and manner that is rarely met with. Actors, politicians, commercial people of all grades and men in high social circles visited him frequently.'

Foley gave back to the community he'd once terrorised, offering boxing lessons at a gym attached to his hotel. He became the greatest Australian boxing trainer of his time and one of his successes was Albert Griffiths, known as 'Young Griffo'.

Columnist Tommy Sullivan, writing in the US newspaper *Tacoma Daily News* on 6 March 1916, said, 'Young Griffo was not known as much of a puncher, but his skill was uncanny. He had wonderful headwork, almost impenetrable defense, dazzling feints, and rapid two-handed methods of attack. The cleverest boxers and hardest punchers were made to look ridiculous when exchanging swats with him.'

Griffo grew up in The Rocks and Millers Point and, when his mother died, his father, who worked the docks and at sea, put him into the care of neighbours – the community looked after its own.

Like Foley, Griffo was a gifted natural fighter and gravitated toward the Rocks Push, where his tenacity and skills with his fists supplemented his income from a string of jobs, including a paper boy, tailor's assistant, helper to a horse trainer and working as a runner at the *Sydney Morning Herald*. In 1886, he began training with Foley and on 27 December 1889 he won the Australian Featherweight Title in a bout with fellow Sydneysider Nipper Peakes. In September the following year, he fought New Zealander 'Torpedo' Billy Murphy in Sydney for the World Title. Young Griffo won, but his victory wasn't recognised outside Australia because US officials believed Murphy had forfeited his title when he'd left their country.

'Young Griffo' had a problem – the booze – and drinking became more appealing to him than training. His problems coincided with the bite of the financial crisis, although that didn't impact on many of the Sydneysiders enjoying a bet on a fight and a drink while watching. On 15 May 1893, Griffo left for the US, which wasn't a wise decision.

In 1894 he lost his World Title, and in April 1896 Griffo fought 'Young Bull' McCarthy in Sacramento, California, and McCarthy died in hospital shortly after. Griffo was charged with manslaughter – at his bail hearing he was 'helplessly intoxicated' according to a contemporary report. However, in June, a judge found the death was 'entirely due to accident in a friendly contest'. In August that year Griffo was charged and convicted of assaulting a twelve-year-old boy while he was drunk. Twelve months in prison didn't resolve his drinking problems or banish the ghost of McCarthy.

In 1898, Griffo was admitted to a home for drunkards – at the age of twenty-six. His career never recovered and his last recorded fight was in Chicago on 10 February 1904 against Tommy White. It lasted just one round, and Tommy White won when Griffo simply gave up. The *Chicago Tribune* reported 'Griffo is pugilistically dead in this town, as no club would dare give him another chance'. The man dubbed 'The Australian Will o' the Wisp', never had another chance anywhere. He turned to doing vaudeville style tricks for cash, relying on meals, shelter and money from his former fans, and begging on the streets around Time Square. He died on 7 December 1927, at age fifty-six.

Shortly after 'Young Griffo' had departed on his journey to the USA in 1893, the pushes of Sydney found themselves the focus of a media furore and a favourite subject of temperance advocates who lobbied parliament and spoke at length on soapboxes in the Domain on Sunday afternoons.

The larrikins had been the subject of public ire after the 1886 'Mount Rennie Outrage' as the case was dubbed by the newspapers. Sixteen-year-old Mary Jane Hickman was in Sussex Street, Sydney, around the middle of the day when she hailed a hansom cab driven by Charles Sweetman. Rather than take her the short ride to Castlereagh Street as she asked, he took her to Mount Rennie, a sandy hill in an isolated, swampy part of what is now Moore Park, where he sexually assaulted her. When a group of around twenty young men, all between seventeen and twenty, arrived and interrupted Sweetman, Ms Hickman thought she was saved from further abuse, but she was wrong. The men were members of the Waterloo Push, named after the nearby semi-industrial suburb, which was nearly as tough and poor as The Rocks.

The men, some armed with knives, dragged Ms Hickman from the cab and the clutches of Sweetman, and took turns in raping her. A passer-by tried to stop the assaults but was beaten up and ran off – fortunately to get help. As there were no police available at nearby Redfern, constables from Darlinghurst went to the scene, arriving belatedly around 5 pm. They found Sweetman boiling a billy for tea, and the dishevelled victim on the ground near him. Outrage at the crime was tempered by reports that Ms Hickman, who had asserted she had maintained her 'purity of person', had recently had an affair with a married man – demeaning the victim in sexual assault cases has a long and unpleasant history.

Fifteen men were arrested for the assault and eleven finally went to trial. Nine were found guilty and Justice Windeyer imposed the death penalty – five later had it mitigated to life and were released around a decade later. Four were executed by hanging in Darlinghurst Gaol on 7 January 1887 while a crowd of around 2000 people gathered outside the gaol's high sandstone walls.

The larrikins' brazen activities and the public's demand for action by both police and government remained in the headlines. In February 1892, members of the Rocks Push had allegedly murdered a 24-year-old Dutch seaman who'd mistaken them for friends and spoke to them. Two men were later arrested but the prosecution failed because they couldn't be identified. Police believed the witnesses to the killing were too intimidated to come forward. In the tight-knit waterfront community, you didn't rat on your own.

Local residents told reporters from the *Sydney Morning Herald* 'it wasn't safe to be in the streets after dark', and that 'the larrikins who banded together would not hesitate to attack anyone who was fair game, and rob him in a most open manner. Of their many misdeeds, the police know absolutely nothing.' The waterfront community was silent even when some of the victims of these attacks were hard-working men from the docks, as the *Sydney Morning Herald* said, 'men after getting paid on the wharf often drank more than was good for them, and while in this maudlin state the larrikins relieved them of all the cash in their pockets.' Around this time, the pushes had been growing rapidly and changing, with younger newcomers taking over and exacerbating the strife.

The government reaction was to increase the number of police on the beat, and to introduce harsher penalties, including the return of whipping and the power for police to stop people associating and have them 'move on'. However the 'whipping' clause in the *Disorderly Conduct Suppression Bill* meant it failed to pass the Legislative Council; it was too much like the bad old days of the colony.

The New Zealand *Daily Telegraph* of 20 October 1892 reported the troubles and the 'stringent proposed measures' with some relish, saying, 'the future men of New Zealand tower above their fellows in Victoria and New South Wales in moral character and while they have quite as much surplus energy, they expend it in athletic exercises rather than cowardly assaults on inoffensive and unprotected people'. The United Kingdom papers also inserted the boot, with the *Leeds Mercury* of 1 October 1892 ignoring the origins of the colony, then only a shade over a century old, and said, 'the larrikin appears to be a particular product of the country; and he has grown with the growth of the population until his present numbers have become an interference with the liberty of the well disposed'.

Events soon took a turn for the worse.

Around 10 am on Sunday 25 June 1893, Thomas Pert, a 37-year-old Scottish-born wharf labourer and seaman on *Royal Tar,* was beaten to death near his brother's home close to the corner of Moore Street and Argyle Street by members of the Millers Point Push.

In the months leading up to the murder, Pert had been repeatedly harassed by the Millers Point Push. One reason given for their behaviour was vindictiveness – about six months earlier two members had demanded free cigars from the publican of the Gladstone Hotel and had been turfed out. They came back for another try later that evening to find two constables waiting. Pert had been at the hotel, witnessed the incident, and called the police. Not long after that, Pert had gone to the aid of a drunken woman who was surrounded by some of the push and helped her to the safety of a constable who was nearby.

On the night before his murder, Pert had been in a scuffle with Henry Doohan, one of the leaders of the push, and was chased home by other gang members. His brother Robert recalled that Tom – a big man who could look after himself – had tears in his eyes and said, 'Bob, what am I going to do, I cannot get out, they are after me wherever I go'.

The next morning Pert told his brother he was heading over to the local store. In spite of his brother's warnings, Pert left the house. A few minutes later Bob saw his brother having a conversation with a man, and also saw a group of youths heading toward them. He heard his brother say to the man, 'Go, I want nothing to do with you', and in an interview with the *Sydney Morning Herald* of 26 June 1893, Bob recalled, 'my brother took his coat off to fight, and I caught hold of the man's wrist and took him aside, and told him to leave before there was trouble – but trouble had already arrived'. In a scuffle with the arriving crowd, Tom Pert fell, picked himself up and both brothers made a dash for the safety of their nearby home, but one of the mob tripped Tom and he fell and the kicking started. He was rescued by his brother and another man and taken home. Bob Pert said, 'We saw he was hurt and I took my brother's overcoat off. We lifted him onto the bed and he died within three minutes. He never spoke after we picked him up on the street.'

The press reacted predictably the next morning, with headlines in the *Sydney Morning Herald* proclaiming 'Murder at Millers Point: A labouring man savagely attacked! The victim kicked to death. Eight men arrested!' The *Daily Telegraph* led with

'A Sunday Morning Outrage – Extraordinary Molestation of a Push', and the article then noted 'the appalling extent to which lawlessness is rife in this city' and warmed to its theme the next day with the headline 'Larrikin Reign of Terror'.

The boys of the Millers Point Push had done a great job of painting a target on the back of every push in Sydney. A day later, eight young men, mainly waterfront labourers, had been charged with the murder. On 7 July, a public meeting at the Sydney Town Hall supported the return of flogging to deal with 'larrikinism and ruffianism'.

Forty more constables were sworn in, and the 'Light Brigade' – a squad of mobile and armed officers – was established to target crime hotspots.

Of the eight men arrested, only two, Thomas Reid and Edward Rich, were convicted for Pert's death. The jury believed there was no pre-meditation and found them guilty of manslaughter; Reid got ten years and Rich got five. The light sentences, a result of the jury's 'recommendation for mercy on the grounds of provocation' weren't popular with the public or the trial judge, Mr Justice Innes, who said he regarded 'the assault as a grievous outrage upon the peace of a civilized community'. Justice Foster, a fellow judge, mentioned that Innes, on reflection, 'in no way found fault with the jury's decision' and considered the sentences to be 'severe and exemplary'.

In the years following the trial, vigorous policing and public support for the tougher police measures, saw the decline of the pushes. There was speculation that community leaders had taken a strong hand to bring the pushes to an end, but crime's association with the waterfront was now embedded in the minds of the public, police and politicians. The *Los Angeles Times* of 4 April 1897 carried a feature article headlined 'The Australian Larrikin Most Brutal of the World's Outlaw' – an interesting call considering the USA's Wild West was in its closing days – and said, 'these pariahs are as much the outcome of Australia's distinctive civilization as the kangaroo, the bushmen and the gumtree are products of its climate and soil'.

Australia was again prominent on the world map – for all the wrong reasons.

13
PLAGUE!

The one thing the Australian Labor Party does better than any other party is to hate and it does so with creativity and vigour – particularly with internal battles. When recently talking to a Labor mate, the subject of Billy Hughes popped up. 'That conniving little bastard,' she said, 'just a bloody opportunist who used the blood, sweat and tears of the workers to get ahead. Unforgiveable.' Donald Horne, who'd had a career as a journalist before succumbing to academia, shared my friend's view of Hughes. In his book *In search of Billy Hughes* he said his subject 'had a gargantuan appetite for lying' and was 'a zealous and talented illusionist'.

Hughes had a different view of himself, writing in his memoir *Crusts and Crusades* that he wanted 'to make the world a fit place for heroes to live in', and with that in mind he turned himself to the battered remains of the union movement.

Whether idealist, opportunist or somewhere in between, Hughes had magnificent timing and a plan. In 1899, economic recovery from the panic of 1893 was well advanced, and on the waterfront the shipping companies had returned to healthy revenues. For the workers it meant jobs and the chance of consistent work with better pay and conditions.

Hughes had been the member for the seat of Sydney–Lang in the NSW Legislative Assembly since the seat's creation in 1894. His employment in 1893 as an organiser for the Australian Workers Union helped with the cash flow needed to enter politics. The seat was bounded by Darling Harbour to the west, George Street to the east, Margaret Street to the north, and Hay Street to the south and included a section of the now bustling docklands. He knew that a key to the future success of both the Labor Party and his own career was to revive the union. On 15 July 1896 a meeting of union members elected an executive and Hughes and a few fellow politicians were there. They became regular speakers at subsequent gatherings, trying to stir the unionists into action, speaking about the need for workers to unite for a common purpose, to organise and the need for an eight-hour workday campaign. The *Australian Journal of Politics and History* said that Hughes' exhortations provided 'a popular turn' at the meetings.

However, they didn't succeed in firing up the union, and by December that year membership had declined to 356 men – about one seventh of the workers on the docks. By 1899, the union was nearly moribund and broke – even the rental on its safe at Trades Hall was in arrears. Fitzhardinge wrote in *W M Hughes and the Waterside Workers*,

> though the union continued to exist, at least in name, its power was broken and it was numerically insignificant. The stevedoring firms and shipowners, on the other hand, were strong, closely organised and united. Members of the union were blacklisted, and its organisers hunted off the wharves. In some cases, 'company unions' were formed to which men had to contribute one and a half pence out of every shilling earned in order to get employment. Unskilled labour in the nineties was superabundant, and the men dared not resist.

Of the plight of the workers, Fitzhardinge observed, 'Wages were very low, work irregular, and employment depended wholly on the superintendent or foreman. Men might work for twenty-four hours at a stretch, then be unemployed for weeks.'

The decisions of the superintendent or foreman were known as the 'bull' system – with the 'bull' being the stronger men who could worker longer and harder, and preferably didn't cause trouble. Buying a drink for the foreman regularly didn't do any harm either.

It was a situation that stirred community leaders to finally act – John Langley, the Anglican rector of St Philips, had many waterside families in his congregation, and John 'Manchester Jack' Kilberg, the publican of Mann's hotel, who catered to their less spiritual needs and was influential in local politics. Kilberg was a large, red-cheeked and engaging Irishman whose hotel was the unofficial meeting place for the unionists. Billy Hughes, their local member, knew an issue when he saw one and, according to the *Australian Journal of Politics and History*, Hughes 'set himself seriously to master the problems of the industry and its workers'. The journal also observed 'the task might well have daunted any man – to Hughes, now at the height of his powers, it came as a challenge and stimulus'.

The stimulus was also timely. Australia was on track for Federation, which meant an ambitious man like Hughes could take his abilities to a national stage – all he had to do was be preselected for a Federal seat then win it. Hughes would not have been the first politician to know the labour movement had the potential to be a political powerbase, and a union representing a chunk of his constituency was the perfect fit – plus it was a union he knew well from his time as a Balmain resident.

During the closing months of 1899, Hughes and his supporters took on the hard work of politics – canvassing, lobbying, persuading – to make sure he had the numbers for the next phase. Frank C. Browne, Hughes' enthusiastic biographer, wrote that his subject 'though differing from them [the dock workers] physically, with his accent strangely ringing in their ears, nevertheless projected himself among them not only as one of themselves, but as the epitome of their aspirations and ideals'. A less enthusiastic observer, with the benefit of hindsight, might think that Donald Horne was more on the money.

On 27 December 1899, the union met and Hughes announced there were now 1300 members of the union, '600 of whom were fully paid up', and he was elected as secretary of the refurbished and renamed Wharf Labourers' Union. There were no other candidates.

Two days later, the shipowners and stevedoring firms got an unwelcome Christmas gift, when Hughes called the union's first public meeting – and he displayed a gift for showmanship. On the platform with him at Federation Hall both Church and State were represented by Premier William Lyne, ten members of the NSW Parliament, Archdeacon Langley, and Catholic priest Father Aubrey.

The *Sydney Morning Herald* reported Hughes was now secretary after 'three months of unremitting work', and the union 'had been formed to enable wharf labourers to maintain their dignity and their rights without harassing employers. The union, having been started by men who were determined to see it through would seek to secure as a member every wharf labourer who was worthy of the name man.'

The report also caught what was going on in Hughes' mind, saying 'it is the intention of the union to be a political as well as an industrial factor in affairs', and foreshadowed the need to 'introduce a Workers Compensation Bill'. Even more importantly for the short term, the union had £200 in the bank, so Trades Hall could expect to get paid for the safe rental.

Browne wrote that as 1900 arrived, his subject 'had changed little physically since the day five years before when he had made his initial bow as the new member for Lang. Increasing deafness was making itself felt, but the strain of internecine party struggle and the constant Parliamentary fight for concessions, both of which involved killing hours, had done nothing towards toning down the boundless energy which at times embarrassed his own colleagues nearly as much as it did his political enemies.' Henry Gullett, then a reporter for the *Sydney Morning Herald,* had a slightly different recollection of Hughes, writing, 'the first time I saw him was on a night at Church Hall in Sydney immediately prior to Federation. He stood at bay, a sallow, emaciated figure in a hall full of truculent wharf labourers, and fogged with the smoke of strong pipes.' In a rowdy meeting with the wharfies keen to strike, Gullett said Hughes 'reasoned and pleaded with them; he ridiculed them; he swore at them and assailed them as a host of misguided idiots. The meeting ended with wild cheers for him and there was no strike.'

While Hughes and the wharfies had grabbed the public attention with the large meeting at Federation Hall, another union in Balmain that would have a huge impact on Australia in the new century was slowly coming back to life. On 31 January 1900 the Balmain Labourers' Union met in the Working Men's Institute in what Issy Wyner described as 'smokey, dusty, grimy, noisy' Balmain 'for the purposes of electing officers'. The union had been around since 1883 but, like the wharfies, had gone through a long period where it had been a union in name only. Manning Clark wrote in his *History of Australia* that one of the problems in building a union to represent an amalgam of labourers and skilled workers – and much of the work on ships at Mort's Dock was skilled – was that 'the skilled tradesmen were reluctant to have any public association with the unskilled workers'.

In August 1900, the union formally changed its name to the Painters and Dockers Union, and by 1901 had 376 members. Their work was miserable – chipping, scraping, painting, rigging and cleaning everything from boilers to bilges – and depended on the arrival and departure of a ship for their livelihood.

Nature has a habit of throwing a spanner in the works, and three weeks after the wharfie union's resounding return to the stage, the waterfront community was hit with a devastating blow – bubonic plague.

Diseases from overseas were part of what Margo Beasley described as the 'hard, unpleasant, dangerous and irregular' working life for the wharf communities.

Australia had been alert to the plague since an outbreak in Hong Kong in 1894, and the risk of it spreading courtesy of rats on ships. What no one paid attention to was a spike in the number of dead rats around the wharves. On 19 January 1900, 33-year-old Arthur Paine, a deliveryman who lived in Ferry Lane in The Rocks and whose work took him frequently to the wharves, was diagnosed with the plague and died at Prince Alfred Hospital. His family were taken to the North Head Quarantine Station just to be on the safe side, as was his body. The following day, sections of The Rocks and wharves were quarantined and health officials and residents hoped Mr Paine's death was a one-off. The *Sydney Morning Herald* reported 'there is nothing to show Sydney is experiencing an unusual season of sickness'.

On 3 February, the *Australian Town and Country Journal* reassured readers that, though there were reports of the disease in Adelaide, Sydney was in the best of hands – 'on South, Middle and George's Heads' the paper said

> and other points of vantage at the entrance to Sydney Harbour, are the hidden batteries designed to give a warm welcome to the militant human invader. North Head possesses none of these ingenious devices of modern military science, but it is nonetheless a fortress designed to delay and destroy the numberless deadly foes, which are ever threatening to storm the great metropolis a few miles away. It has no disappearing guns or torpedo tubes, but its armory is replete with everything

which science can indicate to annihilate the microbe myriads. The Quarantine Station is, in fact, Sydney's first line of defence against bubonic plague.

Unfortunately, by March, Sydney's leaders knew they had a major problem on their hands as more citizens from the waterfront communities were diagnosed with the plague. The community response, according to the University of Sydney's Medical School, 'was one of panic and dread, fuelled by knowledge of the history and ravenous potential of the disease'. On 21 March, a crowd of around 1000 people gathered outside the Board of Health on the corner of Macquarie and Albert streets to make a public display of their fear. According to a report in the *Evening News* of 21 March 1900, 'a foolish panic of exaggerated fear and alarm had obviously set in'. The population of the Blue Mountains swelled with those having both the money and time to flee the city. The Victorian Government cancelled the monthly excursion train from Sydney to Melbourne, fearing that the cheap fares would encourage Sydney workers to escape, and *The Bulletin* took a pragmatic view, reporting, the plague 'isn't a patch on the daily, hourly typhoid as a means of slaughtering the public'.

Religious leaders, fearing the plague may have some biblical cause, lobbied the government for a day of prayer. However they'd misjudged both their knowledge of Sydney's priorities and the city's event calendar, with the Colonial Secretary declining as it would 'be very inconvenient, as the arrangements for the official opening of the agricultural show on that date had been made months ago'. Journalists from the *Arrow* weren't sympathetic to the religious leaders, writing that if they were right about the plague being punishment for the city's 'sins' and 'transgression of Divine laws', then 'why, oh why! have all the alderman so far escaped'.

George McCredie, an architect and engineer, was appointed to take charge of stopping the plague's spread. A large swathe of the city and surrounding suburbs were quarantined and, from 24 March to 17 July, residents and McCredie's workers set about inspecting the slums, bond stores, drains and sewers where they believed rats who'd slipped off visiting ships were breeding and spreading the disease. In *Plague in Sydney*, authors Peter Curson and Kevin McCracken wrote the city had 'through years of apathy, neglect and inadequate regulation, fallen into a dirty, insanitary condition'. They said the plague 'entered the city via the filthy wharves and dirty slums of Darling Harbour'. Houses were overcrowded, often not connected to the sewer, and human waste ran down drains and into the harbour. While many Sydneysiders looked disparagingly at the Chinese and Middle Eastern immigrants that were moving into the waterfront areas, the *Daily Telegraph* noted, 'white people are the worst offenders'.

Stanley Yarrington wrote of the housing conditions in *Darkest Sydney – some incidents in slum life* that 'men, women and children, forced through circumstances to sleep, to wash, to eat in the same room, whose only opportunity of obtaining fresh air is in the lane or street'. Yarrington said these areas were ones in which 'we shall always be faced with sickly immoral and degenerate section of citizens. Though at the same time there are thousands of healthy, noble men and women who have lived a lifetime amidst most unsatisfactory surroundings and have been as beacons to all who have known them.' He was a fan of forcing landlords to improve the properties, writing 'is it not better to inconvenience the wealthy landlords for a time rather than allow a mass of people to drag out a wretched existence?' It took plague, not compassion, to drive changes to benefit the waterfront community.

Properties were whitewashed, disinfected with solutions of lime, carbolic acid, or sulphuric acid. Some houses were pulled apart and sections burned, others demolished whether the occupants agreed or not. Rat trapping was briefly a profitable business, with some local councils paying a bounty of up to 6 pence per rat, which was then disposed of in a purpose-built incinerator. Around 44,000 rats were caught and killed. Down in Melbourne the bounty was 3 pence per head, but by the end of May, with the rat death toll standing at 18,700, the local councils all agreed to double the bounty to encourage the demise of the rodents.

Hughes, comparing it to the Great Plague of London, wrote in his 1947 memoir, *Crusts and Crusades*, that 'I do not pretend it [Sydney's plague] was quite in the same class. But it was pretty bad, and besides putting the fear of God into the hearts of very many people, it put quite a lot in the cemetery.' He took some credit for swift action, later writing 'the plague came from Mauritius in a sailing ship, which, by evil chance, berthed near the foot of Erskine Street, right in the heart of my old constituency'. He described the ship as having a cargo that 'when it reached port it had become the most awful compost of corruption ever generated'. A good story, but more fiction than fact. Hughes also wrote of the fury of his constituents at being quarantined and having their houses destroyed or badly damaged by what they believed to be a 'body of desperadoes hired by a tyrannical Government to carry out the bowelless edicts of the Health Department. Fortified by strong drink these men carried on a veritable orgy of destructions.' He reckoned that when he visited the quarantine area, 'men and women shook their fists in my face, vowing dreadful vengeance'.

One woman, Hughes said, 'tearfully assured me that they had whitewashed her piano', and Charlie Shireham, one of his staunch supporters, complained his bathroom had been taken away – with Hughes drily noting that Charlie didn't have a bathroom, but 'he performed his ablutions, such as they were, under the tap in the yard. For the rest he pinned his faith to beer.'

While both Charlie and Hughes took liberties with the truth, the impact of the plague on the waterfront community was both significant and long term. Work ceased along with the cash flow for most of the families. Quarantine meant they couldn't travel outside a small area – 'cooped up like fowls in crate, exposed to every indignity and denied the opportunity to earn their living' as Hughes wrote. Most declined the government offer of temporary relocation to the Quarantine Station at North Head. With the docks at a standstill, and workers unable to leave the quarantine area to get employment elsewhere in the city, Hughes persuaded Premier Lyne to pay each resident in the quarantine six shillings a day.

The impact on morale, according to Hughes, was immediate, and he described it as 'the sun of this new and better day', he continued, 'swarms of children played cricket in the trafficless streets, knots of men gathered hopefully around the innumerable pubs for which this fertile district was so justly famed, filling in the intervals between drinks with debate, discourse and the occasional song'.

The plague brought into focus the poor state of the city's privately owned wharves – many were almost derelict, filthy and a breeding ground for the rats. Ninety members of Parliament signed a petition, passed in May 1900, for the government's resumption of control of the wharves as part of the cleansing of the city. The plague also stirred anti-immigration enthusiasts who believed Asia was the cause of their recent problem – a sentiment that would grow rather than abate.

By August the plague was gone and the city was back to normal. There had been 303 cases of bubonic plague diagnosed, with reports of the death toll varying from 103 to 112. The Quarantine Station became the burial ground for those killed by the plague with their bodies buried in a specially dug grave around fifteen metres deep. Most of the cases were reported in an area stretching from The Rocks in the north, Elizabeth Street to the east, Liverpool Street to the south, and the Darling Harbour wharves to the west – the heart of the city's maritime community. Peter Curson in *Living in Cities* wrote 'in terms of community disruption, human tragedy, suffering and panic, [the 1900 plague] was the greatest social disaster in the city's nineteenth century history'.

There were cases of plague reported around Australia, as wide apart as Coolgardie and Townsville, and only Tasmania was fortunate to miss out. Sydney bore the brunt of the epidemic. It was the first of twelve outbreaks over the next twenty-five years and each time the disease arrived via the waterfront, hitting the local communities first.

In the aftermath, the government acted to improve the conditions on the docklands, harbour and waterfront communities, particularly The Rocks and Millers Point. The result was the Sydney Harbour Improvement Trust – a name that lasted only briefly until wiser heads realised the acronym and dropped 'improvement' in 1901. The trust was charged to 'make the ocean gateway to the city wholesome, attractive and efficient to meet the requirements of trade, and, as far as practicable, provide for the future shipping and commercial needs'. The government bought around 900 houses, along with commercial buildings like bond stores. Houses in The Rocks that had been demolished were not rebuilt. A rumour doing the rounds in the following years suggested the acquisitions and demolition were part of the early planning for the Sydney Harbour Bridge.

The new century brought with it the prospect of dramatic changes to the politics of the nation and to the working lives of most Australians. In the waterfront communities it would be become a century of equally dramatic changes as they transitioned from the grind of poverty and the uncertainty of work to a life with a whiff of comfort and political clout.

14
A NATION UNITED – SORT OF

Federation arrived on 1 January 1901, and the Duke of York, in Melbourne on 9 May 1901, swore in the first Federal Parliament. Edmund Barton was prime minister, and William Morris 'Billy' Hughes was no longer a state parliamentarian, but the first member for the New South Wales seat of West Sydney – an electorate that took in his old State seat and most of Sydney's waterfront.

One of the first pieces of legislation passed by the new Federal Government was the *Immigration Restriction Act,* ostensibly to keep the arrival of more crooks to a minimum and make sure that people with infectious diseases were also kept out. The Act introduced a dictation test that could be used to exclude a new arrival if they couldn't write a 'passage of fifty words in length in a European language' dictated by an immigration officer – handy if you were keen to preclude Asian immigrants. Speaking in support of the bill, Barton said, 'the doctrine of the equality of man was never intended to apply to the equality of the Englishman and the Chinaman'. Alfred Deakin, then attorney-general and later prime minister held a similar view, saying 'unity of race is an absolute essential to the unity of Australia'. With the Chinese and Japanese squarely in his sights, he said 'it is not the bad qualities but the good qualities of these alien races that make them dangerous to us. It is their inexhaustible energy, their power of applying themselves to new tasks, their endurance, and low standard of living that make them such competitors.' Billy Hughes, union leader and now Federal politician, agreed and years later said the notion of a white Australia was 'the greatest thing we ever achieved'. The first parliament had captured the mood of the country, and for generations it would prove very difficult to change.

Under Hughes' leadership, the Sydneysiders moved to consolidate the waterfront unions into a national body – giving more power to Hughes and his colleagues and building a power base for their political careers. In the lead-up to winning his seat in Federal Parliament, Hughes was busy on the hustings, talking to meetings of workers like cab drivers, marble-workers, fishermen, and store men. Just as he'd done with the union he now headed, he revived the Trolley and Draymen's Union and became president. The union added 'Carter' to its name and later became part of the Transport Workers Union. It was a good fit for Hughes because the union's members were tasked to shift goods from the waterfront to the bond stores and warehouses and their pay was around 35 shillings for a sixty-hour week – significantly less than the wharfies – and they could be used as extra labour on the waterfront rather than have the employers use 'blackleg' labour.

On 7 February 1902, the Waterside Workers of Australia was launched at Parliament House in Melbourne – uniting the Sydney Waterfront Labourers, Port Phillip Stevedores, and workers from Port Pirie, Mackay, Townsville, Thursday Island, Cairns, Brisbane, Geraldton and Maryborough. Fremantle, Albany, Hobart, Strahan, Bunbury, Cooktown and the Melbourne Wharf Labourers Union joined shortly thereafter with the Newcastle Wharf Labourers and Rockhampton signing up the next year.

•

By the close of that first meeting, the Waterside Workers of Australia union had around 6300 members, of which around 2800 were in Sydney. What was unusual about the union was that the first executives were more familiar with the workings of politics rather than the workings of the waterfront.

As the driving force for a federal union, and with the largest membership block in his own electorate, Hughes was elected as president – he'd come a long way fast from those early days in Balmain. Joining him on the executive was the Vice President F. W. 'Fred' Bamford – the member for Herbert (situated in Townsville, Queensland) and a former publican; the treasurer was Western Australia's Senator Hugh de Largie – an ex miner; ex miner Andrew Fisher, the member for Wide Bay (situated in Maryborough and the Sunshine Coast) and later prime minister; and Queensland Senator William Higgs – a former printer. Joe Morris, from the Port Phillip Stevedores' Association, was the sole waterfront worker on the executive, and he got the political equivalent of a 'flick pass' when he accepted the post as general secretary – plenty of work and the princely sum of 10 shillings a week as pay.

One reason for the make-up of the leadership was put forward as a simple matter of economy. The unions weren't flush with funds, travel was expensive and with the Federal Parliament now based in Melbourne it was good sense to have the executive all in the one place at the same time, and so politicians with taxpayer funded travel was an elegant solution. They'd meet during the parliamentary sessions, and then return to their state or electorate and deliver the results of their deliberations on behalf of the wharfies. As Margo Beasley wrote in *Wharfies,* it 'reflected symbiotic relationship between the trade unions and the young Labor Party'. Laurence Fitzhardinge in the *Australian Journal of Politics and History* wrote that Hughes was 'first and foremost a politician' and his 'activity as a union organizer, important as it was, was an extension of his political ambitions'. The probability of a conflict of interest wasn't a consideration.

Less kind was one unnamed writer who took issue with Hughes and his team, commenting that David O'Keefe, the Tasmanian Senator who joined the committee in 1902, had his waterfront experience confined to 'watching the Launceston wharfies loading the Union Steam Ship Company's *Loongana*' – a ship on the run across Bass Strait to Melbourne. The writer also said the executive were 'immune from job victimisation' and as for Hughes, the choice of elegant Kew for his Melbourne residence was a place where the 'horny-handed sons of toil were unlikely to be neighbours'. American writer Isaac Marcosson in his 1916 book *The War After the War* described the formation of the national union and its leader as 'Hughes was the unanimous choice of the husky stevedores. He became The Great Restrainer. Never was the influence of lip and brain over muscle and temper better demonstrated. The wild men of the wharves – the roughest crowd in all labor – were under his spell.'

•

The formation of the national union coincided with two of nature's less desirable traits: drought and disease. Australia was in the grip of the Federation Drought – one of the worst in the country's history. Wheat crops failed, the cattle population dropped by 40%, and sheep dropped from around 106 million in 1891 to around 54 million with the wool trade, the country's greatest export, being savaged. The regular wool trains to Williamstown docks and into Sydney's docklands slowed to a trickle.

The bubonic plague reappeared with reported cases in Sydney, Melbourne, Brisbane and one suspected case in Newcastle. Sydney's GPO was described as a 'potential plague centre' after one worker fell ill, and an inspection found an 'unsanitary state of affairs'. Smallpox followed.

The plague's return visit to Melbourne was blamed on the steamer SS *Coolgardie*. The ship wasn't popular on the Melbourne docks with the 'lumpers' fearing the cargo had been contaminated in Sydney before heading to their city. In spite of assurances the cargo hadn't been loaded in Sydney, the workers refused to budge until it had been fumigated. On 5 March 1902, the *Argus* reported that the *Coolgardie* had brought the plague south from Sydney, saying 'the recent appearance of bubonic plague, which has been followed by a daily list of fresh cases, has prepared the people, in some measure, for some manifestation of its presence in this city'. The article went on to note the manifestation was 'when startling news of an outbreak in Fitzroy spread through the city'. The first victim was James Quantock, a 45-year-old wharf labourer of Argyle Street, Fitzroy.

Mr Quantock and six colleagues had been loading cargo in the number three hold of the *Coolgardie*, which already contained superphosphate fertiliser that, according to *The Age*, was a 'commodity in which rats fairly revel'. The names and addresses of the six wharfies were given to *The Age* and published, along with reassuring news that the plague had come from Sydney and wasn't of local origin.

The newspaper reports provided a snapshot of the life of a waterside worker and his family and of how the broader community viewed them. As reported in *The Advocate*, Quantock was 'the father of five children, four of them are girls. The children are aged 9, 7, 4, 2 and 9 months. They were living in a small wooden tenement with five rooms, and adjoining another cottage. The whole street is unsavoury, and the two houses referred to are the worst in the street.' Quantock's house 'stands a little back from the street, and in the locality there are weather worn and ancient tenements, doomed to demolition sooner or later, under the progressive and insistent march of sanitary science'.

The Melbourne authorities were as aggressive as those in Sydney two years earlier, and while Mr Quantock survived, the family home didn't. On 13 March both the Quantocks' house and that of their neighbour, a Mr Tunks, were burned to the ground on the order of the Central Board of Health. Their landlady, a Mrs Taylor, was paid £20 in compensation, but there was no report of any compensation being paid to her tenants or help in finding a new home.

Joining the plague was smallpox – a disease that had arrived on the First Fleet and in 1789 had quickly spread to the Aboriginal communities near the new settlement. Lacking the built up immunity of the white arrivals, these communities were devastated by the disease, with a mortality rate of around 70%. The later smallpox outbreak was mainly in Melbourne around the waterfront, and had the wharfies understandably nervous. On the positive side, Australia's health authorities were vigilant and quick to act with quarantining and a vaccination program.

If disease hadn't made life on the waterfront even more miserable than the harsh working conditions, poverty and thugs from the pushes, there was a further problem and one that was a cornerstone of the thinking of both the unions – competition for jobs.

At the outbreak of the Boer War in 1899, Hughes, then in the NSW Parliament, attacked the idea of sending of troops from the Australian colonies to fight as 'a war undertaken in the interests of a powerful clique in Africa whose only desire appeared to press on and by fair means or foul, to put their hands on the best lands and the best property in Africa', and said that Britain was 'a great pugilist attacking an infant' and continued the metaphor describing Australia's role as like asking your little brother to 'hold the infant while he gets at him'. The colonial governments ignored Hughes. In July 1899, with war looming, the British government asked New South Wales and Victoria to send troops. Queensland volunteered. War broke out in October 1899, and in November, Australian troops had 'boots on the ground'.

Around 16,000 Australians eventually headed to Africa to fight. As the war drew to a close, Australian shipowners and stevedoring firms began advertising in the British papers for waterfront labourers, promising ample work and good pay to those happy to jump on a ship and head to Australia. It was a tempting offer that also caught the attention of returning Australian soldiers – many of them young men from the bush who, after a few years of war in the African scrub, weren't in a hurry to return to their former lives.

The employers were taking aim at Billy Hughes and his rapidly strengthening union, and Hughes, swapping his parliamentary hat for that of union leader, attacked. In the *Sydney Morning Herald* of 29 May 1901, he wrote that the Sydney waterfront, with more than 3000 men able to work, and with the unpredictable nature of their trade, meant there was no need to recruit. The Boer War veterans returned to an Australia with a brand new Federal Government and high unemployment. If the veterans were looking for a warm welcome after three years of war in harsh conditions – freezing cold nights, scorching days, and a conflict that had descended into guerrilla warfare – they were out of luck. Contemporary technology – telegrams and fast ships – meant the Boer War was one of the first conflicts to be covered by correspondents who filed their story as the battles were happening. The reporting of the British mistreatment of Boer settlers – destruction of farms, rounding up of women and children and their placement in concentration camps where thousands died of malnutrition and disease – soured the Australian public's view.

In August 1902, the Waterside Workers union executive made their first foray as a national body, approaching the Australian Steamship Owners Federation for an increase in wages to 1 shilling 3 pence per hour and time and a half for overtime. The opening gambit of the shipowners was to question the right of the union to negotiate and, in particular, whether the Melbourne Wharf Labourers were supporting them – a clever move as the labourers weren't overly excited by Billy Hughes and his colleagues.

The negotiations didn't amount to much, with the shipowners exploiting differences within the unions. The politics didn't interest the union membership and at Trades Hall on 10 September 1902 one report said, 'angry men and women told of families evicted into the streets because they had no money to pay for rent'. Children were going to school hungry, and there wasn't money for new clothing or, for some, even a shoelace. One wit noted that Cobb & Co – the transport company that had got its start during the gold rush, ferrying hopefuls from Melbourne's docks to the goldfields – who provided much of the transport from the wharves paid £22,000 per year for horse feed, and only £20,000 in wages, with the horses on the wharves looking better fed than the wharfies.

The wharfies' work remained brutal even with modern steamship designs making the job a little easier than in the days of sail. Bags of products ranging from the superphosphate in the hold of the SS *Coolgardie*, coffee beans, potatoes, flour, cement and manure were lugged from the ships. The bags weighed from around seventy to over 100 kilograms. The wharfies usually 'necked' the bags by laying them across their shoulders, carrying them about twelve to twenty-five metres, and a typical wharfie averaged around sixty-seven bags per hour.

Overfilling was common, with freight costed by the number of bags rather than weight, so producers would cram in as much as possible – and the wharfie found out just how much that was when he lifted the bag. The inevitable injuries were called 'bed bugs' because men were often taken to hospital as a result of an unsuccessful lift. With plenty of cheap labour on offer, occupation health and safety concerns weren't high on the list of the employers.

Plague, pestilence and politics at the beginning of the new century had done a fine job in dominating the news cycle.

15
AUSTRALIA GOES TO WAR – AGAIN

Australia's politics in the years immediately after Federation were turbulent – the country had had six prime ministers by the time World War I was declared. Two of those had sprung from the early days of the Labour Party on Sydney's waterfront. Chris Watson, a former newspaper editor and ardent unionist, became the third prime minister, and the first Labour member to hold the post, but it was only a brief tenure. He was appointed after Alfred Deakin, whose Protectionist Party was propped up by Labour, resigned after disagreeing with Watson and his party over industrial relations laws. George Reid, the Free Trade leader, declined to take Deakin's place, and so Watson got the job – but he only lasted from 27 April 1904 to 18 August 1904. The same industrial relations legislation claimed its second government. George Reid became prime minister, but not for long with Deakin returning in 1906.

The wharfies got their first man as prime minister, when Andrew Fisher got the job on 13 November 1908, and Billy Hughes became his attorney-general. Hughes had completed his law studies in 1903 and in 1909 was appointed King's Counsel

– not a bad effort for a barrister who was unfamiliar with the inside of a courtroom. He remained President of the Waterside Workers Federation and like some modern politicians hadn't grasped the concept of 'conflict of interests', or preferred to ignore it.

As usual in those tempestuous days, Fisher wasn't in office long, replaced by Deakin on 2 June 1909 after Labour was defeated in the House. In the merry-go-round of Australian politics, Deakin barely had time to sit down before being ousted, this time at an election when Andrew Fisher and his Labour party were voted back into power on 29 April 1910.

Fisher and his government fared better this time – at least in tenure, and it wasn't until the elections of 31 May 1914 they were shown the door when beaten by a Liberal coalition who secured the House of Representatives by just one seat. However, new Prime Minister Joseph Cook didn't enjoy a lot of luck. While his coalition controlled the lower house, Labor (the spelling changed from Labour to Labor in 1912) had the Senate and used their power sooner rather than later.

There have been six 'double dissolutions' in Australian history, with the most famous involving Gough Whitlam's Labor Government versus Malcolm Fraser's Coalition Opposition. The first was in 1914, when Joseph Cook's Liberal coalition government was thwarted by the Labor-dominated Senate, and so in June 1914, Cook sought a double dissolution and an election was set for 5 September 1914. It was interesting timing with the world on the brink of war.

Both Cook and Fisher, still the Labor leader and eyeing a third term as prime minister, talked up their support for Britain in the forthcoming war with Germany. On 31 July 1914, the day the governor-general received word from Britain that a declaration of war was at hand, Fisher told the nation, 'Australians will stand beside our own to help and defend her [Britain] to our last man and our last shilling.' It was a political promise that came sadly close to a reality. On 4 August 1914, with Australia's political leadership in 'caretaker' mode, the nation went to war. Labor won the election and Fisher began his third term on 17 September 1914 – but by that time the first shots had been fired, and the first men killed.

Drummer E. Thomas of Britain's 4th Dragoon Guards usually gets the dubious credit for firing the first 'British' shot of World War I when he opened fire on the Germans in the Belgian village of Casteau on 22 August 1914. The first shot fired at an 'enemy' target, however, was fired from the Australian waterfront at a German target, and is more generously referred to as the first 'allied' or 'British Empire' shot.

SS *Pfalz* was an almost new cargo ship owned by Germany's Nordeutscher Lloyd line under the command of Captain W. Kuhiken – on his first voyage in command. It arrived at Melbourne's No. 2 Victoria Dock on 31 July 1914. War was imminent and the captain knew that when the declaration was made, his ship, his crew and himself might spend the duration in Australia and possibly not with the comfort and freedoms they enjoyed onboard unless he acted quickly. On the evening of 4 August, the ship was ready for sea, and bound for Sydney – or so the port authorities believed. But Kuhiken had no intention of sailing his ship up the coast, and instead was planning on changing course after clearing Port Phillip Bay and heading straight toward neutral territory in South America.

A last-minute delay meant the *Pfalz* didn't get under way until early the next morning, and that's when she struck a run of bad luck. Early morning traffic in the Yarra slowed her departure even further. Around 10 am when the heads were in sight, she was stopped to allow a launch from the Naval Board's Examination Service to come alongside, and personnel from the service to board and inspect the ship – a common practice in those tense times. Fortunately for the crew and passengers of the *Pfalz,* which included staff from the German Consulate, the Examination

Service hadn't been notified of the outbreak of war, and the ship was given the all clear. As the launch headed back to shore, Captain Robinson of the Port Phillip Pilot service – on board to take the ship down the bay and out through the heads – turned *Pfalz* around as she'd moved during the inspection, and pointed her toward the channel. One report noted 'German consular officials, who had not previously made their appearance on deck, then came on to the bridge, and they and the ship's captain displayed great jubilation' – bye bye Melbourne, hello South America, and just in the nick of time.

However, their jubilation was premature because by the time the Examination Service launch had returned to shore, news of the outbreak of war had arrived. Fort Nepean, on the point that forms part of the heads – a stretch of water that had troubled mariners ever since the early days of white settlement – used flags to signal *Pfalz* to stop, but Robinson was busy piloting the ship through the tricky waters and didn't notice them, and the Germans didn't mention them.

What did get Robinson's attention was a shot fired from one of the fort's guns, which landed close to the stern. Robinson believed the shot was a variation of the classic 'shot across the bows', but it was more likely poor aim. He reacted quickly and ordered 'full-astern' on the bridge telegraph to the engine room, but Kuhiken then acted just as quickly, ordering full speed ahead. As the two then struggled for control, Robinson pointed out the next shot would be at the target –'resistance is futile' or something similar he told the German. Robinson took the ship to Portsea where the crew and passengers were arrested, then sailed *Pfalz* to the docks at Williamstown. Five months later she became the Australian troop ship HMAT *Boorara*.

By 10 August, military recruiting offices were open for business, and the following day, ships from the Royal Australian Navy were scouring Simpson Harbour and Matupi Harbour in New Guinea, in search of Admiral von Spee's German East Asiatic Squadron, which was thought to be lurking in the area. Further out to sea, the navy's flagship, the battle cruiser HMAS *Australia,* under the command of the Royal Navy's Rear Admiral George Patey, was also on the hunt. On 19 August, HMAT *Berrima,* a P&O liner requisitioned for the war effort, left Sydney's Cockatoo Island docks with the Australian Naval and Military Expeditionary Force of around 1000 troops and 500 naval reservists and former Royal Navy sailors.

One of the main challenges for the force was to destroy von Spee's network of wireless stations in German colonies in New Guinea, the Caroline Islands to its north, and Nauru. On 11 September, troops landed at Bitapaka near Rabaul and encountered stiff resistance in the dense jungle but finally overwhelmed their enemy. The cost was five men killed – Able Seamen Walker, Williams, Street, Moffatt, and Captain Pockley of the Army Medical Corps. These were the first Australian casualties of the war.

The task force achieved another unwelcome first – the disappearance of the submarine *AE1* on 14 September. *AE1* had a total of thirty-five men on board and was one of two Australian submarines. It was the nation's first naval loss, and the first 'British' submarine loss of the war. At the time of writing, the hunt for *AE1* has resumed – 100 years after her disappearance.

The Hughes-led union had enjoyed some success by the outbreak of war: an award to set uniform wages. The lead-up had been eventful, with dock strikes and squabbling between the unions involved on the waterfront, and power plays within the Waterside Workers Federation. By 1913, and mostly due to Hughes' strong leadership, a log of claims had been formulated which included demands for basics like increased wages and overtime, payment for breaks like lunch and the 'smoko', and then more exotic requests like special rates for working with refrigerated cargoes, explosives and fertilisers, and health and safety issues.

At the heart of the wharfies' claim was the need for consistency of income in an industry that was at the mercy of employers, the weather and economic fluctuations. They wanted a basic wage and tenure instead of the casual system of pick-ups at the whim of the supervisors or foremen. Justice Higgins summed up his view on the conditions of the waterside workers saying, 'it is lamentable that so many lusty men, mostly in the prime of life, should have to stand about idle, waiting for a job at the usual place of hiring – earn nothing some days, nothing even some weeks, and earning high wages some weeks by excessive hours of toil'. The judge then compared the workers to the better-fed horses of Cobb and Co, saying, 'they [the men] are entitled at least to food, clothes and shelter for them and their dependents during the whole term of this service. If a man keeps a horse, he has to feed the horse on days when he does not use him, as well as on days that he does'. The judge also made an insightful observation, saying 'the frequent bouts of idleness must often lead to bad habits'.

Bad habits, war and the long-standing suspicion of anyone either not white or from British stock collided in the first months of the war. The Germans went to the top of the list of people Australians didn't like and the country had a community of around 100,000 to pick from. Army recruiting posters showed the world in the grip of reptilian looking 'Huns' wearing the pointed military helmet favoured by German officers. Businesses run by Germans, or people of German descent, were boycotted, men were rounded up and sent to internment camps. My great-grandfather, who was born in New Zealand and moved to Australia as a young man, had a lengthy spell interned in Sydney's Darlinghurst Gaol because he hadn't seen a need to change his very German surname. It ruined his business and destroyed the comfortable retirement he'd planned and saved for.

On the waterfront, war hit the community first and hard. The prospect of attack from Graf von Spee's squadron – raiders like

Emden and the latest in naval technology, the U boat – caused the inbound shipping trade to slow dramatically. The difficulty in getting insurance on their ships and cargoes meant shipowners were loath to commit their vessels to risky voyages. When the British Government introduced the War Risk Insurance Scheme to support owners, the insurance didn't run to cargoes deemed to be luxury goods or unnecessary. In 1915, the problem was compounded by sinkings outnumbering shipbuilding, and the following year, the British Empire had around 3500 ocean-going cargo ships, with a little over half requisitioned for the war effort. Short haul routes serviced by 'tramp' steamers collapsed. The Royal Australian Navy's publication *Semaphore* noted in November 2003 of Britain's trade with Australia during the war that, 'due to its isolation at the furthest limit of the Empire, [it] was the first to be abandoned and the last to be re-instituted'.

The damaged trade meant work on the waterfront became even more unreliable – the poor became poorer and the German waterside workers became a target for the anger of their fellow workers. The Melbourne *Argus* of 8 September 1914, headlined 'Trouble on the Wharves – Germans and the Flag – Stevedores' Club Incident', recounted that at the Port Phillip Stevedores' Association club, a German member had threatened to trample a British flag – not a wise move at the time, particularly with alcohol added to the politics. No surprise that a fight broke out and the German was on the receiving end of some 'rough handling'. The paper then reported the response of the club was to drape a ten by four feet Union Jack on a pole above the entrance and 'every member entering the building was compelled to raise his hat and salute the flag. Excitement ran high and a huge crowd gathered in the street. A man with an accordion and another with bagpipes, followed by a procession of fifty men, played patriotic airs and marched in front of the club premises.'

Later that afternoon, more brawls broke out with three German members of the association receiving, according to the

Argus, 'a severe thrashing, afterwards stampeding down Bay Street, followed by a large crowd'. The cause was allegedly that the 'Australians' had decided to refuse to work under the orders of 'German' foremen. Wilhelm Smock was attacked by Cecil Brotherton who 'put his arm around Smock's neck and punched him'. Brotherton later claimed the Germans were rumoured to be carrying revolvers and he'd asked Smock to give him the weapon, Smock 'applied an objectionable expression to him' and the fight began. The Germans, 'white with fear', 'lost no time in making for the police station, where they took refuge, one afterwards boarding a passing tram'. One unnamed commentator in the *Argus* noted the large crowd was more of a 'cowardly mob'. One of the Germans had been in Australia for decades and his children – by then in their late teens – were born here.

The *Argus* reported Constables Boyd and Walsh, while trying to 'rescue Smock from the violence of the crowd, met with considerable opposition. Foul epithets were shouted at them, and Constable Walsh, in addition to receiving face bruises, had a tooth knocked out. In order to get clear, the constable had to make use of both batons and handcuffs as weapons.' The association members weren't deterred by four of their members being carted off by police and charged with assault, with the *Argus* reporting that on the day after the mob scenes, the members gathered again at the club which was 'bedecked with additional Union Jacks and a bold placard outside gave the information: No Germans Need Apply. Three Germans were singled out and were struck violently.'

The Port Phillip Stevedores' Association members were equal opportunity racists, so, as the *Argus* reported, 'foreigners other than Germans have come in for treatment intended for Germans'. Among the other targets were men from Scandinavia, some of who were Australian-born but, like my great-grandfather, hadn't seen a need to anglicise their surname. The exclusion of these 'foreign' workers also meant that there was more work for association members in difficult times – the employers just wanted the job done. The situation worsened with members refusing to work with anyone who wasn't a man 'of British origin' – including long-standing members of their own union. They were joined in their stance by other unions.

On 30 November 1914, the *Argus* reported,

> the antipathy displayed by the Port Phillip Stevedores' Association of Port Melbourne has spread to the Wharf Labourers' Union, and the members of the Union have agreed that from today they will refuse to work with Germans on the river wharves or at Williamtown. The objection to German labourers was not preceded by a repetition of the disturbance that characterized the boycott agreed upon by the Port Phillip Stevedores' Association. There were no free fights, and no Australian flag was hoisted with every foreigner compelled to salute by baring his head as was the case at Port Melbourne.

The unhealthy enthusiasm of the Victorians spread around the nation's ports. One of the few voices of reason was that of Tom Barker. He was an ex British Army soldier who headed to New Zealand where he became involved in unions and joined the International Workers of the World (IWW). After running into some strife in 1914 – he was charged with sedition – he came to Sydney and resumed his union career. In the 1 January 1915 issue of the IWW's *Direct Action* he wrote 'now that the Empire is in danger the Sydney Wharfies have risen to the occasion. They have determined not to allow Germans, Australian, or Turks, naturalised or unnaturalised, to get a living on the Sydney waterfront.'

In an intriguing foretaste of today's complaints of the influence of tabloid media, he wrote,

> we fail to see anything to boast about in this business and the whole matter should leave a nasty taste in the mouths of those militant members of the organization who refuse to have their

opinions manufactured for them by the 'Sunday Times' and other inspired organs of vested interest. It is a reflection upon the intelligence to drive a father off the wharf and to leave his son working there just because his father was born in Germany. The whole thing is childish in the extreme and unworthy of men who pretend to be unionists.

Barker's emotive language fell on deaf ears. He didn't endear himself by shortly after telling the Australian Workers Union, who were refusing to organise 'coloured workers', that 'the Class War is a nobler sentiment than the Race War, for it strives for the abolition of chains and not for their perpetuation'. He also managed to annoy Billy Hughes with his views. In July 1915, Barker achieved a career highlight when he published recruiting posters that shouted 'To Arms – Capitalists, Parsons, Politicians, Landlords, Newspaper Editors, and other Stay at Home Patriots; Your Country Needs You in the Trenches – Workers Follow Your Masters!' He was prosecuted but the fine was remitted by the government. He wasn't as fortunate the next year when, as editor of *Direct Action*, he wrote that Billy Hughes, by then prime minister, had 'offered another 50,000 men as fresh sacrifice to the modern Moloch [the demanding of a sacrifice]. Politicians and their masters have always been generous with other people's lives', which resulted in a prosecution under the War Precautions Act and a sentence of twelve months in prison.

In 1918, Barker was deported to Chile from where he was quickly expelled to Argentina and became a wharfie. By 1927 he was back in London, working as a clerk and involved in local Labour politics as a councillor.

16
MR HUGHES GOES TRAVELLING

Billy Hughes was sworn in as prime minister on 27 October 1915 – moving into the top job unopposed after the resignation of Andrew Fisher that same day. Hughes also kept his job as president of the wharfies' union. Fisher's departure was prompted by poor health and a brutal year. The Gallipoli landings had been devastating and, in September, Fisher had asked journalist Keith Murdoch, then on his way to Gallipoli and London, to secretly report to him on what he'd found. Murdoch reported of the Gallipoli campaign that 'your fears have been justified' and that 'continuous and ghastly bungling' by the British had led to 'one of the most terrible chapters in our history'. For Fisher, it was the final straw, and after missing parliament for three days without any excuse, he resigned as prime minister and from his parliamentary seat. His retirement package was a familiar one – he was appointed as High Commissioner to London, replacing another former Prime Minister, George Reid. However, Hughes' tenure as prime minister was to be brief – at least this time around.

On the waterfront, business had picked up. The intensifying war in Europe and the lack of any sizeable enemy presence in the Pacific and Indian oceans meant that early concerns for the safety of shipping dissipated. Captured enemy ships were replacing Allied vessels that had been sunk. The drought that had plagued the nation was gone by 1915 and the wheat crop that year was the highest for the ten-year period from 1911 to 1920. To take advantage of the bounty and the US crop failure, Hughes bought fifteen ships to export it, with the ships becoming the first in the government-owned 'Commonwealth Line' – a move that appealed to the members of his union. But, as is usual in politics, Hughes' honeymoon was a short one.

In 1915, he'd told the nation, 'in no circumstances would I agree to send men out of this country to fight against their will'. The country had compulsory military service but conscripts could only serve in Australia and its territories.

On 26 January 1916, Hughes left Australia and headed to Britain, via New Zealand and Canada where he stopped for talks on the war effort. He visited Australian troops near the front shortly before the deadly Battle of the Somme, addressing them while standing on ammunition boxes. Around 23,000 Australians would be casualties in the battle, with 6700 killed. Charles Bean, the official Australian War Historian, described Pozières, as 'a ridge more densely sown with Australian sacrifice than any other place on earth'.

Hughes returned to Australia on 31 July 1916, convinced of the need to support the war by sending more troops, which meant ordering conscripts to fight overseas. Laborites who didn't agree with him thought he'd been seduced by the power of the British establishment on his travels. The *Oxford Companion to Australian History* said, 'Hughes was fêted in establishment circles. This, according to Labor legend, turned his head and, forgetting his party and his country, he decided to conscript Australian men for imperial purposes.'

Hughes, who made his career by bringing people together and galvanising them to act, was about to face his biggest failure and establish a reputation in the Labor Party that lingers a century later. By mid August, the media was reporting a reversal of his earlier position and that he

> makes no secret of the fact that he is personally for conscription, without which in one form or another, it is clear that Australia can not do its duty by itself to Great Britain or its Allies. The Prime Minister's declaration has been received with profound satisfaction by the great body of the people who, for the time at least, are above party politics. The many realize that honour is at stake, and that honour is involved in the very life of the nation.

The press, conservative-leaning politicians and the Church, were behind Hughes, but his party wasn't. Hughes pressed ahead with a referendum requiring a simple 'yes' or 'no' to the question, 'Are you in favour of the Government having, in this great emergency, the same compulsory powers over citizens in regard to requiring their military service for the term of the war, outside the Commonwealth, as it now has in regard to military service within the Commonwealth?' and set it for 28 October 1916.

Hughes' campaign was state of the art, with the prime minister using silent newsreel films to push his message to the public. 'Vote "Yes" – Fame Success. Vote "No" – Dishonour Woe.' He used the emotive language of his trade union days, calling those who didn't agree with him 'blacklegs', 'scabs' and 'shirkers' – terms familiar to waterside workers who'd directed them at non-union labourers. Playing the guilt card were slogans like 'Do you want to save men in the trenches from a ninety-six hours shift under shellfire? Then vote "yes",' and 'the only proper backing for Anzacs is more Anzacs. Are you going to scab on Anzacs?'

Rather than sway the workers, the campaign divided the nation. The *Argus* reported, 'on the banks of the Yarra again and again police have rescued anti-conscription orators from the crowd'. In Sydney, the *Sydney Morning Herald* reported that an unnamed Labor Minister had 'told a deputation that 200 policemen had failed to protect the "anti" protesters that so unpopular was their view that short of shooting down the crowd, he could see no way of getting them a hearing'. Among the advocates for the 'no' vote were future prime ministers John Curtin and James Scullin.

The Waterside Workers Federation wasn't a fan of Hughes and his campaign either. On 27 September, a special meeting of the Sydney branch – of which Hughes was still a member – heard a motion to expel their member who was both head of their union and prime minister. The vote in favour of expulsion was a resounding 160 to 42. At their conference the next month, the union passed a motion opposing 'conscription of life and industry in all its forms', along with the passing of a rule preventing serving politicians from being officials.

The referendum vote was close: 1,087,557 to 1,160,003 – in favour of 'No'. On 14 November, the first of the great Labor Party splits occurred with Hughes and his supporters fronting a hostile caucus and a 'no confidence' vote. Hughes, however, was in front of the game – he'd done his numbers, and said to the meeting, 'Enough of this. Let those who think with me follow me,' and walked out with twenty-five parliamentarians following. His next stop was to visit an old ally, Governor-General Sir Ronald Munro Ferguson, and offer his resignation, which he knew would be rejected. The governor-general believed Hughes to be the right man to lead the nation during the war, and disregarded the Liberals, led by Joseph Cook who now had a majority in parliament. Hughes remained prime minister, changing parties from Labor to the brand-new National Labor Party. He was expelled from the party of which he was a founder, but had his own view on the end of his Labor career, saying 'I did not leave the Labor Party. The Labor Party left me.'

The Labor Party were bitter and would take years to recover. They thought Hughes' actions were in part motivated by his need to be a player on the world stage. Robert Manne in *The Australian Century* observed, 'the Labor members gave no thought to whether a National Labor government deserved their support except on the issue which divided them – conscription. They were bent on vengeance against Hughes: they wanted to demonstrate that those who broke solidarity would be destroyed, and persuaded themselves that everyone outside the ranks of official Labor was a pawn of the capitalists.'

The failure of the referendum didn't translate into an electoral backlash – on 5 May 1917, Hughes and his party were returned to power with a significant majority in both Houses. The only notable change was Hughes didn't contest his old Sydney seat – a wise move given his ousting from the union that represented most of his constituents – but instead ran successfully against the Labor incumbent in Bendigo, Victoria, an inland seat a healthy distance from the waterfront.

The two national unions, the Waterside Workers Federation and the Painters and Dockers, decided to flex their muscle and add to Hughes' problems by joining the 'General Strike' of 1917. It ran from early August 1917 until late October and involved nearly 100,000 workers. It didn't start on the waterfront but on the railways of NSW because the NSW Department of Railway and Tramways introduced a US-style card system in their Eveleigh and Randwick workshops to monitor and improve the performance of their workers. In response, nearly 6000 workers walked out of workshops in Sydney, Newcastle and Goulburn on 2 August.

By the end of the next week, around 30,000 workers in various unions, including the seamen and coal miners, were on strike in 'sympathy'. The first of those on the waterfront to join the strike were the Melbourne wharfies, followed soon after by their Sydney comrades. In Melbourne, they began their campaign by refusing to load food for export – believing that shortages at home of staples like flour should be addressed first. Exports to Holland or Dutch colonies came in for special attention, with wharfies suspecting them to be a convenient wartime shipping address, with Germany the real destination. This targeted industrial action annoyed Hughes, who said on 3 August that 'it is absolutely essential that stoppages of work should cease. There is hardly a day on which work in some wharf in Australia is not stopped', and then blamed a 'militant minority' who were an 'absolute curse to Australia'. The wharfies ignored their former leader. The media were on the PM's side, with *The Age* editorial of 11 August echoing the concerns of would-be exporters of products like flour, meat and dairy, saying the wharfies 'claims the right of ruling as to what exports shall or shall not leave the country; and quite a number of collateral unions concede that right and applaud the exercise of it', and that their actions were 'subversive of the democratic principle of government'.

The strike was crippling Australia's east coast, and on 17 August *The Age* reported, 'not for many years has the Melbourne waterfront borne such a deserted appearance as that which was presented yesterday. The long lines of closed sheds and the silent ships with their covered hatches spoke volumes. Not a wharf labourer was to be seen.'

On 19 August 1917 wharfies met and confirmed their will to continue the strike, in defiance of their leadership, who were counselling against it. The wharfies were spurred on by the government's introduction of the National Service Bureau, where workers would register so they could be allotted work. Shipowners seized the opportunity to use these men in preference to union members. When the national bureau was closed at the end of the strike the shipowners and stevedores opened their own bureau and gave preference to the men who'd been registered.

The *Argus* said of the strike that 'no rational person can believe that rational men have worked themselves into this rebellious fever upon an issue so trifling'. While the issue may have been 'trifling', it came at a complex time. The nation had been divided over conscription and was heading to the polls yet again to vote on that subject; the slaughter of thousands in the Somme was fresh in everyone's mind; and, in spite of the USA's recent belated entry to the war, victory was not in sight. Closer to home, the evergreen fight for shorter working hours and better money was still creating conflict and was exacerbated by soaring food costs and imported goods in short supply.

Just as before, the solidarity of the wharfies wasn't as solid as they'd hoped. The government wasn't going to countenance a strike while prosecuting a war on the other side of the world, and used the War Precautions legislation to build and unleash strike-breakers – a mix of waterfront union members, farmers, country people, members of sporting clubs and the like. In Sydney, they were housed in purpose-built barracks at Taronga Park, Circular Quay, in the heart of the waterfront community in Kent Street and at Walsh Bay, and at the Sydney Cricket Ground. To the annoyance of the local waterfront families, the accommodation was a good standard and food plentiful. The strike-breakers were escorted to and from the wharves by police.

One Sydney wharfie, known as 'George B', wrote to his union to tell the story of what his family faced, and why, as a loyal unionist, he'd been forced to go back to work. In a letter dated Thursday 15 November 1917, he wrote,

> the only food in the house was a bit of bread when I left home this morning and an extension of the gas bill which I enclose not paid. About 300 men stood at the gas works gate this morning and 32 were engaged after the card system [a permit to work] and third degree had been gone through. Name, address, where you worked last, how long. He walked us through the gas works to their wharf. Shovel coal, drive winches, work eight and three quarter hours per day, forty eight hours per week, two to three shillings wages – ten shillings

and three pence in the gas yard. We never got the choice. Have I not been driven to something? I knocked off work Wednesday, August 7th. Had one coupon for fifteen shillings [union strike pay]. First job November 15th – 14 weeks later. I have a wife and three youngsters that would have had no supper only for Jack Gavin sending his wife with a parcel of groceries and a few shillings.

He finished his letter saying 'in conclusion fellow members, if you think I am not worthy to retain my medal (membership medal) then I know. This is the hardest blow that has ever fallen on me mentally,' and 'PS please show my letter to all who come up to curse me'.

There is no record of a response from the union. Adding to the problems of George and the waterfront families was that returned servicemen were given preference for work, and in Sydney they formed the Returned Sailors and Soldier's Shop and Wharf Worker's Union NSW.

The railway workers returned to work in late September, with the wharfies drifting back between late October and the end of November. One senior Sydney wharfie said of their stance in support of fellow unionists that 'we discovered to our sorrow that they were so weak or disorganized that they either ran back, or, in some cases, offered to take the place of the wharf labourers who had come out in sympathy with them'.

Later that year, on 20 December, Australia again voted on conscription but this time Hughes didn't have the backing of the Catholic Church. The *Australian Dictionary of Biography* said

> Hughes had promised not to reopen the conscription issue unless 'the tide of battle which flows strongly for the Allies turns against them'. In November 1917 this seemed to have happened and Hughes, under strong pressure, announced another referendum for 20 December. This time passions rose even higher, inflamed by mounting hysteria in Hughes

and by the cold, Irish logic of [Melbourne's] Archbishop Daniel Mannix.

Hughes literally became a target while on the campaign trail in Warwick, Queensland. The *Argus* reported, 'on a hot dusty afternoon, a man threw two rotten eggs at Billy Hughes – the Prime Minister and Attorney General. One of the eggs missed and the other broke on Billy's hat as he harangued the crowd. Angrily, Billy as Attorney General of the Commonwealth called on senior Queensland Police Sergeant Kenny to deal with the egg thrower. The sergeant refused, saying he recognised only the laws of Queensland and would act under no others.'

The Queenslander's attitude was one of the reasons Hughes established the Commonwealth Investigation Service – the forerunner of the Australian Federal Police. Hughes lost the second referendum as well – 1,015.159 votes to 1,181,747.

The Federated Painters and Dockers were also strongly opposed to conscription and became a national union in 1916.

The woes of the waterfront community were added to when the influenza pandemic arrived. The flu killed over an estimated fifty million people around the world – more than World War I's death toll of around sixteen million. In 1919, nearly 6000 died in New South Wales and around 3500 in Victoria. The national total of deaths was 12,000 in a nation with a population a shade under six million. Travel between New South Wales and Victoria halted, and many citizens took to wearing facemasks.

As usual, the waterfront communities were hit first. The disease spread quickly through the communities. Waterside workers reacted by declining to unload ships for fear of infection, with fear triumphing over the need to earn an income.

In the first wave of the epidemic doctors noted that twice as many males were affected, which shouldn't be surprising with the disease being carried by passengers on ships – and in many cases they were returning soldiers – and their first local contacts being with the workers and waterside communities.

Dr Cawley Madden, then a medical student, described the scenes in Sydney's inner city and waterfront areas:

> it was a dreadful time. Very short of doctors. Emergency hospitals everywhere – the Deaf and Dumb Institute, the Showground. I hadn't been in a hospital yet. I couldn't take a temperature but they showed you what to do. We went out on rounds to the people. I suppose we looked like doctors. The doctors were so busy. A lot still hadn't come back from the War so they had to use us. I worked from a Depot in Flinders Street, Darlinghurst, a church there, then from Woolloomooloo, down the Stanley and Palmer Street brothels – I was only 19. You'd go into these houses and there'd be no one up and about and they had no food. Volunteers used to come with food but they couldn't keep up with it.

17
A SPOT OF PILLAGE

The recent wartime strife on the waterfront, and defiance of Billy Hughes and his now rather conservative government, came to a head with the 'Bloody Sunday' incident in Fremantle on 4 May 1919 when a brawl between police and wharfies over the use of non-union labour escalated to a riot. Tom Edwards, a wharfie, was badly injured and died three days later. It was time for Hughes to address the broader issue of waterfront strikes, and to take the heat off his government.

On 7 June 1919, a royal commission was formed to investigate 'the cause of industrial troubles now existing on the Melbourne wharfs'. Royal commissions are one of the most effective weapons in a government's arsenal. A well-crafted set of 'terms of reference' along with a tightly managed budget give the government control of a commission and its direction, provide an opportunity to make the troublesome issues someone else's problem, and give the impression the government has actually done something.

The 1919 royal commission was going to particularly look at the employment of returned servicemen in preference to members of the Waterside Workers Federation. It was an astute political and media savvy call – men returning from a fight for their

Empire were clear winners in a dispute with militant wharfies, and Hughes made sure the commission started with the strike of 1917 and moved forward, thus neatly putting the boot into his former colleagues. Heading the Commission was Melbourne barrister George Dethridge who didn't waste any time and had finished his report within three weeks. Dethridge, later described by Sir Robert Menzies as having 'a sort of barking and emphatic manner of speech which concealed beneath it a quick mind and a somewhat Rabelaisian humour', was appointed as County Court Judge the next year, and in 1926, as the first Chief Judge of the Commonwealth Court of Conciliation and Arbitration.

He found 'the substantial cause of the industrial troubles now existing on the Melbourne wharfs is the great insufficiency of work combined with the preference given by the bureau of the Yarra Stevedoring Company [one of the organisations who'd set up an employment bureau following the closure of the federal bureau] to men who were registered there on or before the 3rd of December 1917'. This finding of the obvious was one reason why the commission had been quick to report. Dethridge also found that discrimination against the non-registered men 'has not been proved'. He concluded that 'I am unable to say that any alteration of the present system of engaging labour for work on the Melbourne wharfs is desirable'. Employers one, wharfies nil. While the commission didn't mention crime, that issue was about to take centre stage.

War, starvation, unemployment and disease had provided a stimulus to waterfront crime. Any successful criminal network requires not only opportunity and motive – which waterfront communities had in spades – but logistics management, which is another reason that made the communities perfectly suited to criminal enterprise. They were well-established, and had strong personal ties forged through years of adversity, common goals, church and family – police and informants were easily detected and the rabbit warren of streets, houses and warehouses meant that stolen goods could be easily hidden, and then moved through connections in the pubs and drinking dens. Profits – the other problem that confronts criminal operations – went back to the community for food and clothing. Criminal investigation thrives on information, and cracking a community like the waterfront wasn't going to happen.

Crime on the waterfront had kept well below the radar since the days of the pushes, with the exception of a brief stirring of public interest a few years before World War I. In 1911, one unnamed Melbourne merchant complained that out of thirty-six shipments he'd received from overseas, thirty-three had been tampered with and goods were missing. Melbourne merchants, the *Argus* declared on 18 July 1911, were 'at their wits end' to prevent pillaging and were having trouble finding someone to blame. The clerks on the wharf were turning a blind eye to cargo being damaged or pilfered, and the stevedoring companies were ignoring cargo stolen from either the wharf or their sheds. The merchants, unable to point the finger of blame at anyone specifically, were left to shoulder the losses. A year later, the *Argus* reported that little had changed, and said that cargo pillaging was common in Sydney and 'prevalent to an astonishing extent in Melbourne'. The Sydney Chamber of Commerce was quoted as saying the losses locally were 'disastrous', and 'aggravated by negligence in Adelaide, Melbourne and Sydney'.

Favourite targets for the light-fingered wharfies were 'biscuits, tea, silk and laces to pig iron' according to the *Argus*. 'Nor are the thieves any respecter of persons; the present Governor-General's belongings were tampered with.' Reports had a sliver of respect for the thieves, saying their methods were 'ingenious' and

> all kinds of 'accidents' happen to cases of tea and preserved fruits. Tins of fruit are pierced with a nail and the syrup extracted. In January last a case containing dress goods was opened on the Melbourne wharves for Customs inspection

and found to be intact. An hour later it was in the importer's warehouse and it was then found that £10 worth of goods had disappeared. Sixteen out of sixty rolls of silk were missing from another case when it was opened.

The *Argus* article raised the spectre of organisation creeping into crime, saying, 'there is sometimes an understanding between the thief and the packer, by which the most valuable goods are indicated. A zinc lined case containing valuables is marked on the outside, and the thief lifts the marked board, cuts a hole in the zinc, removes the goods, and covers up his work so neatly there is no outward sign of a crime being committed,' – a trick that still works perfectly with contemporary shipping containers.

The innocence of the times was highlighted by the conclusion of that article that 'perhaps some of the offenders do not realize fully that what they do is theft just as much as it is if they broke into a shop and stole the contents of the safe'. It's a fair bet they knew exactly what they were doing – and some of Australia's most notorious safe-blowers learned their skills as painters and dockers or wharfies.

In 1917, the issue of pillaging made a brief return when James Fielding told the Sydney Chamber of Manufacturers that £100,000 of cargo had been pillaged from Sydney's wharves in the preceding year. Fielding foreshadowed the future of crime on the waterfront when he told the chamber 'there was organisation behind the men who stole the goods in transit' and 'they co-operated to a large extent in both the stealing and disposition of the articles'. The clincher was his comment that 'when a man was charged with pillaging he was defended by the most expensive legal talent'. Fielding finished his address by pointing the finger at the businesses operating the wharfs, stevedoring companies and merchants for their inaction. The chamber responded by forming a committee to consider Fielding's allegations – and nothing happened.

Shipowners and the stevedoring companies finally bit the bullet and acknowledged the growing problem of cargo losses. In 1920, the annual loss of cargo to theft was estimated at around £386,000, of which £317,000 was in cargo coming in from overseas – enough to get the attention of the corporate bean counters. Adding to the issue's growing traction was the waterfront community's response to those who'd been unlucky enough to be either caught stealing or receiving – the hat was literally passed around in hotels, there were dockside 'tarpaulin musters' and contributions from local businesses to pay the fines imposed or to support families if the man had been given a short prison sentence. It was also common for the thief to be re-employed on the waterfront after his case had been finalised.

The royal commission had brought focus to the waterfront, and given the employers a clear win. The unions still suffered from internal power struggles, the revolution in Russia was putting communism on the map and providing an appealing philosophy for some key waterside workers, thus fuelling further conflict, and politically, the unions were dead in the water. Billy Hughes and his government weren't planning on holding out an olive branch – instead, they were nodding in agreement at the complaints by the employers, reading the front pages, considering the list of pluses and absence of minuses, and planning another royal commission to rid them of these turbulent wharfies and their ilk.

The *Argus,* in early 1921, further stirred the government into action saying,

> hitherto the detection of this form of crime [waterfront pillaging], which for many years has been responsible probably for a greater loss than any other branch of thieving in the city, has been left principally to private watchmen and a few patrolling constables along the waterfront. These have been more or less

successful in detecting a number of minor cases of the pillaging which is constantly taking place but they haven't been able to cope with the chief offenders operating on a big scale.

To deal with the usual problem confronting police – getting the Mr Bigs rather than the Mr Littles – in 1921 Victoria's Chief Commissioner Sir John Gellibrand appointed a special patrol of twelve constables, along with two experienced detectives. The shipping companies agreed to a levy on the cargoes to pay for the extra police. It was a good step, but didn't stop the Federal Government's national plans.

On 7 February 1921, barrister William Macpherson Macfarlane, who'd previously shown a safe pair of hands as a royal commissioner inquiring into hospital deaths in NSW, was appointed to investigate the 'evil of cargo pillaging'. Macfarlane's terms of reference were sweeping. He was charged to find if pillaging was 'carried out to any serious extent on cargoes from overseas and interstate cargoes' to find out where the pillaging took place – from prior to shipping to 'delivery to the wharf'; 'whether persons convicted of dishonesty are employed on the wharf, and if so, under what authority, by whom, and to what extent'; if Customs officers were involved in the shenanigans; to find if 'receivers' or 'fences' were involved in offloading the stolen goods; and then what to do – was there a need for 'concerted action' and what 'special measures, if any, are necessary to prevent pillaging in the future'.

The government provided a healthy budget that allowed the commission to 'take evidence' in Melbourne, Hobart, Launceston, Adelaide, Perth, Fremantle, Sydney and Brisbane. The tour didn't make it to Townsville because of 'difficulties there in connexion with obtaining official accommodation and the necessity for taking one or more shorthand writers to record the evidence' but the commissioner also noted that 'ample evidence had been obtained at the other ports in Australia'.

Macfarlane presented his report on 12 July 1921. The good news was he couldn't find any hint of complicity by Customs officers. The suggestion of their involvement was

> promulgated by the editor of a newspaper, who was questioned on the subject, and said he received his information indirectly from a private detective who was also examined on the questions and said he knew of no conspiracy between Customs officers and others to enable pillaging to be successfully carried out. The private detective admitted that he had a grievance against a certain Customs official.

The rest of the commission's findings gelled into three key issues: pillaging was on a grand scale; the extent to which it happened at the time of loading overseas, on the journey or at the final destination couldn't be nailed down; and, finally, that the police knowledge of the waterfront had been thwarted by the silence and solidarity of the local communities. While the problem was rife around the nation's ports – Sydney and Melbourne, the two largest ports, were batting way above the national averages.

In Melbourne, the commissioner commented that pillaging of interstate cargoes was 'carried on to a serious extent' when compared to overseas cargoes. The problem with the imports was the cargo was often plundered at the port of embarkation, with the valuable goods replaced by rubbish of similar weight. Boxes of liquor were stolen, and often eased the thirst of the wharfies while they worked, resulting in 'empty bottles being found lying about the hold, and stevedores being found in a partly intoxicated condition' – not a great idea in a workplace as potentially dangerous as theirs. One witness told the commission, 'I should say that waterside workers are around 20 to 30 per cent criminals'. In the year ending 31 December 1920, Melbourne's losses through pillaging were estimated at £101,000.

The commission didn't comment on the rivalry between Sydney and Melbourne but found the Emerald City had achieved a stunning victory over Melbourne with £181,000 of cargo being pinched. Macfarlane heard from one Sydney witness that 'about 80 per cent of persons who have been convicted are working on the waterfront' and that 'from 20 per cent to 80 per cent of the persons convicted were re-employed on the wharves'. Like their colleagues around the nation, 'money was forthcoming and no difficulty is found in payment of a fine if a man is convicted'.

Some of the responses to questions about criminals working on the wharves were intriguing – workers offered that a conviction was 'a bit of bad luck to be found out' and that 'all convicted persons are re-employed while they are members of the union'. One union official grudgingly offered, 'I am aware that members of my union have been convicted.' Employers weren't as committed to cleaning up the waterfront as they might have been, taking the pragmatic view that 'where we can do without them we do so' or 'we do not take them unless we absolutely have to'.

The solidarity of the waterfront meant that Macfarlane couldn't find 'actual evidence' of where the stolen cargoes went 'but there is no doubt that pillaged goods are disposed of to receivers or fences'. The commissioner's recommendations were lengthy and based substantially on suggestions from those who'd given evidence and submissions he'd received. Many were practical; many were pie in the sky. Broadly, he recommended improved security and supervision from the time ships arrived until the cargoes had departed the wharves and warehouses and became someone else's problem.

Among the recommendations was the employment of a 'detective agency' – the forerunner of today's security companies – to have 'its own men, with a head man on board and a man in each hold, to be present the whole time a ship is discharging', and 'shipping companies should employ sufficient men to search each man who leaves the ship at any time', including the searching of all bags and parcels carried by the labourers. The recommendation for such a hefty force of detectives was prompted by one witness who'd suggested that if only a single detective was on the job and 'didn't look the other way, his life would not be worth living'. The commissioner recommended 'there are no sufficient tally clerks employed. There should be supervision over tally clerks, delivery clerks and watchmen.' The commissioner also suggested a user pays system in which

> special police were detailed for duty on the wharves, the shipping companies or wharf owners would be prepared to pay for them in preference to employing men of their own. Importers should club together to subsidize Police. Shipping and insurance companies and importers should raise a fund by paying 5 per cent of their losses for 1920 and appoint a detective at each port for £500 per annum.

With a whiff of despair, he noted the culture of those employed on the docks meant that 'even children of waterside workers must know that it [stealing of cargo] is carried on; and what kind of an education is it for them'. With that in mind, he recommended that 'educational propaganda is undoubtedly necessary. There must be education for the rising generation to stop pillaging. Publicity of a reliable nature must be given regularly as to the pillaging that is going on.'

Macfarlane observed, 'a direct appeal to the waterside workers as a body would be successful in stamping out pillaging of cargo – the remedy must come from the unions and the men themselves'. While it was a laudable idea, Macfarlane didn't have a grip on how crime or the docklands worked. His suggestion that 'bonuses or rewards should be made to induce persons to give evidence which would convict cargo thieves', wasn't going to work in small, close-knit communities – to 'grass' on your workmates, friends and other families brought with it a punishment from the community that cash couldn't compensate. Many lawyers don't understand the loyalty in a community like the waterfront. The commissioner heard evidence that with pillaging, 'imposition of monetary penalties for this offence is not a deterrent, and that direct imprisonment should be imposed in every case', but fortunately the commissioner didn't add this to his recommendations. Harsh penalties have little deterrent effect, and on the waterfront, the risk of being caught was low.

The commissioner's final rosy hued recommendation was that

> representatives of the shipping companies, insurance companies, underwriters, merchants, manufacturers, Lloyd's agents and the unions connected with the handling of ship's cargoes and also the head of the police force should be held in each state to fully consider the Commissioner's recommendations which have not at the time been carried out, and all other suggestions that are embodied in this Report, and after full consideration appoint one of its members to meet the representatives appointed by each other States in a further conference.

On an upbeat note he added, 'if this proposal is carried out, it will insure that this difficult question will be fully considered and dealt with by some of the ablest business brains in Australia'. It wasn't. Co-operation, education and cultural change didn't happen – and the lack of action provided an incentive for the criminals rather than a deterrent.

Some of the 'ablest business brains' did meet – the Associated Chambers of Commerce from around the country decided in 1921 to lobby their respective State governments for mandatory imprisonment of anyone convicted of pillaging from the waterfront. In support of the idea, Mr J. A. Boyd representing Melbourne pointed out that the Melbourne Harbour Trust had a staff of eighteen police on the wharves and had been paying them a reward of £5 for each successful conviction and yet, after thousands of pounds had been paid out, 'no stoppage of evil had resulted'. Fines, he pointed out, could be paid by nearly everyone and that showed a 'systematic organization to help get the fellow thief out of his difficulty'. On a practical note, the chambers of commerce decided that enclosing the cargoes in wire might deter some of the thieves.

Mr A. E. Clarkson from South Australia mentioned that a meeting to discuss what could be done had been held earlier in Adelaide, and while the Waterside Workers Federation had been invited along and had accepted the invitation, they failed to front.

Up in Brisbane in July 1923, Justice Lukin was making a point about 'crime is rife' on the Brisbane wharves when sentencing Henry Foxcroft, who'd pilfered collars from the wharves, and grocer Norman Fox, who'd received them. The jury recommended leniency – Fox was a first offender (or it was the first time he'd been caught, as most coppers would think to themselves) and Foxcroft had a family – with the result that Fox received twelve months imprisonment and Foxcroft three years behind bars instead of the seven that was the maximum. The *Courier-Mail* of 19 July 1924 reported the judge noted that 'an extraordinary amount of pilfering had been going on. Of course, only a very small proportion of the Brisbane waterside workers shared in the plunder.' The report said the judge 'really wondered why the honest majority of workers did not exercise some reign of terror over the thieves'.

In Melbourne, more tally clerks and supervisors were employed, and patrols on the wharf were beefed up, resulting in a temporary slump in losses. In Sydney, there was a promise of fifty specialist police to work the waterfront, but ultimately, nothing of any worth happened, with the Sydneysiders deciding to keep their cash and take a risk on losses. Six years after the royal commission, the *Sydney Morning Herald* of 25 August 1927 reported the British Government had made the 'startling discovery' of 'amazing figures concerning cargo pillaging in vessels in Australia and New Zealand'. The London insurance underwriters found that ships unloading at Australian ports accounted for 50% of all cargo pillage claims, and 30% for New Zealand – a fine effort from the Kiwis considering the comparative size of their market.

18
SNORTS AND RORTS

While the royal commission had been diligent with its investigation of the loss of profits by the nation's merchants and waterside employers, one aspect of crime on the waterfront hadn't been in its terms of reference, nor was it on the political agenda, yet it was something infinitely more profitable than stolen silk or booze and used the same networks to smuggle and distribute – drug trafficking.

From the mid 1920s until the beginning of World War II Australia had the highest per capita use of cocaine in the world. In 1936, the League of Nations reported that, with a population of only 6.7 million, Australia accounted for 14% of the world's legal supply.

The problem started when the British trading houses operating in Asia used opium from Bengal to barter for silks and tea in China. Opium had been used medicinally in China for centuries, and by the seventeenth century was being mixed with tobacco. The first major British opium shipment from Bengal arrived in China around 1773, and quickly became a money-spinner for British companies, but the Chinese Government weren't dazzled by the effect the drug was having on the locals and the 'Opium

Wars' of 1839–42 and 1856–60 were fought, in part, over the Chinese refusal to legalise the opium trade.

Opium arrived in Australia with the Chinese heading to the goldfields, and in spite of antipathy toward them, the white population joined in their addiction. Aside from offering a break from reality, opium was readily available and legal to have, supply or use. Between 1871 and 1905, it became so popular that imports increased fivefold and colonial governments put a tax on the drug in 1857 – Australia's first drug laws – and were profiting from the trade. Users enjoyed the relaxing effect of the drug but, as use increased, its addictive qualities and the long-term effects like irritability, mood swings and a need that became a driving force – like modern heroin addicts in search of a 'fix' at any cost – were more obvious to the public.

S. D. Yarrington, a clergyman, wrote of his observations in a 'Sydney opium den':

> after admission has been gained, the scene depicted is one of the most degrading and disgusting imaginable. Picture to yourself a large room with shutters down, and six or eight benches on either side of the room. Then as you look closely you will see Chinese and white women, some black men and women, and also at times, white men lying on the hard surface of the benches because it is necessary to have the bench of hard surface to produce what is termed the 'fascinating effects' of the smoke.

Yarrington was horrified when he observed 'the women are almost nude, while the Chinese are scantily clad. There they lie – a man and woman sometimes on the very same bench, smoking from, in many cases, the same pipe. It is a disgusting sight to see a yellow-fanged Chinaman sucking at his pipe, and then passing it on to a white girl who takes it with the greatest relish possible.'

The leading anti-opium campaigner in the country was not a member of the clergy or even a white Australian. Mei Quong Tart was only nine when he arrived in 1859 with his uncle and both headed to the goldfield near Braidwood in NSW. He became a successful businessman and was appalled at the effect of opium on the Chinese he'd met in rural Australia. In 1883, he presented the NSW Executive Council with a petition of 4000 signatures seeking a ban on opium imports, and he offered a pragmatic view that if there wasn't the political will for banning, then perhaps the government could license opium sellers – in order to control the market and still profit.

His idea was practical – Australia had a taste and tolerance for patent medicines that relied heavily on opiates and were available without a prescription. Popular choices were Bonnington's Irish Moss, Godfrey's Cordial – both containing opium – and Ayres Cherry Pectoral, which had a morphine base. It makes today's discussions over sugar and sweeteners in popular beverages a little tame. The popularity of patent medicines was still evident into the 1960s when housewives were encouraged in television campaigns to ease the afternoon with a 'Bex and a good lie down'.

Godfrey Carter, a member of the Victorian Legislative Assembly and a man who didn't mind a drink, took aim at the non-drinking temperance advocates in 1898 and said, 'when I think of what little joy they have here at present [in Victoria] is derived, to a great extent, from the use of morphine, chlorodyne, painkiller and a variety of other preparations of opium, why should we prevent them from going to their chemists and getting these things?'

In 1894 South Australia became the first colony to prohibit opium imports.

After Federation, the other states gradually joined South Australia, and in 1910, Commonwealth legislation made it illegal to possess opium without a reasonable excuse (escaping from the trials of a hard week wasn't one). Labor heavyweight William Holman described the banning as 'not an act of humanitarianism but an act of absolute brutality'.

The problem with prohibiting something the public enjoy is that it creates a profitable black market – and, like rum back in the early days of the colony, opportunity was knocking.

Investigating the opium trade in the early 1920s, police found the biggest suppliers were legitimate chemist stores. When the Minister of Customs threatened to limit the allotment of medical opium to certain chemists, and cancel import licences for those thought to be feeding the illicit market, the Pharmacy Board of NSW complained loudly.

Opium is derived from the opium poppy, and German firms Merck and Bayer, noting the effects of the drug, were tinkering with derivatives for medical purposes, and inadvertently laying the foundations for a profitable market in illicit drugs. In 1805, Friedrich Serturner, an apprentice pharmacist in Germany, isolated an alkaloid from opium, and after some self-experimenting, found it caused drowsiness so he called it morphine, after the Greek God, Morpheus. He also found other medical uses for it, such as a painkiller, and noted it was a 'remarkable substance'. Merck, the German pharmacy giant, began commercial production in 1827. When the syringe was invented in the 1850s, morphine became easily useable and was the world's leading painkiller and a popular cure for a range of ailments, ironically including opium addiction. People soon realised it was as addictive as the drug addiction they intended to cure.

With that problem in mind, Charles Alder Wright – a researcher at London's St Mary's Hospital – came up with a partially synthetic alternative when he bonded morphine with acetic acid and created diacetylmorphine. It was a more effective painkiller and didn't, Wright believed, have the addictive problem. Case solved, and the folks at Bayer in Germany took Wright's creation, developed it, and found it was a fine painkiller but also excellent for respiratory problems. The marketing department decided that with its 'heroic' abilities it deserved the catchy brand name 'heroin'. In 1900, the *Boston Medical and Surgical Journal* said, 'it's not hypnotic and poses no danger of addiction'. The American Medical Association was so impressed that in 1906 they approved it for use 'in place of morphine in various painful infections' but added that a 'habit' was 'readily formed'. By 1902, heroin accounted for 5% of all Bayer's drug sales, and was tying with 'aspirin' as the company's biggest money-spinner.

However, the magic was rubbing off and in 1913, with hospitals on the US East Coast, particularly in New York and Philadelphia, reporting a spike in heroin-related admissions, and hefty recreational use, Bayer quietly removed it from their product list. Some of the addicts treated in the US had been so desperate to maintain their supply they'd been forced to try to sell items they scrounged from the streets for cash, which gave them a nickname – junkies.

By 1924, 98% of drug addicts in New York were heroin users. Prohibition of its use, except with a prescription, stimulated illegal supply for addicts. Organised crime, particularly the Mafia with their smuggling and distribution networks honed by supplying booze during Prohibition, added heroin trafficking to their product list.

Australia's recreational drug of choice in the 1920s and '30s was cocaine and it came with a superb marketing pedigree. The Swiss naturalist Johann von Tschudi headed to South America in 1838 and on his travels noted that the Andean Indians who were his porters could keep going for five days with little rest or food if they chewed coca leaf. His book *Travels in Peru* caught the attention of the clever folk at Merck who concentrated the leaf's active ingredient into a crystal form, called it 'cocaine' and put it into production in the 1860s. Other companies followed. In the US it was used as a remedy for morphine addiction suffered by Civil War soldiers. Sigmund Freud was a fan and said in *Über Coca*, his 1884 study of cocaine, 'I take very small doses of it regularly against depression and against indigestion and with the most brilliant of success.' It was used as an anaesthetic, and even an additive to wine – Vin Mariani came onto the market in the 1860s with coca leaves added to give it a little more oomph. Pope Leo XIII and Pope Pius X reportedly kept a hip flask of Vin Mariani – purely for medicinal purposes – under their cassocks.

Cocaine in Sydney and Melbourne was responsible for the nation's first real gang wars – rather than just brawls between pushes – and added the word 'organised' before 'crime'.

The timing of cocaine's rise in popularity coincided with a time of greater regulation and technical change. The early closing of hotels – starting in 1916 in Sydney and 1919 in Melbourne – created the 'six o'clock swill' in which the thirsty would do their best to drink as much as possible before the pub closed at 6 pm. For many drinkers a cleansing ale or three for the road was needed after closing time – which prompted the arrival of sly-grog dens, ranging from the stylish restaurants where liquor was allegedly ordered when you booked your table, to the back rooms of pubs, and squalid houses in close-knit communities where tip-offs of a police raid arrived well before the coppers.

Drink and prostitution have always been playmates, and it was common for sly-grog establishments and brothels to be operated by the same people. Adding to the criminal mix was SP bookmaking where the bookmaker, usually lurking in a hotel with access to a telephone, accepted bets on race meetings and if the bet was a large one, he'd contact another SP to 'lay off' the bet (passing it on to a larger operator to minimise his risk). The arrival of live radio broadcasts of horse races in the early 1920s revolutionised the SP business – no more waiting for results in the newspaper or fluctuating odds on track.

The impetus for the cocaine market sadly came from soldiers returning from World War I. Cocaine had been commonly used on the battlefields, not only as a medication to counter psychological effects of battle, but also as a recreational drug. In 1916 Harrods was selling a 'Welcome Present for Friends at the

Front', which was a kit containing syringes, needles, morphine and cocaine.

Cocaine in Australia was available from chemist shops and though a prescription was required, plenty of chemists were happy to supply it with a nod of the head and no documents. In January 1919, a man approached a chemist in Collingwood in his army uniform with a chestful of medals that indicated a long and tough war service. He asked the chemist for 'snow' – the slang for cocaine – and when questioned if he'd bought the drug from the store before, he told the chemist that he hadn't but it was common knowledge it was easy to get in Melbourne. The chemist then asked which other chemists he'd visited and the man told him 'no names, no court martial'. Due diligence done, the chemist sold him 4.5 grams of pure cocaine for 5 shillings – 'Mum's the word,' he told the man in uniform.

That same day in Russell Street, Melbourne, another similarly dressed man made a similar request and was sold 3.5 grams of cocaine, then returned a few days later and bought a further 4 grams. The problem was it was a police sting operation. Both chemists were charged, but the penalty was only £20 each for failing to record the sale in the register used to record the sale of poisons and prescription substances.

By the early 1920s cocaine was commonplace among the prostitutes operating in the brothels around the waterfront of both Melbourne and Sydney. Since supply through chemists was dramatically reduced by legislation and vigilance, alternate sources were needed. The *Australasian Journal of Pharmacy* noted, 'the cocaine habit *is* assuming alarming proportions in Australia', and 'one does not easily associate this continent, whose people are noted for their love of sport and outdoors life, with surreptitious drugging'.

In 1923, with the chemists still squarely in the police sights as the main suppliers, the media entered the fray with *The Daily Guardian*, on 17 July, sending a reporter to a chemist, Mr Caines, at his store in Pitt Street, Sydney, to make a buy. Cleverly, they used a female reporter at a time when women weren't well represented in either the media or in policing so the chances of her being rumbled were small.

She had no difficulty in buying 'snow', and returned the next day and bought more. *The Daily Guardian* reported in July 1923, 'if you have the money, you can buy cocaine. If you are a girl, young and good looking, the man who sells you the poison will stroke your shoulder and call you "dear".' Mr Caines was later fined the sum of £2 and 10 shillings for his crimes, with the Magistrate, Mr A. J. Peisley, quipping that as the buyer was a young lady, it might account for the chemist 'being so weak'. The paper, owned by the proprietors of *Smith's Weekly* and edited by Robert Packer – founder of the Packer media empire – attacked the magistrate for his 'vaudevillian patter', and agreed with NSW politician Sir Thomas Henley that 'there should only be one penalty – gaol without option'.

Chemists weren't the only ones involved in the shenanigans – medical practitioners and dentists were doing a very lucrative sideline in drug peddling. Errol McElroy, a dentist of Carlton NSW, was arrested for selling 57 grams of cocaine, and when police dug deeper they found he had enough stock to dull the pain of 12,000 tooth extractions. He was fined £100. What police also found was that one ounce (28.5 grams) of pure product, bought from the ethical professionals for around 22 shillings, was then diluted – or 'stamped on' – using boracic acid (often used in eye wash) that offered a bit of 'taste', which stretched the single ounce into around 250 deals that were sold on the streets and brothels for an average of 5 shillings each.

The official version of Melbourne's cocaine trade was that the prosecutions of chemists brought it to a standstill – unlikely given the market was driven by addicts in need of consistent supply and criminals keen to maintain their cash flow. The main market for the drug was prostitutes – some spending around £7 per week – and it was peddled by people involved in sly grog and vice around the waterfront. Superintendent M. J. Bannon, heading the Victoria's Detective Service, said of the Melbourne crooks, 'they found Melbourne too hot for them and looked for a more congenial climate. A few have gone to Adelaide, but Sydney appears to be the happy hunting ground just now.'

James Mitchell, the NSW Police Commissioner, agreed and said, 'trafficking in drugs is a much more extensive business in Sydney than in Melbourne', adding, depressingly, that 'there is a correspondingly large number of addicts in Sydney'. Larry Writer in his 2001 book *Razor,* said there were around 5000 cocaine addicts in Woolloomooloo, Darlinghurst and Kings Cross in the late 1920s and its use crossed social boundaries: from the rich at their parties; businessmen at 'snow parlours where each table had a bowl of the drug in the centre' to 'vagrants in alleyways . . . mobsters needing a belt of courage before pulling a job', and 'prostitutes seeking fortification to get through a Darlinghurst night'.

The problem was the police, with barely any resources – the NSW Drug Squad Bureau had two officers – were busy cracking down on the cocaine supply through almost legitimate suppliers, but the source of all cocaine in Australia was the vulnerable waterfront. Victoria was making a token effort following Macfarlane's royal commission recommendations and NSW hadn't bothered at all, so pillaging cocaine from cargoes was easy. Similarly, the regular shipping routes from South America – where cocaine was cheap, plentiful and easy to get – meant seaman could buy the drug and offload it in the drinking dens and brothels of the waterfront.

The period marked the emergence of the first batch of notable Australian criminals since the demise of Ned Kelly in 1880, and they weren't diplomatic in protecting their business.

In Melbourne, Joseph 'Squizzy' Taylor, a diminutive career criminal, was top dog of crime, catering to everyone from visiting seamen to the leading lights of the city with gambling, sly grog, prostitution and cocaine. Taylor had started his working life as an apprentice jockey, then improved his income by becoming a racecourse pickpocket, before moving into robbery, blackmail, and crimes catering to the illicit needs of a large port city. The Hobart *Mercury* of 29 October 1927 said of Taylor that some Melbourne people regarded him as a 'sort of gay and cavalier like outlaw' but 'according to a Sydney man who knew him well, he was anything but a picturesque villain. He was probably a traitor to many of his friends, and was absurdly vain and fond of bravado.'

Taylor's career was shortened on 27 October 1927 when he and two colleagues called at the Carlton home of rival gangster John Daniel 'Snowy' Cutmore, in a row of terraces called 'Custom's House' in Barkly Street. Cutmore had been part of Sydney's 'razor gangs' and he and Taylor had a long history of mutual dislike and rivalry. There were stories of a fight over a woman, but both men were involved in the cocaine trade and a fight over criminal opportunities in the booming drug trade was more likely.

The Hobart *Mercury* said of Taylor's demise, 'when Taylor heard that Cutmore was in bed and suffering from a bad bout of the flu, Taylor decided it was time to settle up'. Taylor and his men pushed their way past Cutmore's sister and into the bedroom where Taylor opened fire. What he didn't know was that Cutmore was paranoid and kept a gun on him at all times. Contrary to what happens on television, revolvers are not particularly accurate unless you're standing right in front of them, but if you fire enough bullets in a confined space like a bedroom, there is a fair bet someone will get hit. The first to fall was Snowy's mother, nailed by a bullet in the shoulder from her son's gun. Taylor later died in St Vincent's Hospital from a bullet to the chest, and Snowy died from five bullet wounds. Police described the incident as a 'revolver duel'.

19
SLASH

Matilda 'Tilly' Devine, with her empire based in Darlinghurst and Woolloomooloo, and Kathleen 'Kate' Leigh in Surry Hills were the grand dames of Sydney crime. Competition came from Phil 'The Jew' Jeffs in Kings Cross – then the city's bohemian precinct and not the crime-sodden 'Golden Mile' it became – and Norm Bruhn, one of Squizzy Taylor's lieutenants who'd headed up from Melbourne when the water there had become rather too warm for his health.

Jeffs, Devine and Leigh were products of a tough background. Jeffs was a Latvian who'd grown up around London's docklands and, like Devine, headed to Australia for a better life. He worked his passage on a steamer to Australia and arrived in Sydney in 1912. He started out his new life as a small-time thief and moved into the big time with nightclubs, illegal gambling, sly grog and abortion.

Devine was born in London and began her working life as a prostitute around the docklands south of the Thames. Tilly was an attractive, vivacious woman who knew how to market her talents and in 1917 met James Devine, a digger from Victoria on leave in London who became a regular. He was Tilly's opposite – a quick-tempered and sullen man, but one who was useful as her protector on the dangerous streets of London. The two married in 1917. Tilly kept working and chalked up arrests for theft, assaults and the predictable prostitution. She followed James to Sydney in 1920, leaving their son to be looked after by her parents.

By 1925, Tilly had a string of convictions for prostitution and assault, and at her trial for 'malicious wounding' in May that year, the court was told she was 'a prostitute of the worst type and an associate of the worst type of prostitutes, vagrants and criminals. The only existence she and her husband has is on her prostitution.' An indicator that she may have been a little more organised than the average streetwalker was that she and her husband owned 'meter car' – a taxi – that was 'not used for hire but only to drive the offender and other prostitutes during their calling as prostitutes'.

Devine ran her operations from a terrace house at 191 Palmer Street, Darlinghurst – conveniently located near her brothels and diagonally across from the Tradesman's Arms hotel, the preferred watering hole of Sydney's most vicious thugs and gunmen. It was a place where gunshots, bashings and plotting were as common as ordering a schooner of beer on a warm afternoon.

Kate Leigh was born in Dubbo, NSW, child number eight to parents who neglected their family to the point that Leigh spent time in a girls' home. Unlike her competitor, Tilly Devine, she didn't get the looks – plump, dough-faced and with a large gap between her teeth, she was, at best, plain. She married a small-time Sydney criminal, James Leigh, in 1902 but the two were forcibly separated in 1905 when he went to prison for robbery, and Kate was convicted for being an accomplice and for perjury arising from his trial. By 1919, Leigh was making large profits from Sydney's vices. She ruled her empire from a scruffy terrace house at 104 Riley Street – deep in the slums of Surry Hills, surrounded by thugs.

Norm Bruhn was different. Born on Geelong's waterfront in 1894, he'd spent his early working life on the docks of Corio Bay, followed by enlistment, at the age of twenty, in the army.

Back from the war he returned to work briefly on the docks before moving into a career in crime. In July 1920 he was arrested for assaulting a police officer investigating a series of robberies. Bruhn and his colleague, William Miller, knocked the man to the ground and took off, but ten days later both were caught. A little over a year later, Bruhn and fellow wharfie Harold MacDougall were arrested for 'loitering with intent to commit a felony', and a month after for 'assault and robbery' – the term of the time for a mugging.

Bruhn wasn't a master criminal because he stole his victim's Stetson hat and wore it to court for his first appearance – it made pleading not guilty tricky. A month later he got his first prison sentence: six months for a collection of crimes including stealing, assault and receiving of stolen goods. Bruhn added indecent exposure to his record of crimes and was reputed to be handy with a leather garrotte that he tightened around his victim's neck while rifling their pockets.

James Morton and Russell Robinson, in their book *Shotgun and Standover*, placed Bruhn – the 'ugly, bad-tempered, a beater of women, thief and pimp' – as one of the 'founding fathers' of the Painters and Dockers. He achieved that dubious honour courtesy of his son Noel Ambrose Faure, a criminal who racked up seven convictions before his twentieth birthday, and spent much of World War II in Pentridge Gaol for receiving stolen goods. Faure became a member of the Painters and Dockers – a membership that didn't impede his criminal career. Norman's grandsons would carry on the family traditions, and be key players in Melbourne's ganglands in the last decades of the twentieth century.

In November 1926, Bruhn skipped bail after being charged with shooting and wounding a man. Sydney offered an escape from the police and reprisals. The Victorian Police had issued a warrant for his arrest – a matter of procedure – but weren't chasing him with any vigour, believing his victim would opt for the silence of the underworld rather than give evidence, and one less vicious crook to deal with was a bonus.

Bruhn brought his wife Irene – a prostitute – and young sons to Sydney with him. He became a member of the Waterside Workers Federation, working initially on Sydney's docks – establishing connections with the networks that smuggled or pillaged cocaine, while he looked around for opportunities in his preferred profession. It didn't take long.

Irene wasn't happy in her new city and returned to Melbourne, and so Bruhn took up with prostitute Nellie Cameron, both as her lover and her pimp. Cash flow was strong with Cameron taking around £335 per week, around ten times the average wage. Bruhn assembled a gang of some of Sydney's most unpleasant men, including Squizzy Taylor's soon-to-be nemesis John 'Snowy' Cutmore, along with George 'The Midnight Raper' Wallace, Lancelot 'Sailor the Slasher' McGregor and 'Jack' Hayes.

The Truth relished the stories men like these brought to the pages, and reported the gangs were 'terrorizing the underworld of Darlinghurst, that region of bohemia, crime and mystery'.

Bruhn and his gang focused on becoming the most powerful criminals in Sydney – specifically at the expense of Devine and Leigh's cocaine business. He didn't interfere with the network of seaman and dockworkers who smuggled the drug from the ships and out of the docks to the middlemen in the pubs or nearby houses that were the first steps in the supply chain. He targeted their sly-grog houses, brothels, and the easy pickings of the 'runners' who moved cocaine from safe houses in East Sydney and Woolloomooloo, where it was stashed after being smuggled in from the docks, to the distributors. Journalist Hugh Buggy, writing in the *Argus* in 1950 of his experiences as a young reporter covering crime in Darlinghurst in the 1920s and 30s, recalled, 'deals in cocaine were to be conducted on a strictly cash basis. There were no credits, no lay-bys, and no time payments. That being so, the cocaine runners or distributors, who saw their clients only at night, returned to their principals with solid wads of Treasury notes.'

The battle for dominance was fought in the seedy terrace houses and laneways of the inner east, described by the *Argus* as 'the most forbidding slum belt in Australia. Replanners had nibbled out only a slice of a jungle of crumbling tenements that had become decrepit long before 1900. It was a labyrinth of dank courts, blind lanes and stone stairways.'

Guns were scarce on the streets and there were hefty penalties if you were caught with them, so gangs resorted to something easy to get, simple to use, and delivering 'shock and awe' – the cut-throat razor.

Hugh Buggy wrote, 'gunplay invariably brings the police. Some other form of terrorism had to be devised. They had not long to wait for inspiration. In a brawl in a sly-grog flat in Womerah Avenue, Darlinghurst, a diminutive thief cowed an aggressive and burly enemy by marking his face with a razor. Here was the weapon against which the drug runners would have no counter on a dark night.' Tilly Devine was a fan of the weapon, and resolved a dispute with a man called Sidney Cork by slashing him, with the wounds requiring seventeen stitches.

The Truth reported, 'the razor is more effective than the revolver as a cash extractor. The sheen of its bright blade close to the cheek puts a deadly fear into the heart of the victim. Men who defy the black muzzle quail before the bright blade held threateningly to their cheek.'

The razor was brutally effective not only in getting results, but as *The Truth* pointed out in terrorising the victim to the point that 'even with their faces slashed open, victims refuse to speak to police. They know too well the fate that awaits them once the gang learns they've allowed resentment to get the better of their discretion.'

The other comfort Bruhn and his thugs could take from their attacks was the cocaine runners they were targeting were unlikely to run off to the police to complain. In the underworld, violence was an occupational hazard you had to accept. In the first weeks of 1927, Bruhn's gang had terrified Sydney from the underworld through to the politicians and lawyers of Macquarie Street.

Buggy wrote, 'at St Vincent's Hospital Darlinghurst I saw some of the early victims of the Razor Gang. Their faces, or their heads or their necks were horribly gashed by the swift sweep of the blade. Those scarred men would never tell the police or their doctors who had slashed them. They usually achieved their revenge in their own way, and so the bitter gang war intensified.'

Bruhn had the dubious honour of being the first to die in the gang war he'd started. He met his end deep into the night of 22 June 1927. It was damp and misty, the sort of winter night in Sydney where you could feel the chill seeping up from the pavements as you walked along. But the dismal conditions didn't deter the drinkers heading to sly-grog houses. Buggy reported 'snatches of song and babble floated out in to the fog'.

The scene of Bruhn's departure was a sly-grog venue in a tiny house in Charlotte Lane – a narrow street of identical two rooms up, two rooms down with kitchen and rudimentary bathroom hanging on to the back of the property – on the side of the hill running from Hyde Park down to the wharves of Woolloomooloo, and around the corner from Bruhn's home in Francis Street. Around 11 pm Buggy said, 'in one house voices were not raised in harmony but in violent recrimination. Then five revolver shots echoed down the lane.' Constable Blanch, walking the beat a few blocks away in Stanley Street, heard the shots and raced uphill where he was drawn to the murder scene by the sight and sounds of women in fur coats 'some shrieking hysterically, others were weeping and moaning'.

On the pavement was Norm Bruhn, shot five times. He was rushed to Sydney Hospital in a taxi, but his condition was obviously fatal and a magistrate was called to take his dying deposition. Bruhn wasn't talking. 'I do not know who shot me,' he lied to the magistrate. Bruhn lasted the night and died at 7 am. Back at the scene, only one man was prepared to talk to police – the rest of the drinkers had a case of collective amnesia. Robert Miller, from nearby Dowling Street in Woolloomooloo, was Bruhn's mate and not big on detail, telling police that Norm had been 'menaced' by two men and one said to Miller, 'You get out of the place, you're not in this.' Bruhn's mate didn't argue. A few moments later he heard shots, and then Bruhn's body was dragged through the door, dumped in the grimy laneway, and the murderers fled into the fog.

Police rounded up the usual suspects, but no one saw anything – the code of silence, and fear of a slashing in reprisal, left public duty a poor second. The coppers speculated the killing was payback for Bruhn and his gang's cocaine rip-offs and demands of cash from sly-grog operators in return for 'protection'.

In the following months, the war was predictably quiet – murder is a crime that stirs the maximum effort from police, and with 'loading and verballing' (fabricating evidence) common practice along with 'the biff', Sydney's criminals wisely chose to keep a low profile. The *Sydney Morning Herald* of 24 June reported, 'as the result of Bruhn's silence, there is now little probability of his murderer's arrest', but in the pragmatic way of police they shared the view of their Melbourne colleagues that Bruhn's departure – this time permanent – meant there was one less crim to worry about.

On Monday 27 June 1927, the NSW government responded to the gang violence by announcing another fifty police would be recruited to keep the public safe. At the coroner's inquest a month later, Mr Miller's memory took a turn for the worse. He told the court he couldn't remember making any statement to police, couldn't remember where he'd met Bruhn than night, and could only remember when the fatal shots had been fired but not the direction from which they'd come. When pushed, he offered the shooter was about fifteen yards away and was a slim man in a grey suit – which narrowed the suspect list down to around half the males in Sydney. When pushed harder, Miller's memory failed completely and he reckoned he could only remember meeting Bruhn at a pub earlier that night, and then being with him at the hospital hours later – the bit in between was a blank caused by exuberant drinking. Or so he tried to get the court to believe.

Noel Inman, the taxi-driver who'd taken Bruhn to hospital, wasn't suffering from Miller's recent onset of memory failure. Inman gave evidence of picking up Bruhn, Miller and a couple of other men near the Paddington Town Hall – about two kilometres away – and driving them to Charlotte Lane. All were carrying beer bottles and Bruhn was the most sober of the lot. Inman was nearby and waiting for a fare when he heard shots, and shortly after saw two men fleeing from one end of the street as a police officer came around the corner at the other end. He told the court that while Miller was drunk he was capable enough to help Bruhn into the back of the cab.

At a line-up of suspects at the Darlinghurst Police Station, Inman could only identify Miller, but he told the coroner that the day after the line-up he was approached by a man with 'side-levers' and wearing the inevitable grey suit, but this time with a hat, who said to him, 'Just as well you didn't identify anyone at the line-up today. There will be another one tomorrow; be equally careful or you'll find yourself in hot water.' While the description fitted a large slice of the NSW male population, given the inside information, it was not unreasonable to suspect that the gentleman doing the threatening was a member of what later became known as 'the best police force money can buy'. Cocaine, cash and power are the best corrupters you can get.

•

Norm Bruhn was the first of a crime dynasty. Norm's wife had a long-term relationship with a man called Faure, and Norm's children took the Faure name.

One child was Noel Ambrose Faure – a painter and docker in his spare time and safecracker by profession. Noel's sons – Les, Keith and Noel – took after their grandfather. Keith was an armed robber with a sideline as a docker, among his crimes was shooting Constable Michael Pratt in the back during a bank robbery at Clifton Hill, Victoria in 1976. He was the top dog in Pentridge's notorious H Division during his time behind bars and leader of the imprisoned Painters and Dockers members in Pentridge, of which there were many. Les was convicted for the killing of his girlfriend Lorna Stevens in what he alleged was a game of Russian Roulette, and Noel, aside from killing and robberies, was convicted of the murder of gangland kingpin Lewis Moran at the Brunswick Club on 31 March 2004. The Bruhns were among the first of the nation's prominent criminals to rise out of the waterfront, and a stellar cast would soon join them.

•

Norm Bruhn's murder was the first of four in Sydney's cocaine war, and when 1928 arrived the battle for dominance in the cocaine business was back on. The government response was predictable. In addition to more police on the beat, mandatory penalties for gun possession were introduced, and laws beefed up to give police the power to arrest criminals for consorting. It was a response that would echo for the next ninety years.

The game changer was the arrival of the Consorting Act, which made it illegal for criminals to associate, or if you weren't a convicted criminal, illegal to associate with someone you knew to be a crook. In a time where telephones at home were rare, criminals had to meet to plot their enterprises, and the popular spots were pubs and sly-grog shops – you could get a drink, have an open conversation, and not embroil your family.

Enforcing the consorting laws were some of the State's toughest detectives who had an intimate knowledge of the criminal fraternity: where to find them and how best to deal with them

– strategies ranged from a solid beating, arrest and a robust interview (a solid beating), or a fine (imposed and collected by police and slipped into their back pockets).

By 1932, Hugh Buggy reported the NSW consorting laws, 'certainly broke up coteries of criminal who were wont to compare notes and plan new coups in certain nightclubs and beer flats around Darlinghurst. Some of the really "big shots" felt the time had come to move to another state which didn't have a Consorting Act. Others decided to do some honest work, even though such a prospect was repugnant to them.'

However, Buggy may have committed the sin of many police reporters over the years – giving too much credit to his sources in suits of blue. In 1935, the police claimed a combination of the recent laws and vigorous policing had put an end to cocaine smuggling. The next year, the Commonwealth Government statistics were reporting a different story. Australia had the largest per capita usage of cocaine in any English-speaking country – 12.4 kilograms per million people annually. The US was running a distant second at 6.8 kilograms, followed by the UK with 5.3 kilograms and Canada at 4.9 kilograms.

The tough police measures curbed the criminals' interest in cocaine and razors – and they looked to other, less risky ventures to make money, with protection rackets, standing over bookmakers and burglary popular. These were crimes that appealed to the criminal leaders who came to prominence after the Second World War, and many were from the waterfront.

The threat of powerful enemy raiders and submarines on the prowl saw shipping between Australia and South America grind to a standstill. At the same time, the Germans' march through Europe meant that medicinal cocaine pilfered from the laboratories in Hamburg and Amsterdam and smuggled to Australia by seamen also stopped. War killed the cocaine business in Australia.

The kingpins of the gang war – Kate Leigh and Tilly Devine – had made millions from their mix of booze, drugs and brothels, but not without some trouble. Devine had over 200 convictions for prostitution, drugs, assaults and even attempted murder. Leigh had over 100 arrests and thirteen sojourns behind bars for a similar range of crimes, but missed out on being arrested for murder when she killed John 'Snowy' Prendergast, a 23-year-old Melbourne boy who'd come to Sydney to try his luck in the vibrant market, on 27 March 1930.

Like the Bruhn clan, the Prendergasts became well known for their role in Melbourne's gangland, with Laurie Prendergast ending up as a painter and docker, armed robber and assassin, and who disappeared in 1985 with police presuming he was murdered.

The hold that cocaine, and its profits, had on Sydney endured the biggest financial crisis in world history, and came at a time when another man, destined to become the Mr Big of Australian crime, was spending his childhood in Balmain.

20
IT'S ALL IN THE TIMING

By the close of the 1920s the waterside communities were displaying a capacity for organising crime, hard work, political awareness and, unfortunately, a poor sense of timing. Margo Beasley, writing in *Wharfies,* described it as the beginning of a decade that was 'the most disastrous in the Federation's history'.

Conditions for the waterfront workers hadn't greatly improved. During summer heatwaves, with temperatures soaring past the Fahrenheit century, some wharfies who'd been working in refrigerated holds were hospitalised with frostbite. Cargoes of sulphur and cement were still shifted by the shovel-load, and explosions and fire from volatile substances were not uncommon. Overtime was common, and some men worked shifts of up to forty-eight hours without a break – both exhausting and dangerous given the hazards. Fractures, hernias and respiratory illnesses were part of the job.

Lew Hillier in his 1981 book *Meet the Ship Painters and Dockers* painted an equally grim picture of what confronted the dockers every day they went to work. He said they went to the 'pick up' to 'try to get a job cleaning out the filthy holds of ships infested with rats, mice, and other vermin', or clean putrid bilges with 'tons of water containing urine, oil, spillages of every known chemical, dead rats, cockroaches, all of which have been swilling around for months till it has been concocted into the vilest smelling and most dangerous brew a man could ever cook up'. He added that for everyday Australians to understand the life of a waterside worker they should see them working 'covered from arsehole to breakfast time in every describable filth known to man'. Hillier recorded that Robert Mahony, Painters and Dockers union secretary, in a conference with employers on 6 June 1905 commented on the cleaning of an oil-carrying ship – the dockers had to use a lime wash to clean some of the compartments. 'We lime washed all that [the compartments]. She had had kerosene in her, and the effect on the men, when they were lime washing her, was something cruel. Half of them were stupefied from the effects of the kerosene and the lime. What with this small entrance [3'9" by 3'6"], using candles on the job [to provide light] in this confined space, with about 100 men on the job, some of them had to knock off.'

James Gaby, a stevedoring foreman, wrote in his 1974 book *The Restless Waterfront,* 'times without number, the waterside or wharf labourer as he was generally known in those early days, walked in through the gate at eight one morning and walked out again at seven o'clock the following morning, tired and dirty after a long twenty-three hour shift'. Advance notice wasn't part of the deal, with Gaby noting the man might be told 'at four thirty that the ship was working right through the night. No tea money was advanced, so it was bad luck if his tucker-bag was light or he only had return fare in his pocket. He had to keep working with or without tea or supper. Anxious wives must often have gone to bed really worried about the safety of their husband.' Gaby also said, 'amenities was a word yet to be recognised', and described filthy toilets with a grimy concrete trough for washing and drinking water, and 'midnight supper breaks were dismal affairs on the best of nights. Men perched around on cargo sacks in the gloom of the sheds, at their cold sandwich, drank their billies of tea and fell asleep until roused by the foreman's "*on again*" shout. Horse-drawn carts were still common on the wharves, and the smell of manure was ever present.'

In 1928, strikes on the docks were a regular occurrence, exacerbated by the national tour of the Arbitration Court's Justice George Beeby, who was taking evidence for a new award. By July, Beeby's proposals, which included a strengthening of the 'bull' system of worker selection (where the foreman picked workers who were less troublesome and who could work hard and long) to allow two pick-ups per day, and removing the right for local negotiations, infuriated the wharfies and they were unified in calling for its rejection. The wharfies argued the system was unfair and prone to corruption, but Beeby found 'there was not one scintilla of evidence that the bullying ganger of the old days is now tolerated on the waterfront'. The wharfies disagreed and Gaby was on their side, writing the bulls had their own regulars who were loyal to him and 'the men could be moved from one job to another at the boss's convenience; rules may have been in the book, but the book was seldom read'. He also wrote that the foremen were 'cracking the shipowner's whip' and that 98% of them were ex wharfies who had 'forced their way through by toughness and often ruthlessness. To watch some of them in action was like watching a circus boss bawling and shouting at his roughnecks when the big top was going up or coming down. One Sussex Street firm was satirically called the "Callan Park Stevedoring Company" [a reference to a Sydney mental hospital] because of all the crazy shouting that went on whilst a ship was working.'

Lew Hillier, writing in *Meet the Ship Painters and Dockers,* said of the 'pick-up' system that 'men followed the gates of the various wharves along the waterfront. If they missed out at one wharf they'd run to the next and so on.' He said, 'each foreman had his bulls. Other favourites would work some of their wages back to him later. These men he gave first preference to.' After a flood of demands, the pick-up was moved to outside 'The Big House' hotel on the waterfront – an establishment that, in my memory as a young detective working the inner city, was an 'early opener' to ease the thirst of men who'd worked the night shift, and offered other services in the men's toilet.

In Melbourne, the pick-up was outside Duke & Orrs dock in Lorimer Street; in Brisbane outside the South Brisbane dry dock; and in Newcastle in a park at Carrington not far from the woolsheds.

The Beeby Award, as it became known, came into force in September, and the waterfront greeted it with a strike. The shipowners, sensing another victory against the Waterside Workers Federation, weren't responding to the union's overtures to negotiate and reach a compromise. They knew they were in front and told the WWF, 'the new award represents the law which must be obeyed by both employers and employed'. A sting in the tail of the award was that there were financial penalties for non-compliance.

Adding further annoyance to the workers was the introduction of a piece of Commonwealth Legislation – the Transport Workers Act – popularly known as the 'Dog Collar Act' because of its controlling effect on the workers. It was rushed through parliament during an all-night sitting on 25 September 1928 by the Nationalist government under Prime Minister Stanley Bruce. Bruce had replaced Hughes in 1923 when the government was forced into a coalition with the Country Party under Earle Page, who was no fan of Hughes and his flexible political values. Hughes stood down as prime minister and Bruce, his treasurer, stepped into the top job.

The legislation was designed to control how workers were employed, how they did their jobs and how an employer could sack them. In practice, it introduced a system of licensing for workers like the wharfies and painters and dockers. The licence cost one shilling per year and could be cancelled by the licensing authorities. Union members received a pink-coloured document, and non-union members a brown one. No licence, no work.

If the government had had any commitment to clearing up the criminal problems identified on the waterfront in Macfarlane's 1921 royal commission, the licensing process would have been a fine opportunity to check the criminal records and character of those applying. Unfortunately, the royal commission's findings had been forgotten.

Predictably, the strike's first impact was felt by the waterfront communities. Les O'Shannessy, then an eight-year-old son of a waterside worker living in South Melbourne, recalled of his local area that, 'most of the male population worked on the wharves' and his family was 'living in an old weatherboard house with boards missing where kids pulled them off the wall to make cricket bats and kites. There was a stable at the back for three horses, belonging to a rag, bone and bottle merchant. The horses were a help when people had to shift house because they couldn't pay their rent.' He recalled his father and his colleagues plotting 'how they could attack and drive off the scabs. I used to open my bedroom door a little and listen to the battle plans.' Food was scarce and 'porridge and bread and dripping were the staple diet. We children did not suffer as much as our parents because we were the first fed: parents survived on leftovers.'

Elsie Davidson, the daughter of striking Melbourne wharfie Joseph Baldwin, recalled the strike provoked a deep bitterness in her father, and he drummed into his family they should 'never forgive them [the shipowners] for what they did to us'. He was a staunch union member, and with the family completely broke during the strike, he pawned his son Clifford's bike – bought with money earned from selling newspapers – to pay his union dues and remain financial. Elsie recalled, 'the kid never complained, though he'd lost his most treasured possession'. With working on the docks out of the question, Baldwin 'lived in a tent in

Gippsland where he got odd jobs on timber to send a little money to his family'.

By mid September, financial penalties against the unions were looming and the WWF voted overwhelmingly for its members to return to work. There was resistance, but in the ensuing month, workers in most states had capitulated – except for Melbourne where the situation was becoming more troubled. Beeby handed down a decision that 10,000 licences – around double the number of jobs available – were to be issued in Melbourne with only 40% going to unionists. The Melbournians took aim at the Carters & Drivers Union who'd declined to join the strike – demanding the docks be declared 'black' – off limits to those not on strike – and not letting them on. Carters, fearing intimidation, were given police protection when heading to the docklands. Railway workers, who'd been supported by the WWF during their strike in 1917, declined to return the compliment and noted the wharfies strike was 'an absurdity'.

The strike became one of the most bitter and violent in Melbourne's history. 'Scab' labourers were assaulted, and later housed under guard in the depot of the Vacuum oil company to ensure their safety. They were escorted to and from the wharves each day by police. Protesting unionists clashed violently with police, two 'scabs' died after being thrown from a railway bridge and others were ostracised in their own communities.

Heightening the tension was a bombing campaign that saw eight attacks in three months, including the homes of two foremen stevedores and shipping agent William Swanton.

In the early hours of 10 October a homemade bomb built from gas pipe with gelignite sealed tightly inside – later popular in the Spanish Civil War and with the IRA – exploded in a house in West Melbourne. The bomb was attached to the front door, and inside were thirteen Italians – men, women and children – who were asleep at the time of the explosion. The *Canberra Times* reported, 'the front door was blown to pieces and the flooring in the passage way ripped up. The walls were stripped of plaster and all windows broken. A portion of the bomb was stuck in a door on the other side of the street.' Ceilings collapsed on sleeping couples and children, and power lines in the street were blown down.

Bombs are the most indiscriminate of weapons, killing or maiming with the explosion and the flying debris, and it was pure good fortune no one was injured. The paper noted, 'the outrage is thought to be an act of malice against the Italians who have been working on the wharves as volunteers. It is surmised that a miscreant placed the bomb inside the house.' Anthony Barbaross, who was sleeping with his wife when the ceiling dropped onto their bed, told a reporter that Mussolini would have 'speedily secured a confession from those responsible'. The Victorian Police weren't as vigorous but the reward of £250 for information about the bombing was doubled and the homes of shipping company executives put under police guard.

On Friday 2 November, a riot broke out in Port Melbourne as non-union labourers were escorted onto Princess Pier. Newspapers reported, 'about 2000 unionists, angered by the protection afforded anti-strikers, made an attack on Police. The officer in charge warned them that any attempt of intimidation would be suppressed, but stones were thrown and the mob moved toward the police.' The police reacted by drawing their revolvers and firing shots into the air. When the warning shots proved futile and the mob surged forward instead of retreating, police fired directly at the advancing men.

It was impossible to miss, and Allan Whittaker was shot in the jaw and 'in a bad way' according to the news reports; James Williams, Jim Nagel and George Dray were shot but the wounds were relatively minor. The police had begun with blanks, but switched to live rounds for greater effect. Nagel recalled seeing Whittaker walking near the waterfront, when he was shot through the back of the neck. In his statement to the Coroner, Nagel said, 'I saw Whittaker fall. The bullet came out of his mouth, and I turned around and said, "You dirty bastards, are you fair dinkum?"' The constable then shot Nagel in the arm. He said, 'the blood was squirting out. Another feller by the name of George Dray, he got shot through the back of his shoulder. A chap picked us up in his car and took us to hospital.'

Whittaker had been shot before – around 8.30 am on 25 April 1915 at Gallipoli – and recovered. This time he wasn't so lucky, and died of the wound from the police bullet on 26 January 1929.

Victoria's Police Commissioner Thomas Blamey was quick to defend his men, saying, 'I have no hesitation in saying that the action of the officer in charge was fully justified.' Bob Haldane, a former superintendent with thirty-four years in the Victoria Police wrote of Blamey in his book *The People's Force* that Blamey was keen to crush any public protests and, 'it could be said that Blamey's style of dealing with public protest was confrontationist, readily violent, and generally ruthless'.

At the inquest into Whittaker's death, the coroner disregarded the wharfies' assertions they were shot in the back and agreed with Blamey, finding that it was a case of 'justifiable homicide'. Whittaker's death, and the ongoing social misery, robbed the strikers of much of their will. Some younger men ignored their parents' commitment to the cause and returned to work; alienating themselves from both family and community.

Jack Kiely, when interviewed in the mid 1980s by Rupert Lockwood, commented, 'it was bitter. Some sons who scabbed were banished from their homes by fathers loyal to the Federation. Mothers would sneak from their homes at night and meet with their scabbing sons on street corners or dark lanes,' and if they were spotted, the father would quickly find out, often with dire consequences. Kiely recalled, 'this resulted in fights and arguments in the homes. Some mothers suffered physical injuries inflicted by husbands crazed with anger at the stigma of having sons who betrayed unionist fathers and workmates by scabbing, and wives who refused to disown scabs in the family.'

Men weren't the only ones protesting. A week after Whittaker's death, wives of waterfront workers were in the Victorian Parliament making their presence felt. Armed with umbrellas to fend off police or parliamentary staff, they stood in the public gallery and shouted at the politicians on the floor of the House, 'we are the wives of the stevedores of Port Phillip, and our children are starving while the scabs are scabbing'. Opposition Leader Sir William McPherson called for the police on duty in the House to remove the protesters, telling them 'this is not a place where ladies may interject'. The women were removed from parliament without being arrested or unfurling their umbrellas.

With work in short supply and Christmas looming, the will for striking was replaced by reality, and the men straggled back to the waterfront to try and find work. One of the last acts of defiance came on Saturday 1 December, when a bomb was detonated at the Greek Club in Lonsdale Street. Twenty men were injured – six seriously. The *Argus* reported,

> a little before 10 on a busy Saturday night, four bombs exploded in the club, including one in the ceiling above the billiard table. The ceiling was blown out and the top floor extensively damaged. Police and firemen arrived to a scene of utter chaos as men scrambled to escape the crowded club, the growing fire and debris. It was a spectacle of harrowing sights. Men bleeding from wounds to their faces staggered into the street, dazed with the effects of the explosion and half blinded with the blood streaming down their faces. Less fortunate men who had been wounded in the legs and body fell as they tripped on the footpath. Over these, other men fell. The groans of the injured and the hysterical screams of others were painful to hear.

Five men were arrested within forty-eight hours, and one was found with a bomb in his car. Among them were wharfies and brothers Norman and Alexander 'Sandy' McIver, and Timothy O'Connell, a man with a few prior brushes with the law who'd been arrested at a waterfront protest a week before.

At the subsequent trial, Francis Delaney, who'd been caught with the bomb in his car, Alexander McIver, and Timothy O'Connell were convicted. Over the following decade the rumour mill was busy, suggesting the explosion may have been caused by a battle between illegal gambling operators over a casino allegedly on the second floor of the Greek Club and was a well-timed copycat crime, or the police had 'verballed' some of their suspects.

After months of the terror of a bombing campaign, strikes turning violent and the senseless death of a Gallipoli veteran, the waterfront community could only hope for a better new year – but they'd be hoping in vain because the following year was going to be far worse not only in Victoria but around Australia and most of the world.

21
THE HUNGRY MILE

Black Tuesday – 29 October 1929 – was the day a plunge on the New York stock market rocked the world financial markets and the Great Depression began. Around $30 billion was wiped off the value of stocks on America's mightiest exchange. A security guard on the trading floor of the New York Stock Exchange recalled of that day, 'they roared like a lot of lions and tigers. They hollered and screamed, they clawed at one another's collars. It was like a bunch of crazy men.'

There is a popular notion that financiers reacted to the destruction of their fortunes by strolling to the nearest window and stepping out. However that's an urban myth that may have its origin in a column written by satirist Will Rogers, who said, 'when Wall Street took that tail spin, you had to stand in line to get a window to jump out of, and speculators were selling space for bodies in the East River'. But when the depth of the crash became obvious over the next few months, the suicide rate in New York did spike. Wellington Lytle, reportedly left with only four cents to his name, committed suicide with a gun, and left a note saying 'my body should go to science, my soul to Andrew W Melon [Secretary of the US Treasury], and my sympathy to my creditors'.

Australia wasn't in the best of shape when the Depression hit. While the recreational drug market was doing a brisk trade, 10% of the nation's workers were unemployed – a figure felt particularly in the waterfront communities where men's only asset to sell was their ability to work hard. Coming out of the 1928 strikes, the shipowners were putting further pressure on the unionists by giving employment preference to the labourers who'd kept them trading during the strike. Adelaide, Melbourne, Newcastle and the Queensland ports were the hardest hit by the employers' decision.

A week before the Wall Street collapse, Australia had gone to the polls, and, as usual, Billy Hughes was up to his neck in the plotting. Prime Minister Stanley Bruce had tried to pass the Maritime Industries Bill, which was designed to abolish the Federal Arbitration Court and flick the arbitration powers to the States. The union movement, having worked so long to become national powers, were not pleased and believed the bill gave even greater strength to employers. Hughes, with his long history in fostering a national approach, wasn't pleased either. He'd annoyed Prime Minister Bruce on 22 August, when he'd crossed the floor to vote with Labor on a censure motion – the government had recently dropped a prosecution against the Newcastle coal 'baron' John Brown who'd locked out his miners and closed down mines. Bruce retaliated and locked Hughes out of meetings on his Maritime Industries Bill.

In tit for tat politics, Hughes did what he did best, and organised some of his Nationalist colleagues to join him and vote with Labor against the bill when it came to the House on 10 September. Bruce and his party lost by one vote – 34 to 35. Bruce wanted a mandate from the public and called an election. In a speech delivered at Dandenong on 18 September, he laid the nation's arbitration woes squarely at the feet of the union movement, saying, the death blow to Federal arbitration has, however, been struck by the extremists who have been allowed to occupy positions of power and authority within the labour movement. They have defied the awards of the Court, and have used the machinery of trade unionism to compel tens of thousands of moderate unionists, who have been working contentedly under awards of the Court, to subscribe to the support of strikes against the fundamental principle of arbitration. They have exploited for their own ends the spirit of loyalty in trade unionism.

On 12 October, Labor won in a landslide victory. Bruce became the first prime minister to lose his seat.

Labor's James Scullin was sworn in as prime minister one week before the crash.

In the waterfront communities, it was misery as usual. Author and journalist Rupert Lockwood, writing in his *Ship to Shore* of Port Melbourne at the time, said the 'swingeing cuts in earnings, black-listing and mass unemployment forced the Port families into a sort of tribal communism' sharing fish pulled from the grimy waters of Port Phillip Bay, or rabbits caught in the shoreline scrub. Les O'Shannessy told Rupert Lockwood, 'a wharfie's wife who acquired a loaf of bread would slice it up and give to the neighbours' children as well as her own. Never a crust was thrown away. Some families were forced to shoplift to eat. Port Melbourne magistrates, none of them ever having missed a meal, were harsh on those caught.' Simple comforts like a roof over your head and bedding were sold to buy food, and O'Shannessy noted, 'plenty were sleeping on bags and tables under hessian, and not all had roofs over their heads. Rents could not be paid. Evictions of families into the streets were a commonplace social atrocity. My brother Jack's heart was broke. For the first time he could not feed his children.'

As the Depression deepened, businesses closed and workers were laid off in thousands. By the middle of 1930, unemployment reached 21% and continued climbing for the next two years when it peaked at almost 32%. Women from the waterfront community, often the only ones in the family making any money during the strike periods by working in factories making and assembling products like confectionery, biscuits and textiles – all industries heavily affected by the economic disaster – found themselves out of work. Women at the time weren't eligible for unemployment benefits. It was tough to maintain basics like food and clothes for their families. The union movement didn't help matters either as the male-dominated organisation was not supportive of the notion of women taking jobs that could be given to the men.

Shipping was in sharp decline and jobs for experienced dock workers and the 'scabs' became even more difficult when men who'd lost their jobs in other sectors joined them. Dawn Gietzelt, in a living history recorded for the Museum of Sydney, recalled food was short and parents made sacrifices for their children. She said, 'Mum would call my sister and myself for the evening meal and there would be two places set at the table and we would have a bowl of – a slice of bread with a little bit of sugar on it and milk. And I can often remember saying to Mum, "Where's yours and Dad's? Why aren't you sitting down and eating it with us?" And Mum would always say, "Oh, Dad wanted to have his later on and I'll have mine with him."' It was a common story from the waterfront through to the middle class suburbs. In The Rocks, the hardwood blocks that were laid as roadways in the late 1880s were stolen by local children to provide heat for their home and kitchen stoves. On Sydney's Hungry Mile – the northern end of the eastern side of Darling Harbour – white-collar workers lined up with tradesmen and labourers in the hope of a day's work.

I remember stories of my paternal grandfather – a senior captain in Sydney's tug fleet – queuing for work on the Hungry Mile after he'd been temporarily put ashore as shipping slowed to a trickle. He'd take the ferry at dawn from genteel Cremorne and most days he'd return at dusk – no work, no money.

My paternal grandfather was joined on the Hungry Mile by my maternal grandfather – an accountant who'd never done a day's labouring in his life but had been laid off by the bank in which he'd hoped for a career. Both men were the product of exclusive private schools but the search for work to feed their families was a great social leveller. Men from middle-class backgrounds could be found rubbing shoulders with wharfies, painters and dockers, clerks, managers, and businessmen on the docklands in every major port.

Arthur Brown, who had a long career on the wharves, said that in Sydney during the Depression he was 'lucky enough' to get work and it often meant a twenty-four-hour shift, carrying seventy-five kilograms of sugar or flour – ten kilograms more than Arthur weighed. The work was literally back breaking, and he ended up with fingers that were 'broken and bashed'. He recalled, 'to be honest, sometimes it felt like you were going over bloody Mount Everest. But we considered ourselves lucky enough to get more than two shifts like that per week. The rest had to go home hungry; there were no jobs for them. The bosses picked the bulls – the strong blokes who were known – the rest had to hope like hell.'

He remembered the brutal physical work that followed for anyone lucky enough to be picked, and said, 'we'd get into the ship holds and lift out these bloody enormous loads of wool, pig iron, soda ash and asbestos – that's another one. They've dropped like flies the old wharfies. They all got asbestosis. That's their reward.'

Poet Ernest Antony wrote of the Hungry Mile in 1930,

They tramp there in their legions on the morning dark
   and cold.
To beg the right to slave for bread from Sydney's lords of gold;

They toil and sweat in slavery, 'twould make the devil smile,
To see the wharfies trampling down the hungry mile.

The Depression was written into the lore of the waterfront with rousing words like Antony's, sometimes signalling the rise of the docklands' flirtation with communism:

And through the revolution's smoke, ascending to the skies,
the master's face shall show the fear he hides behind his smile,
of these his slaves, who on that day shall storm the hungry mile.

However, the labourers didn't storm anything – most of the nation was in the same boat.

The Communist Party of Australia was formed in 1920 and by the end of the Depression had become a strong voice in the union movement and one that would last for decades. The WWF's British-born Irishman, the strapping and quietly spoken James 'Big Jim' Healy was a dominating figure in Australian communism. Police were no fans of communism, with the *Police News* of 15 February 1930 reporting, 'the unemployable who preach the advantages of revolution and wiping out police – the guardians of the people against revolutionaries, lunatics and criminals – are windy half-wits likely to become a serious menace if not checked'.

Police, under William MacKay, the man responsible for the creation of the Consorting Squad, took an aggressive approach. A nine-month strike by coal miners at Rothbury in the Hunter Valley over a range of issues including 'scab' labour turned violent shortly after dawn on 16 December 1929. Four thousand miners, armed with sticks, stones and bricks marched to the colliery to confront the scabs.

Unfortunately for the miners, police, fearing that communists might be stirring the strike, had been tipped off and arrived in force from Sydney and surrounding areas. They were armed with batons and revolvers with MacKay in charge. When the miners surged forward, the police opened fire. While the order was to aim over their heads, someone obviously hadn't heard, and miner Norman Brown was killed by a shot. The *Sydney Sun* of 16 December 1929 dramatically reported, 'Smoking Revolvers in Fight at Rothbury', and 'a volley of gunshots rang out, supposedly aimed above their heads and at the ground. One miner, Norman Brown, was killed instantly and nine others were seriously wounded. The police suffered their own casualties in the ensuing melee from miners throwing stones and wielding sticks.'

The following day 7000 unionists, many of them from the waterfront and maritime unions, converged on Sydney's Hyde Park, then marched on State Parliament in Macquarie Street. The sturdy gates and fence, along with a large contingent of armed and baton-swinging police, kept the protesters from getting into the building.

The *Police News* was more vocal than the major newspapers and on 15 February 1930 pointed the finger of blame for the entire debacle at the communists, saying 'reds' were responsible for 'despicable tactics' and that swift and decisive action prevented a 'civil war – the aim and hope of vicious and foolish communists'. The police may have been spurred on by reports in the *Sydney Morning Herald* in the weeks following the riot, in which a letter from the Third International in London to the Australian Communist Congress, declared that 'large sections of Australian workers have been defeated with the aid of capitalist agents, who are the allies of the Labour party and trade union bureaucrats'. The letter went on to stir the Australian worker, saying 'the main task is to penetrate the masses and begin the organization of an independent revolutionary leadership for the working classes'.

The Sun stirred concerns of a class war on 8 November 1931 when it published a hypothetical 'If revolution came to Sydney – Death, Fire, Plunder . . . Gunswept Streets and Mob Rule . . . What Communism Really Means'. The paper cleverly added the Church to the debate by commissioning a foreword for the piece from Canon Howard Lea, the Rector of St Marks in leafy and affluent Darling Point – a suburb high on the target list for any marauding communists.

By 1931 an alternative to communism was also emerging – the New Guard – and it wasn't attracting workers, but rather appealing to former military officers. On the application form was a statement of values and among the New Guard's goals were, 'sane and honourable government throughout Australia; suppression of any disloyal and immoral elements in government, industrial and social circles; abolition of machine politics; and maintenance of the full liberty of the individual'. Cynics, or the experienced, might suggest the first was unobtainable.

Eric Campbell, an Army officer in World War I with a distinguished service record for bravery, led the New Guard. When he returned from the war to civilian life he followed his father into the law, and married into the squattocracy. He became a prominent businessman, and in 1925 organised 500 ex officers to break up a seamen's strike. By 1930, he was the recruiter for a group of businessmen, ex-army officers and graziers called the 'Old Guard' who'd been rattled by the Depression, the rise of communism, and the arrival of Labor firebrand Jack Lang as NSW Premier. Campbell later wrote in his 1965 book *The Rallying Point* that the New Guard's aims were 'First to preserve law and order and maintain services in case of civil strife breaking out as a direct result of the economic crisis, and second, to foil any attempt, constitutional or unconstitutional, by the government to foist socialisation upon the people'.

A year later in 1931, disappointed with the lack of action by the Old Guard, Campbell formed the New Guard, and ran it on military lines with himself in charge. The New Guard peaked with around 50,000 members, mainly in Sydney. The *Australian Dictionary of Biography* noted that the New Guard 'rallied in public, broke up "communist" meetings, drilled, vilified the Labor Party and demanded the deportation of Communists'.

However, the rise of the working class didn't happen – the vocal minority were far outweighed by families trying to survive, and Campbell's militia became more isolated from reality and more volatile. With the New Guard recruiting men with military training and knowledge of where to find stockpiles of arms and explosives, Australia had a genuine internal terrorism risk. Campbell also had the unfortunate habit of using the fascist salute, similar to that made famous by Hitler who was then on a rapid ascent to power in Germany. 'Shock Troopers' from the New Guard prowled Sydney, targeting meetings of groups they decided were left-wing – they'd try to push the speaker from the podium to start a brawl, and reportedly came with iron bars and guns.

Campbell again turned his interest to the waterfront in the 1931 seamen's strike. Prime Minister Scullin called the strike a 'wanton disregard of national welfare' in Parliament on 21 October 1931 and Campbell entered the debate, in a speech that same day to the Millions Club (later renamed as The Sydney Club) offering volunteers to man the ships and that his New Guard would protect volunteers replacing the strikers against 'basher gangs'. He also claimed that many seamen had joined his organisation. The strike ended shortly after without Campbell's assistance.

Campbell's views and his militia's propensity for cowardly and violent attacks didn't gain traction with the public. The actions of one of their members, Francis de Groot, added impetus to their decline. De Groot committed a major public relations blunder on 19 March 1932 at the opening of the Sydney Harbour Bridge when he arrived on horseback in full uniform and used his sword to slash the ribbon about to be cut by Premier Lang. Police dragged him from his horse, he was arrested and taken to Darlinghurst Police Station.

What Campbell and his cohorts didn't know was that MacKay's approach to policing was even-handed and he targeted any person or group who might be considering interrupting the peace of his state. His officers had infiltrated the Guard. On 10 May 1932 they raided the New Guard's headquarters in Hunter Street, Sydney, and found plans to kidnap Lang, his ministers, and senior police and hold them in Berrima Gaol. The idea was to isolate the city and as the *Sydney Morning Herald* reported on 11 May 1932, 'form up with other forces in the city, overthrow Parliament and the constitutional government, take possession of all government departments and set up a dictatorship'. Curiously, charges against the New Guard were quietly dropped. Like the waterfront communities, the city's well-to-do – many sympathetic to Campbell – had closed ranks.

By the end of 1932, the New Guard was sliding into history. Campbell made an unsuccessful attempt to become a Member of Parliament, and eventually returned to Young in rural New South Wales and resumed practice as a solicitor.

Communism fared better, with Jim Healy – who'd visited the Soviet Union in 1934 where he was, according to Rupert Lockwood in his *The Story of Jim Healy*, 'impressed with what he observed: free medical services and worker's rest houses as well as plenty of work for everyone' – taking over the WWF as General Secretary in 1937 and later appointed by Prime Minister John Curtin to a significant role in the World War II effort.

The Depression's effect on the waterside unions had been significant with 20,000 members at the end of the 1928 strike plummeting to nearly half that by 1934. The good news was that, as the world recovered slowly from the Great Depression, life on the waterfront began to improve again as well.

Crime was also changing. During the hard times, policing had been focused on maintaining order. The drug trade was in decline but what police weren't investigating was the network of crime that started on the waterfront and wound its way back into the city. Policing in the late 1930s was focusing on sly grog and gambling – two criminal enterprises that provided magnificent profits at low risk to their purveyors, and for police the twin bounties of photo opportunities of places being raided, and the opportunity to make a quick 'quid' to ensure some establishments weren't raided, or raided with plenty of notice.

22
THE BOUNTY OF WAR

War brings opportunity, and for the waterfront communities of wharfies, painters and dockers and seamen, the connections, networks, loyalties and infrastructure were about to combine with that bastion of capitalism, market forces. The result would be a thriving black market and the first big steps to what James Morton and Russell Robinson in their book *Shotgun and Standover* described as 'criminal infamy'.

In the lead-up to the war, Menzies encountered the ire of the waterfront when in 1938, as attorney-general in the government of Prime Minister Joseph Lyons, he dusted off the Transport Workers Act to break boycotts on the docks. The issue that brought him into conflict with the waterside workers was Australia's export of iron to Japan – and Japan's track record of aggression in China. Australia's attitude to Japan was the same as Britain's to Germany and Italy – don't rock the boat.

Australia was providing the Japanese with scrap or 'pig' iron made from smelting iron ore in a blast furnace that can be refined into a sheet, and had just leased an iron deposit in Yampi Sound, off the coast of northwestern Australia, to them. The fact that the iron was essential to Japan's military industry was politely overlooked. Business as usual. The wharfies, under Jim Healy, took a different view. The Australian Council of Trade Unions had denounced the Japanese attacks in China. The WWF took it a step further and declined to load the iron onto ships bound for Japan. The strike was most aggressive at Port Kembla – home to the vast BHP steel plant and the major exporter of iron.

Menzies used the heavy-handed approach to dealing with the dispute in early December 1938 and invoked the provisions of the 'Dog Collar Act'. Unlike a decade before, there was plenty of work and no 'scab' labour around to load and unload cargo so the Act was pointless, and thus the port was quiet. Negotiations continued over Christmas and by early January around 4000 BHP workers had been laid off. On 16 January 1939 Menzies visited and was greeted by a jeering crowd of wharfies and ironworkers. Fortunately a compromise was in the air. A few days later, the men agreed to load one ship, the British-owned *Dalfram,* on the understanding it would be the last export to Japan.

Wharfie E.C. Roach, talking to the Labor History Conference in Newcastle in June 1993, said, 'Members [of the WWF] were incensed at the Japanese rape of China' and had seen a document 'which contained maps showing projected Japanese expansion in the Pacific, which included Australia'. Roach said one of the reasons for their actions was to 'alert the Australian people to dangers inherent in the Japanese policy and to force an alteration in government foreign policy'. Sir Isaac Isaacs, a former governor-general, agreed, and wrote 'the Government applied to the men and their families what I would describe as the economic pressure of possible starvation unless, contrary to their conscience, the men helped to dispatch the pig-iron for the use by the Japanese Government. For myself, I honour the men who stood out as long as they could and those who supported them.' Sir Isaacs concluded by writing that the actions would 'find a place in our history beside the Eureka Stockade with its more violent resistance of a less settled time'. Rupert Lockwood, writing in *The Story of Jim Healy,* said one Sydney wharfie was told by a Japanese officer on a ship in Sydney, 'never mind, we shall be back to make you load it'. He came perilously close to making good his boast.

At the beginning of World War II, Robert Menzies was in his first tenure as prime minister, and his government reflected Britain's notion of a 'twilight war' – the name coined by Winston Churchill for the first months of the war – that would soon be over by saying that for Australia it would be business as usual. Australia was poorly prepared for conflict, and after hasty training our first troops left Sydney in January 1940 for the Middle East where they waited, and waited, and waited. If nothing else the waiting time allowed them to build on their initial training in which recruits were turned into soldiers in a month.

The great stimulus for the waterfront and the black market came on the morning of 7 December 1941 when Japan attacked Pearl Harbor. Prime Minister John Curtin, in office since 7 October that year, broadcast on radio to the nation, saying, 'Men and women of Australia we are at war with Japan. This is the gravest hour of our history. We Australians have imperishable traditions. We shall maintain them. We shall vindicate them. We shall hold this country and keep it as a citadel for the British-speaking race and as a place where civilisation will persist.'

Japan entered World War II match-fit – like its Axis cohorts Germany and Italy it had had some recent practice. At nearly the same moment as their planes were wreaking havoc on the US naval base at Pearl Harbor the Japanese armed forces were attacking Southeast Asia. Their progress was brutal and rapid. Hong Kong and Thailand were attacked on 8 December 1941. Two days later, the British battleship *Prince of Wales* and battle cruiser *Repulse* were sunk off the coast of Malaya by land-based bombers. For an Empire built on the might of its capital ships, it was a devastating blow to the British Navy, to regional security and Britain's pride. Hong Kong fell on Christmas Day, and by the end of January, British Empire forces had been driven to Singapore. In January 1942, the British code-breakers decoded a statement from a meeting of Axis Ministers, in which the Japanese told their European colleagues that, 'attacks are to be expected on Darwin, Sydney, Melbourne and other Australian ports to destroy bases'. On 15 February 1942, Singapore surrendered to the Japanese. Four days later, the Japanese bombed Darwin, targeting the harbour, which was poorly defended and heavily congested with ships. Suddenly, it was no longer Churchill's 'phoney war' on the other side of the world.

US economist Mark Perlman wrote on the impact of the war, and particularly the entry of Japan, on Australia's waterfront in his 1954 book *Judges in Industry*. In the years prior to the war the waterfront was a 'dismal work place', where 'steady employment was hard to obtain and labour conditions were degrading'. He also noted the WWF 'has a tradition of fractiousness, which can be attributed to Mr Jim Healy, its general secretary since 1937. Mr Healy is a member of the Communist Party.' Not a surprising comment given Perlman was writing in the early part of the Cold War when communists were the target of Senator Joseph McCarthy.

Perlman didn't blame Healy alone, and noted that the wharfies in Australia were similar to their colleagues around the world: all subject to the 'twin evils of casual employment and hard physical labour or because there is little craft pride, in the nature of their work'. Wharfies 'have a grudge' and this 'industrial distemper has a tendency to manifest itself whenever the economic situation so permits'. As a backdrop to Perlman's comments, Paul Hasluck wrote in *Australia in the War 1939–1945* that Australia had lost an average of 666,000 days each year to industrial disputes from 1933 to 1939, but in 1940 that jumped to 1.5 million days with just under a million Australians members of a trade union. To put that into perspective, he also reported that in 1940 the nation lost around 11 million days to sickness and 18 million to unemployment.

Jim Healy when talking about the strikes that beset the nation in early 1941, in which his union had flexed their muscle for a three pence increase per hour, said that Justice Beeby 'classed their action as subversive and aimed at the security of the country, and he demanded that the Federation take some action against these elements'. In June 1941, the wharfies prevailed, getting a three and a half pence per hour increase, with a four-hour minimum engagement. But the win, and the acknowledgement of growing power didn't bring industrial peace. Hasluck said the 'Waterside Workers Federation sought to use a period of sustained high demand for labour to redress the accumulated grievances of the 1930s'.

The war was a boom time for the waterfront, and the first months of 1942 were marked with delays, strikes, a spike in thefts and a new problem. Healy wrote after the war that Japan's entry 'brought about a much more serious position on the waterfront'. Healy's problem was that the boatloads of refugees fleeing the swift Japanese advance, and the arrival of American forces en masse, meant 'further congestion [of Australian ports] and great fear expressed for the safety of our members', because 'ports are always a strategic target, and with the development of more destructive weapons, it is our members who will assuredly be in the first line, not the politicians in Canberra'. Healy observed his belief was spurred on by 'our traditional opposition to war [which] must be maintained and every effort devoted to the cause of maintaining world peace'.

With the US now calling Australia home for their Pacific operations against the Japanese, any problem on the waterfront that affected supply lines was intolerable and it provoked clashes between allies. On Melbourne docks, wharfie Tom Hills in *Under the Hook* (1982) said that on Station Pier, they'd 'knocked off in heavy rain as we were entitled to do under the award for health and safety reasons. Yank sentries pulled their guns on us, in contempt for Australian law, and ordered us to keep working in the rain.' The Americans, however, received a quick lesson in local customs and 'were told, with no shortage of adjectives, just where they could shove their guns. There was nearly a riot.' Hills had no love for the 'Yanks', describing them as often from 'poor white communities of the Deep South – racist, arrogant and stupidly so'.

Prime Minister John Curtin had little tolerance for the delays, and sympathy for the growing American irritation about the speed and reliability of the ports – heightened with the arrival in Melbourne on 21 March 1942 of General Douglas MacArthur, who was about to be appointed as the Supreme Commander of Allied Forces in the South West Pacific.

Australia was the hub of preparations for the war in the Pacific, with Cockatoo Island and Mort's Dock in Sydney the focus of shipbuilding, conversion of merchant vessels into naval vessels, and repairs. Among the conversions was the pride of the Cunard Line, the *Queen Mary,* which morphed from luxury liner into a troopship that carried more than three quarters of a million troops – many of them Anzacs – by the end of the war. Melbourne was the centre for US military supplies, and its smaller dockyard facilities at Williamstown did smaller scale conversion work like fishing trawlers into minesweepers.

US officials complained bitterly about the speed and attitude of the wharfies, noting that their soldiers, without the benefit of generations of training, could unload at four to five times the speed. One US military official observed of the Australians that, though the day started at 8 am, many arrived over the ensuing hours, with their day punctuated by regular 'smokos'. Lunch was leisurely and took around an hour and a half to two hours, and 'knock off' time was usually around half an hour before the official time. Working in the rain was forbidden for health reasons. Strikes were frequent and for little reason or purpose. The wharfies weren't fond of the US soldiers they dealt with either.

The wharfies had growing affluence and political power, and they were in demand. For the first time ever, they had muscle and weren't afraid to flex it. Jim Healy wrote in a *A Brief History of the Waterfront* that the 'increased volume of shipping led to a serious shortage of labour and waterside workers in the main ports were in a position of being able to choose when they would work and for whom they would not work'. Employers' complaints, Healy wrote, resulted in an 'immediate squeal to the Government' and a chat between Healy and Prime Minister Curtin resolved the problem. Healy observed, without a trace of irony, that 'the well being of the nation has always come second when the shipowners have their own immediate interests under consideration'.

The Painters and Dockers were also in equally high demand but took a less militant line. Lew Hillier said, 'with the outbreak of war in 1939, things changed very quickly. The NSW branch, which had about 800 members, jumped to around 4000.' They were diligent and not prone to strikes, and as Hillier wrote, 'the union had a stroke of luck when the government froze wages. Our rates were loaded by 35% because of the casual nature of the work, and this gave us a high rate of pay when the men were working full-time as well as a great deal of overtime.' Their reward after the war was an industrial agreement that made them a 'closed shop' with the union controlling all hiring. It seemed like a good idea at the time, but history would paint a different picture. Hillier noted 'when the war ended was when the disputes started'.

Curtin warned the waterside workers, saying, 'the men who are not in the fighting forces and who, at the same time, will not work are as much the enemies of this country as the directly enlisted legions of the enemy', but added, 'the Labor Government stands for justice for the workers'. Eddie Ward, his Minister for Labour and National Services, and a former boilermaker and prize-fighter, was more direct, and the *Sydney Morning Herald* of

16 January 1942 reported him saying 'sections of the unionists, in many cases in defiance of their leaders, have taken action leading to delays in production and interruption to essential services. Men have been released from the obligation of military service because they have been engaged in important war work. Obviously if they cease to be so employed the ground for their exemption from service ceases to exist.' The wharfies ignored the implied threat. In the following eighteen months the waterside workers contributed to more than 900,000 working days being lost to industrial disputes.

Curtin was a politician with a deft touch, and in April 1942 set up the Stevedoring Industry Commission to control the docks. On the commission were members of the stevedoring companies and unionists including Jim Healy, Jack O'Connell from Melbourne and Barney Mullins from Sydney. The appointment of Healy, an avowed communist, along with the entry of the Soviet Union into the war on the side of the Allies in 1941, brought with it, according to Margo Beasley in *Wharfies,* 'a profound turnaround in the Communist Party's attitude to the war'.

Writing in *Australia in the War 1939–1945*, Hasluck said the communists' anti-war sentiments, prior to this point, were particularly notable in Darwin, where they found the port to be a 'profitable field' made more vulnerable by 'bad facilities on the harbour and railways, dishonesty among wharf and railway workers, industrial troubles, shortage of labour, a low output due to climate, procrastination by civil authorities and general lassitude and malaise', and problems heightened by a 500% increase in freight landing in the port. Curtin's action brought the party, and the wharfies who were members, into the tent – far preferable to them standing outside and pissing in. By late 1942 the Communist Party in Australia had around 15,000 members, rising to 23,000 in 1944.

The Stevedoring Industry Commission made a few major changes. The old pick-up, where labourers were at the mercy of the 'bulls', disappeared and was replaced with an equitable 'rotary' system in which men all had to be registered, were able to form their own 'gangs', were given work in rotation and pay became regular and predictable. In what Perlman had accurately described as a 'fractious' group, not all wharfies were pleased with the new system. Some of the 'shonks', who worked under a variety of fake names to minimise their tax, or keep below the radar of police or creditors, weren't happy with the more fair and formal arrangement, nor were those who'd benefited from the favouritism and kickbacks of the bull system. In Melbourne, when the rotary system was put to the vote, only 60% were in favour, and in Sydney, rumours that the new system would lead to a loss of freedom of choice, and the possibility of being drafted to other docks around the country, led to disputes and stoppages. Curtin dealt with the Sydney situation by ordering troops onto the wharves to do the work of wharfies.

One task of the commission was to investigate the credibility of the disturbing number of workers alleging disability. Malingering rather than genuine health issues was suspected, and eminent Sydney physician Dr Ronald McQueen was appointed to delve into the issue. His report provided the first serious look into the physical impact of work on the docks.

In November 1944, he reported to the Stevedoring Industry Commission

> I was under the impression, when commencing this survey, that its main object was the detection of malingerers. Having encountered only one of these crafty undesirables among the first 130 cases I examined, I realized I was dealing with quite a unique collection of genuine and serious disabilities. I was forced into a real and surprised admiration, for a body of men earning a more or less arduous living and handicapped by gross and serious physical abnormalities.

He went on to note that 'my chief impression of these was that all of them were prematurely aged. It was rare to find any man who did not look at least ten years older than his stated age', and he commented on the role of pubs in their lives, saying 'the obesity, characteristic of many enthusiastic beer drinkers, was however, frequently seen'.

The new gang system had another benefit that has never been fully acknowledged. Margo Beasley observed it became a 'core feature of the WWF strength' and promoted 'deep and personal relationships' – further strengthening the strong bonds of a community that had been through poverty and plague. The flip side of those positives was it was also an environment in which crime could flourish – particularly if there was a strong market for the illicit.

Senior Constable P. B. Wilson of the Victoria Police writing on crime prevention for the Melbourne Chamber of Commerce, observed of those involved in theft that 'the Professional steals to re-sell for profit, so he must have a market. The Amateur steals when the opportunity offers. So he must have the opportunity.' The constable went on to observe,

> to the professional thief, stealing is a matter of business and he calculates the risk against the profit. Having stolen the goods, the thief must get rid of them so his market is of prime importance. Many professional criminals conduct their deals in hotels, and often the word goes around that certain goods can be obtained by contacting a certain person in a certain hotel. Only too often do we find that while the 'word' is widely spread, it does not come to our notice until too late.

When I was a young detective, I walked into a hotel near Sydney's waterfront – one of Constable Wilson's 'certain' hotels' – where an intriguing mix of locals gathered. I was meeting with a journalist and trying to be discreet and not look like a copper, a task at which I failed dismally. The game was up when I opened the door, stepped inside, stopped and instinctively scanned the public bar. The pool game stopped, drinkers paused in mid sip of their schooners, and one wit said, 'Careful boys, the coppers are here' – a crack that got a laugh, and a hasty departure by me to the ladies lounge. Pubs, along with sly-grog shops and gambling dens, were the ideal place to find a market for pillaged goods, with coppers or outsiders 'sticking out like the proverbial [dog's balls]'.

War brought with it the chance for some of the workers on the waterfront to go professional.

23
ACCIDENTAL INCENTIVES

In mid 1942, opportunities for a spot of skulduggery increased dramatically. First up was the arrival of rationing of food and clothing in May – joining petrol, which had been rationed since 1940. Austerity became one of Prime Minister Curtin's favourite words. He told the nation, 'austerity means a new way of life; a new spirit of action to do things the nation needs. I am convinced that the aspect of our national life which gives the greatest scope for the further development of our war effort is the human element.' Unlike many contemporary politicians, Curtin practised what he preached, with Hasluck noting that he was 'living severely, permitting no indulgence, devoting his life unsparingly to the duties of his office'. As part of the austerity campaign racing industry meetings were cut back to Saturdays only, with one race-less day per month, however 'holiday' and 'carnival' meetings like the Melbourne Cup were untouched – a relief to the waterside workers for whom a punt [bet on the races] was a favourite pastime. Curtin also tried to reduce 'the disproportionate spending on drink' by reducing alcohol production, and hotel trading hours to seven hours per day. These measures provided even more stimulus to the sly-grog trade. Hasluck wrote, 'they may have saved some manpower and materials in the breweries, but may have lost manpower not only to black marketers but by reason of the fact that drinkers either waited for the beer to come "on", or when it was "on" hastened to the pub so they didn't miss their share'. He also wrote 'wartime experience makes it clear that beer and betting mean more than anything else in life to a considerable number of Australians'.

The austerity drive also had some quirks. Restaurant diners were only allowed three courses, newspapers were asked to stop printing the social pages or pictures of people not involved in the war effort. The 'Fashions for Victory' campaign saw men's double-breasted suits being reduced to single, waistcoats and trouser cuffs disappeared, and in regulations for 'female apparel', 'evening wear' was prohibited.

The second reason opportunity for crime increased was the arrival of the Japanese in Sydney Harbour. On 29 May, five large submarines arrived around fifty-six kilometres northeast of the Heads. Around 3 am the next morning one submarine launched its reconnaissance aircraft, which flew over the harbour and reported rich pickings of 'battleships and cruisers' – targets of military and public relations significance. On 31 May, the enemy closed to around eleven kilometres from the Heads and around 4.30 pm three of the large submarines, *I-22, I-24* and *I-27,* released one midget submarine each. The two-man crews were tasked to penetrate the harbour's defences and sink the plumpest targets they could find.

The defences were a series of electric cables on the harbour floor to detect vessels passing above them and an anti-submarine and torpedo net boom that was opened and closed by craft on the surface. Like Australia in the first days of war, Sydney's harbour defences weren't quite ready to repel the enemy. The first cable near the Heads wasn't working, and when the midget sub from the *I-27* – the first through – was picked up by an inner cable, it wasn't recognised owing to other harbour traffic like ferries motoring around as well. However the submarine's good fortune didn't last and it was caught in an anti-submarine net. An alert nightwatchman from the Maritime Services Board decided to investigate in his skiff, and found the catch of the decade. HMAS *Yarroma* was quickly on the scene and around 9.30 pm opened fire with depth charges, however the submarine's crew beat them to it, destroying their own craft and killing themselves in the process.

The second submarine motored past shortly after, but thanks to the plight of its predecessor, received a warm but not hospitable welcome. When it was about 200 metres from Garden Island, the heavy cruiser USS *Chicago* – it had been mistakenly identified as a 'battleship' by the reconnaissance aircraft – opened fire but the submarine was untouched and managed to fire its two torpedoes then escaped. One torpedo ran ashore on Garden Island and didn't explode, and the other passed under the Dutch submarine *K9*, then hit HMAS *Kuttabul* – a former Sydney Harbour ferry made obsolete by the Sydney Harbour Bridge in 1932, and commissioned as a depot ship into the navy when war broke out. Nineteen Australian and two British sailors were killed in the attack, and ten more wounded. Recreational divers found the wreck of the submarine on a reef off Newport Beach on Sydney's northern beaches in 2006.

The third submarine was attacked by the patrol boat HMAS *Yandra*, who initially rammed it, then attacked with depth charges, which damaged the *Yandra* which was a little too close to the explosion. The submarine was later found at Taylors Bay with both men dead – it appeared the commander, Lieutenant Matsuo, had shot Petty Officer Tsuzuku, then himself. A week after the attack, two of the large submarines briefly bombarded both Sydney and Newcastle's harbourside suburbs with their deck guns. Coastal artillery drove off the Newcastle attacker after a twenty-minute exchange of fire, and the sub's target – the shipyard – was undamaged. In Sydney, ten shells were fired, with only one exploding in salubrious Bellevue Hill but the Japanese did achieve something the city has always feared – a drop in real estate values.

Rupert Lockwood, writing in *Ship to Shore*, observed that Melbourne faced a different threat. The army had prepared the port for destruction in preference to falling into enemy hands, by placing gelignite charges around the wharves at Port Melbourne, Altona, Williamstown and down at the former wool wharves in Corio Bay near Geelong. Stocks of combustibles like petrol, oil and coil were ready to be ignited, and working boats like tugs and ferries were to be scuttled to prevent access to the wharves. However, the preparations for the destruction of the port were done without the knowledge of anyone working there, and as Lockwood said, 'Melbourne ports would have been a mess after the holocaust' but the workers were 'unaware that the engines of the tanks, heavy trucks, jeeps and armoured troop-carriers roaring off the wharves emitted sparks near the massive charges of gelignite'.

Melbourne waterfront wag Les O'Shannessy when interviewed by Lockwood in the mid 1980s also recalled that a plane flying over the wharves one evening startled his co-workers. The anti-aircraft batteries opened fire but missed their target, which was fortunate as it wasn't an enemy aircraft. He said, 'we were mystified. The Japs were a long way away. The explanation that went around the waterfront was that the authorities felt the workers weren't digging deep enough to support war loans and it was advisable to let them know there was a war on.' It might have also stimulated them to work, faster, harder and more diligently. What was clear was Australia's ports and sea lanes were vulnerable to attack – and the shortages and rationing started to bite deeply.

The greatest boost for the black market was the arrival of US servicemen on leave – with Sydney as the favoured destination. In the course of the war around one million men would visit. Hasluck wrote that 'as shortages, particularly of drink and tobacco became more acute black marketing became more profitable and attracted and nourished an increasing body of criminals'. Many of the most desirable and profitable products on the black market came via the waterfront.

Scotch whisky was part of a lucrative interstate trade and was often stolen on the Sydney or Melbourne waterfront, then trucked to the other city for sale, depending on the market demands, or if the product was too 'hot' to sell in the home city. Unlike policing of the time, crime didn't respect state borders.

Empty bottles sold for 5 shillings a piece and were refilled with whatever the black marketer could find that could be passed off as Scotch – a boon to crooks working at Australian distillers like Corio on the shore of Port Phillip Bay whose unspectacular whisky was at least the right colour and packed a punch. Less fortunate buyers found themselves with a bottle of ginger ale or cold tea or some concoction of cheap spirits. With the real stuff in short supply and selling for £24 anyone buying a bottle of Scotch for £8 should have known better.

Senator Richard Keane, the Minister for Trade and Customs, issued a warning statement in 1942, saying that some of the dodgy whisky contained 'some essences mixed with "the spirit", which was almost raw, in an effort to provide it with some sort of character'. He also offered advice on wine which had been sold on the black market to servicemen and was so dreadful they thought they'd been poisoned – 'prepared by Fascist sympathisers' the Senator speculated.

Later in the war, journalist Keith Newman writing in the *Sydney Morning Herald* observed that the government could have averted boosting the black market in booze if they had 'followed the British example of making adequate supplies of beer available even in the darkest days of the U-boat blockade.'

By September 1942, the authorities were finally waking up to the existence of a booming black market trade based on Sydney's waterfront. The *Sydney Morning Herald* reported, 'Cargo Pillaging – heavy loss in Sydney – the Biggest Criminal Racket', with shipowners predicting a loss of 'hundreds of thousands of pounds this year through cargo pillaging' and unsurprisingly, 'many of the goods stolen are making their way onto the black market'. Thieves were targeting the goods that were now rationed. The article was probably written by one of the police roundsmen of the time as it noted the thieves had succeeded 'despite the vigilance of Police, wharf watchmen and patrolmen' – there was a fair chance that some of the watchmen and patrolmen were either asleep or complicit in the thievery.

The only solution, according to police sources, was the set piece 'more police and greater powers'. Unfortunately for the shipowners, the greater powers never came, and more police was always going to be a problem when a large number of potential recruits were volunteering for service instead. Female police in those days were confined to school lecturing, and dealing with female offenders, female victims and children – all of which weren't highly represented among the crooks on the wharves or their colleagues in the black market.

The *Sunday Sun* in 1943 reported another major problem confronting police was the complete lack of any information coming out of the waterfront. Ray 'The Blizzard' Blissett, who was a young detective during the war and rose to lead the Criminal Investigation Branch of the NSW Police, once commented that 'information from inside the gangs of crooks' was the 'life blood of a detective'. Motivations for slipping tasty morsels to the police included being paid, getting a favour or 'get out of gaol free' card, being caught in a compromising situation and trading information for freedom, revenge on the person you're informing on, or that old favourite of criminals – informing on your competition. There is honour among some thieves, but not all.

Blissett was on the money. The *Sun* said that 'no underworld wall of silence was as thick as that on the waterfront – no grapevine system of warning so efficient'. With the arrival of the police – conspicuous in most places but particularly in the narrow streets and cheek and jowl terrace houses – word spread rapidly over fences, and via local kids scurrying throughout the neighbourhood.

Blissett recalled in an oral history recorded in 1988 for the National Library of Australia his time working around Sydney's waterfront in World War II, and said the prime target for the light-fingered wharfies on any arriving ship was the manifest, which helped them target the most desirable goods. Wharfies left the ship with their plunder in CSR suitcases (a reference to sugar bags used by the Colonial Sugar Refinery) over their shoulders.

Coppers who'd been around at the time were united in the belief that, manifest or not, wharfies would 'steal anything that wasn't nailed down', but common targets were goods in short supply locally and goods that were easily transportable, whether by sugar bag, or in bulk from the warehouses. Popular items were tea, coffee, razor blades, shoes, American cigarettes and tobacco, and 'luxury' products like silk stockings – popular gifts from US servicemen to local women – and canned salmon.

Wharfies and dockers working on the arriving ships that were regulars on the Australian run developed relationships with the seamen or knew a kindred spirit when they saw one, making the transactions on goods relatively easy. The seaman could either hand over the goods directly if they were brazen, or leave them in a pre-arranged hiding place on the ship like engine rooms for painters and dockers or in the hold or a lifeboat for wharfies.

Stealing from the warehouse was also straightforward. Security was lax and with the volatility of the industrial scene, confronting wharfies with no more than suspicion was asking for trouble, so items could be easily walked through the gate in a kit bag, or slipped onto a truck with the connivance of the driver.

US entertainer Bob Hope on one of his regular tours to entertain the troops in the Pacific had stopped in Sydney for rest and recreation of his own, which invariably took him to places that offered gambling and liquor after hours. Hope wandered into the kitchen of the gambling club where a few of the club's 'security' staff were enjoying some prime canned Canadian sockeye – 'like gold' one of the men told me in a chat some years ago. Hope joined them for a snack and was returned to Sydney three days later after spending his time with the lads at their Central Coast retreat. His minders were most displeased but the men recalled that every time Hope visited to do a show in Sydney there were tickets at the door for them.

Blissett wasn't a fan of the WWF and believed the union was nothing more than a 'front for organized crime' – an intriguing remark as he'd been a senior detective at the CIB when it was magnificently corrupt and his peers had been men like the notorious Fred Krahe and Ray Kelly – some of the most corrupt police in NSW history. Blissett's regular public comments after his retirement omitted references to crooks in blue uniforms.

24
SILK STOCKINGS

The hub for any black market is a port city's red-light district, where the underworld can network, have a fine time and do a little business, and in Sydney it was conveniently located adjacent to the civilian and naval docks of Woolloomooloo.

Wharfie Alan MacMillan when interviewed for the Australian War Memorial summed up Australia's attitude to the black market that thrived during World War II, saying 'you asked no questions, got no answers; everybody knew it was going on'. Paul Hasluck noted the notion of a black market 'did not become part of the Australian vocabulary for perhaps a year because the thing itself was of minor importance. As much as any people Australians had always regarded the Government as fair game.'

Until World War II and the 'overfed, oversexed and over here' Americans arrived, Kings Cross was a place for Sydney's sophisticates, artists, musicians, and émigrés who'd decided that hanging around in Europe with the Fascists wasn't a great idea – the Cross provided them with a glimpse of the salons they'd once enjoyed. One Cross resident in an interview remembering her youth there just before the war, said, 'you could wear and do whatever you wanted without anyone bothering you'.

It was dramatically different to the brothels and laneways just a short stroll down the hill in East Sydney, described by artist Robert Eadie as 'like a scene from Dante's Inferno, around fifty girls working in two laneways. Men, drunk and sober.' Nightclubs had sprung up around the CBD and prostitutes worked the streets, particularly King Street where the Ziegfeld Nightclub was a hit with the visiting servicemen. The girls would strike a deal, bundle their client into a taxi and head for East Sydney to consummate the deal. By 1943 eight nightclubs and cabarets had opened in the city and the Cross. The Roosevelt, owned by Sammy Lee, was home to US officers, and for the African American enlisted men, it was around the corner at the Manzil Room.

Though legal liquor sales were forbidden after 6 pm, the trick was to 'order' before six so it could be delivered to you after – orders, of course, were often backdated. The *Sydney Morning Herald* reported that some servicemen 'take their own liquor much of which is obtainable on the black market'. The leading lights of the black market were an unlikely pair – Richard Gabriel 'Dick' Reilly and Reginald Stuart-Jones.

Reilly was a streetwise tough who'd been acquitted of shooting a man to death in 1937. He ran illegal casinos around Kings Cross, had a vigorous black market business supplying essentials for the inner city crowd and visiting US troops like whiskey, silk stockings and cigarettes – all conveniently available through his casinos, and a sideline in arranging robberies. Reilly was one of the gangsters who introduced the game of baccarat to Sydney and became known as the 'King of Baccarat'. Stuart-Jones was a surgeon and a playboy who'd made a fortune from abortions carried out in his Macquarie Street clinic, and had gone into the sly-grog business with Reilly. Stuart-Jones was famous for his lavish parties held on his yacht moored in Elizabeth Bay. The pair were instrumental in keeping the visiting servicemen well sozzled, with a by-product being a spike in Stuart-Jones' abortion business.

Abortions could be procured in a range of places from the seedy backrooms of inner-city houses and done by women with scant if any medical training through to the consulting rooms of Macquarie Street – then home to some of the nation's most prestigious medical practitioners. If you had the money, Stuart-Jones would perform an abortion in his rooms. The arrangements were handled discreetly with referral by word of mouth and Reilly – well known around the Cross as a man who could arrange most things – the main contact with much of his business done in the casinos or after-hours drinking establishments. He'd make the arrangements and Stuart-Jones would do the procedure, and the pair kept police away with regular bribes.

The booming black market finally came to the attention of the government, who introduced the Blackmarket Act in 1942, but nothing much happened. Michael McKernan in *All In* said 'throughout 1944 and 1945 the determination to prosper out of the war grew' and that 'commentators were dazed by the pursuit of pleasure and the large sums of money some people would spend for poor quality alcohol or still dreary meals'. The *Catholic Weekly* wrote that the black marketeers were 'engaged in treasonable activities' and 'sabotaging the nation's war effort', but the article didn't mention the vigour of the market – and there were no stories of the clergy being short of a drink.

By early 1945 there had only been fifty-nine prosecutions under the Black Market Act, most for sly grog or fuel rationing breaches, with only twenty-five convictions. Paul Hasluck wrote that 'high potential spending power combined with weaknesses in the law and its administration made conditions ideal for illicit trading'. Curtin's call for austerity hadn't worked and as Hasluck wrote, his 'Cabinet simply noted serious instances of black marketing that were brought to its attention'. The other problem was there were insufficient police and little will to investigate what were really victimless crimes – unless your bottle of Scotch had been filled with something that gave an even viler hangover than you'd expected.

During the closing moments of the war in June 1945, crime on the docks again emerged briefly as an issue, and the responses were predictable. The police in Sydney wheeled out their old and unfulfilled promise of 1942, and announced that when the force was 'strengthened by enlistments and discharges of men from the services' that the 'pillage patrol' on the wharves would be boosted from the present paltry fifteen men to 180. The coppers would also be doing a criminal record check on all the tally clerks, gatekeepers and watchmen – an acknowledgement that these chaps might have been complicit – who would have to be approved for employment by the Commissioner of Police. Finally there would be 'stricter checks' on the wharfies and dockers to get rid of the criminal element which was 'a very small percentage of men employed'. The problem with that assertion was that to be part of that criminal element the labourers would need to have been caught and successfully prosecuted first to make the 'stricter' check viable. The WWF's Tom Nelson defended his men, denying they were the key players in the black market, and insisting the union 'discouraged' pillaging. He also reckoned that men who'd been convicted could work hard on the wharves to rehabilitate themselves, and that men with convictions '10 or 12 years back' shouldn't be denied the opportunity to work.

The Painters and Dockers didn't miss a chance to get their slice of the black market. Their connections onboard ships, fostered through the dockers' work on board, common interest in making cash, and regular visits by the ships meant that illicit goods like opium from India, silk stockings, liquor and cigarettes could be hidden onboard in machinery, storage rooms, fuel bunkers and lifeboats – from which items were easily removed from the ship.

The waterfront, as an essential service with its workers protected from being called up for military service, became a haven for people not keen on serving their country. Well-heeled families looked on it as a place for their sons to avoid military service – a few pounds in the right hands, and suddenly you were a bona fide unionist and a member of the working class. The oceans of cash being made, plus the shelter offered, inevitably attracted men with a serious criminal pedigree. As contemporary criminals have found, trafficking in products the public greedily demand is more profitable and less risky – both in being caught or being shot at by police – than crimes like armed robbery.

The Painters and Dockers in Melbourne led the cultural change from petty thieves to professional. During the war, the emerging kingpins of the Melbourne underworld were men like Harold Nugent and his cronies Joseph Turner – a gunman and standover merchant who usually gave his occupation as 'caterer', Freddie 'The Frog' Harrison who enjoyed similar pursuits with his sidekick and driver Norman Bradshaw, and John Eric Twist – a gunman, standover man, pimp and competent boxer. They were all members of the Painters and Dockers, but it is unlikely any of Nugent's crew had seen the inside of a ship other than on a ferry ride.

Nugent was a reasonably good-looking man of average height, with wavy hair and a dapper dress sense. Like Norm Bruhn in Sydney during the Cocaine Wars, his taste for brutality was perfectly suited to the underworld protection business – why make cash from hard work when you could 'tax' the hard workers instead? In the mix were the usual crimes of opportunity like rip-offs, robbery and assaults.

Nugent had grown up in the dockland community in South Melbourne and was recruited by the dockers during a stay in Pentridge. On release, he joined the union. His reputation as a thoroughly unpleasant criminal crystallised at the age of twenty-four when at around 1 am on 27 July 1943 a nineteen-year-old waitress called Pearl Oliver was shot to death outside the Fitzroy boarding house she lived in. A fellow resident of the boarding house, Melbourne wharfie Joe Fanesi, and US Navy enlisted man

Peter Croft were with her. Nugent and his mate were lying in wait for the men – Pearl just happened to be in the wrong place at the wrong time. One witness heard Nugent ask Fanesi, 'Joe, I want to have a word with you,' then asked what he was going to do about 'the blue'. As the conversation deteriorated, Nugent shot Fanesi who told Pearl to run, which she did. The men then shot Croft. Fanesi later gave evidence that one of the men said, 'Get her, don't let her get away.' She didn't – the men opened fire on Pearl, hitting her five times in the back at close range. When she collapsed into the gutter one of them beat her head twice with the butt of his pistol. She died quickly and brutally.

Both Croft and Fanesi were shot in the legs, with Croft also wounded in the body and arms and, like Pearl, pistol-whipped, but both survived and later told their tale to the court. Police believed that Nugent's accomplices were Leslie 'Lair' Brown, a gambler, horse racing fan and drug addict whose most notable feature, according to police, was 'cysts in the region of the testicles'. Police believed the getaway car was driven by Cecil Bobbs, a 'skilled metal worker' from Newcastle NSW, and, like Brown, a 'snow man' – slang for a cocaine fancier.

Nugent was arrested in Geelong on 19 August that year and charged with Pearl's murder. However, at his trial a few months later in November, the jury took only sixty-five minutes to acquit him. His liberty was short-lived and he was arrested leaving court and charged with being a 'rogue and a vagabond who consorted with convicted criminals', as well as with the shooting of Fanesi, and possessing an automatic pistol. He was convicted for the wounding of Fanesi and sentenced to three years.

The other two men were on the run; with Brown caught two years later and receiving the same sentence as Nugent. Bobbs was found in Brisbane nearly two years after the murder and extradited to Melbourne, but he was luckier than the other two as the attorney-general decided not to proceed with the prosecution. The motive for the attack wasn't clear, but the confluence of waterfront crooks and a US serviceman suggested a business deal turned deadly.

Nugent and Freddie Harrison became the leaders of the Melbourne underworld in the postwar period, but Harrison didn't live long. Professional criminals value control and don't like having attention drawn to them; by the early 1950s Harrison was not under control and police believed he had a persecution complex and was 'trigger happy'. In the criminal world, if you believe someone is after you, you're generally correct.

The growing disenchantment among the members of the underworld with Harrison came to a head when a group of crooks went pig shooting in southwestern NSW, not far from Balranald, at the beginning of February 1958. In the group were Nugent, Harrison and Twist. Alcohol, firearms, testosterone and a persecution complex are a recipe for disaster, which duly occurred when Harrison and Nugent got into a heated dispute which ended when Harrison allegedly told Nugent he was 'too big for his boots' and turned his shotgun on him. Nugent grabbed the barrel of the gun, it fired and he lost a few fingers and a little of his hand. Harrison then turned the gun on Twist – witnesses could be a real problem for men like these – but fortunately for Twist, the gun jammed and, after a brief wrestle, Harrison drove off. Nugent later turned up at the Balranald Hospital with a story about an accident. The injury was so severe that he was transferred to Melbourne.

A few days later, on 6 February, it was payback time. Around 4.40 pm, Harrison was on 13 South Wharf in Melbourne, with docker Bobby Hayes, uncoupling a trailer from his Ford Customline sedan. A man carrying a twelve-gauge shotgun walked up to Harrison and said, 'This is yours, Fred', then shot him in the head at point blank range. While there were reportedly around thirty dockers on the wharf at the time, no one saw anything, not even Hayes who was covered in the grisly remains of Harrison's head. Investigating police heard that around twelve of the potential witnesses had gone to the toilet around the time of the shooting, and as Detective Inspector Charles Perry of the Homicide Squad drily observed, 'it is a two man toilet'. Hayes told the coronial inquest that 'I stood up, turned right and walked away, I didn't look back,' which was probably a wise decision. One docker told the *Truth* in the days following the murder. 'Harrison was involved in every type of racket and made enemies in them all.'

Nugent and Twist were on top of the list of suspects even though a teenager was seen fleeing the scene of the crime. When the young man was caught and searched police found he was carrying a cardboard ammunition box of twelve-gauge shotgun shells hidden in his cardigan. The box had room for twenty-five and they found twenty-two in the box, two in the teen's pockets. The teenager was Nugent's stepson, Charles Wootton. No one was ever charged with the murder.

Both Nugent and Twist continued their criminal careers.

The rivalry between Australia's biggest cities touches many areas, even crime. When I was a NSW copper the traditional view was that our Victorian counterparts were lightweights, and the Victorians traditionally thought we were more corrupt. Oddly enough, some of my peers took that as a compliment. Criminals are frequently similar to those on the other side of the blurry line that divides them from police, and Sydney crims looked down on the Victorians as unruly and not as slick.

Sydney was where the 'A' game, was played and home to the man ready to take on the national title of Mr Big.

25
MR BIG'S BIG BREAK

Leonard Arthur McPherson was born in Balmain on 21 May 1921 – one of generations of Balmain's boys who didn't cry, to paraphrase the quip of Neville Wran, QC, the former Balmain boy and later Premier of NSW.

McPherson was one of ten children to father William – a metalworker at Mort's Dock – and mother Nellie. Though very bright, Lennie didn't get much formal schooling, but in crime, rat cunning is more useful than good grammar, and Lennie was adept at maths as some criminals who'd done business with him could attest. He was thrifty and loved to remind people that during the Depression he and his siblings had survived on 'bread and dripping'. In the criminal world, Lennie was commonly known by NSW Police and his underworld associates as a man who'd 'take the fillings from your teeth if he had half a chance'. Malcolm Brown, the *Sydney Morning Herald* journalist who has written for decades about the city's more intriguing criminals described in the *SMH* of 29 August 1996 the tall (nearly six feet), heavily built and bloodhound-faced McPherson as a man who 'always had that bit extra, a greater degree of cunning, a ruthlessness, to rise above the level of the common crook'. Richard Neville, writing in *Oz* magazine in 1965, described a visit from Lennie, as a 'bear-like brute came to the door'.

Lennie was first arrested at the age of eleven – one year above the age of criminal responsibility in NSW – for stealing, and as it was the first time he'd been caught, he got a bond to be of good behaviour. The magistrate at the Children's Court was an optimist. Eighteen months later Lennie was in court again for stealing and the magistrate extended his probation for a further year – magistrates prefer to offer a child every chance to come to grips with the difference between right and wrong. However, Lennie wasn't that keen on the notion, and was back in court one month later, again for stealing. Magistrates also don't like someone who fails to take advantage of an opportunity or two, and this time Lennie's lack of good behaviour resulted in him being sent to Mt Penang – a juvenile detention centre near Gosford opened just before World War I. On first view it was like a holiday camp with a series of wooden houses on top of a steep hill, and a central hall where films were shown. While it didn't have the high walls, barbed wire and armed guards of an adult prison, the two had much in common. Places for 'wayward boys' as governments liked to call them, were finishing schools for many of the criminals of the '50s, '60s and '70s, with a regimen of deprivation, violence and sexual assault. The boys learned lessons, but not the right ones.

At the recent Royal Commission into Institutional Responses to Child Sexual Abuse one witness who'd been at Mt Penang in the supposedly more enlightened '70s, said it was

> more like a jail than a home, and the boys who lived there called it "The Pound". I was physically and sexually abused at Mount Penang almost every day. Routinely, the Officers, stripped my clothes off, hosed me down, and flogged me – with a piece of 4 by 2, or a garden hose, whatever was available. This would lead to anal intercourse. If I screamed loud enough it could deter the officers from attacking me, but not very often.

Among the Mt Penang alumni were George Freeman, the SP bookmaker and shoplifter par excellence; and Arthur 'Neddy' Smith, one of the nation's biggest heroin traffickers, as well as an armed robber, assailant and murderer.

McPherson left Mt Penang both older and wiser, with his education reflected in a notable lack of convictions for anything serious until after World War II. However, he was busy locally, leading a ragtag gang who made cash from theft, burglary and the like, and the money was sufficient to keep him in cars, booze and that great Australian pastime – betting on the races. In his book *Mr Big*, Tony Reeves observed Lennie had a 'lavish lifestyle for a lad who had no steady job', and a cousin who described him as a 'mug lair'.

Lennie wasn't a man you'd call 'public spirited' and so when Australia declared war on Germany he didn't rush to join the armed forces.

With a father working at Mort's and no particular desire to learn the basics of soldiering, Lennie took advantage of the family connection, and got his first real job – a driller at Mort's Dock. McPherson was now exempt from military training when he hit twenty-one, and any other ideas the government might come up with as the war progressed.

McPherson's employer was focused on building Bathurst-class corvettes and River-class frigates for the navy, which were mainly used in coastal defence, anti-submarine and convoy work. Mort's was only eclipsed by nearby Cockatoo Island in production for a navy that, prior to war, had been depleted in both ships and personnel – unlike the navies of Germany, Italy and Japan.

In 1940 Lennie married a local girl, Dawn Allan, and moved to nearby, and a little more upmarket, Gladesville. Lennie made it through the war without any troubles but the honeymoon ended on 22 January 1946, when he was back in front of the magistrates, this time for receiving stolen goods. For his first time charged with a crime as an adult he was fined, but when arrested shortly after, again for receiving, he wasn't so fortunate and on 15 February 1946 he was sentenced to one year in prison. Two weeks later he was before a judge in Quarter Sessions (today's District Court) on more serious receiving charges for which he got eighteen months. He spent the first part of his sentence in the relative comfort of an afforestation camp at Glen Innes on the New England tablelands, before his 'unsatisfactory' conduct caused him to be transferred down the hill to Grafton Gaol – then the favoured place to send intractable prisoners.

McPherson learned his lesson about poor behaviour and how to repair boots. In October 1946 he was back in Sydney enjoying the balmy sea breeze at Long Bay – or the Malabar Motel as police joked – then home with his wife and baby Janelle on Christmas Eve that year after serving ten months of his sentence. Good behaviour had its rewards.

Lennie resumed his criminal career but not his career at Mort's, and began a handy sideline as a police informer – a fine way to curry favour, eliminate his opposition, and revenge himself on those he didn't like or who didn't like him. Receiving stolen goods and protection rackets were the staples of the McPherson cash flow, and he'd fenced some major hauls of jewellery, etc. that had drawn him closer to the centre of the underworld.

He and the criminal Dick Reilly were on good terms, with Reilly putting opportunities McPherson's way for him to organise and take a cut of the profit. Reilly used friendships and relationships forged through his gaming interests to pinpoint affluent targets for McPherson to pillage.

With Lennie's relationships with police, the risk of being arrested was minimal unless the coppers were in a mood to make a point. Coppers of the time would rather have turned a blind eye to the actions of a reliable source in return for the 'drum' (information) on crooks planning serious crimes. McPherson was also hitting the booze, and according to Tony Reeves in *Mr Big*, hitting his wife and the women with whom he was often involved. His marriage was on the way out and Lennie was all about Lennie.

In 1949, Darcy Dugan re-entered his life, and for Lennie it was his first step into the big time. Dugan was one of the most well-known criminals in Australian history. Police use the term 'good crim', without any sense of irony, to describe men like Dugan, but the reality was that Dugan, while busy and violent, wasn't all that good because he was frequently caught. He spent much of his adult life behind bars for serious crimes like armed robbery.

Dugan was a year older than McPherson and the two had known each other since childhood. Dugan recalled in *Catch Me If You Can* (1992) they'd 'knocked about together' around Annandale and Balmain, dabbling in minor thefts. The two had a brush in their late teens when Lennie hadn't taken 'no' for an answer from a young woman, and Dugan had intervened and 'punched him to the ground' – while Lennie had relied on his bulk and menace, he wasn't much of a fighter, unlike the lithe and quick Dugan.

McPherson needed an experienced operator, and Dugan was on the hunt for profitable jobs, so the two put the incident behind them and got down to business. Dugan recalled he met Lennie in a hotel in Rozelle, where McPherson talked about another Reilly tip – burgling a harbourside mansion owned by a businessman who was a big punter. Ten thousand pounds in the safe on an average day, and up to £50,000 if it had been a good day at the races. Dugan was a competent safecracker or 'tank man', and McPherson thought a team of five was appropriate for the task, but Dugan was surprised when McPherson put himself on the team. However, the robbery was a dud. On the upside was the fact no one was home but when Dugan opened the safe, he found only £2500 – four hundred each after Reilly's £500 commission. A few days later Reilly was back with plans to make up for the shortfall.

The target this time was an Elizabeth Bay penthouse with a safe containing at least £12,000. The five were armed with automatic pistols, and this time the family were home. When the owner declined to open the safe, McPherson pistol-whipped him. Dugan recalled, 'the man had guts', but rather than encourage the vicious streak in McPherson, he told the man that failure to comply would result in them beating his son. He capitulated, but the safe was empty. Either the victims had seen the robbers arriving or they'd got a bit of inside information themselves. There had been £17,000 in the safe but they'd taken the cash and hidden it in a wastepaper basket. The robbers left empty-handed.

The gang took a brief break when Dugan was arrested for an assault and robbery. Dugan became famous for his regular escapes and earned his nickname 'Houdini' when he escaped from Long Bay Gaol on 20 August 1949. He was soon recaptured, but that didn't stop him. His fourth prison escape happened on 15 December 1949 when he and William Mears – his partner in crime – escaped from the cells under Central Police Station, after cutting through the bars with a hacksaw. It was cunningly planned, with Mears appearing at Central Court that morning to defend a charge of possessing a pistol, and Dugan called as his witness. No one could explain whether the hacksaw had come from the prison with Mears, had been left for him in the cells at Central, or arrived baked in a Christmas cake. In rumour hungry Sydney, there was a strong suspicion that police had 'taken a few quid' to help Dugan flee. The pair's timing was perfect – the streets were packed with Christmas shoppers and Central was moments from bus routes and the busy Town Hall train station with multiple lines and exits. Dugan and Mears disappeared.

On 8 January Dugan and Mears, both armed, raided the beachside home of jockey Jack Thompson at Coogee, with McPherson driving the getaway car, which had been stolen earlier in Elizabeth Bay. This raid was nearly deadly and a dud as well. The robbers got around £170 in cash along with two bottles of beer, two bottles of Scotch and two radios. As their getaway car accelerated from the kerb, the plucky jockey, dressed in his pyjamas, opened fire with a double-barrelled shotgun but only caused some minor damage. Police initially played down the involvement of Dugan and Mears – and didn't know about McPherson – until Mrs Thompson was shown photographs and later told reporters she'd pointed at Dugan's and said, 'I had no hesitation in recognizing him'. Dugan spiced the investigation along by sending letters to newspapers denying his involvement – a tactic that only served to keep his crimes on the front page and spur on the detectives.

Dugan and Mears were desperately short of money and luck, so they planned something almost guaranteed to succeed – the old reliable bank robbery. As Dugan said in his book *Bloodhouse,* 'Len, true friend, made the necessary arrangements.' Among Dugan's numerous failings was his lack of ability to correctly judge McPherson's character. Their target was the Commonwealth Bank in Ultimo – a small branch with, they hoped, around £20,000 on site. McPherson provided the stolen car, and followed them to the job as a 'cockatoo' to keep watch outside.

At 10 am, opening time, on Friday 13 January 1950, Mears and Dugan entered the bank, and, though both had pistols, Dugan later asserted his wasn't loaded however Mears' was. A smarter criminal would have waited until near closing time on a Friday when all the local businesses had delivered their cash for safekeeping over the weekend – in the 1970s and early 1980s, when bank robberies were at their zenith, coppers dreaded the hour between 3 pm and 4 pm on Fridays.

The robbery was proceeding quite well – there were four customers, a teller, the bank manager and a female cleaner, all of who obeyed orders and put their hands in the air. Mears then shot Leslie Nalder, the manager, in the chest. According to police, he 'went berserk and fired three wild shots,' with one also hitting a customer, Roger Joseph, in the arm. The two very rattled robbers backed out the door of the bank with only a handful of notes Dugan had scooped from the teller's drawer. On the way out he said to Mears, 'Why did you do that, you silly cunt?' The cleaner, Blanche Anderson, told police that Nalder had reached for the gun in his desk 'and the bandit shot him in cold blood', but fortunately Nalder survived his injuries.

Dugan and Mears were picked up by McPherson, with Mears telling them he'd shot in defence of Dugan – a story Dugan didn't believe, thinking that it was panic rather than protection. Mears was armed with a Webley Scott pistol, nicknamed a 'Wobbly Scott' by police who had them as their service weapons – 'more dangerous if you throw them' – though Mr Nalder may not have agreed. McPherson was furious, telling Mears, 'I shoulda got seven grand outa that. Instead there's a murder rap,' which accurately displayed the order of Lennie's priorities.

While the trio didn't have much luck with robberies, they were luckier with police and though around 100 detectives poured into the area, the men managed to get away and plan another venture. This time it was a payroll job on home turf – Mort's Dock. McPherson was well connected at Mort's and had no trouble getting something they'd been missing out on – accurate intelligence on the job they were planning. Friday 3 February 1950 was payday for the 1000 workers at the dock and McPherson expected around £12,000. McPherson and Dugan both had doubts about using the erratic Mears, but Dugan was 'too hot' and so finding someone keen and brave enough to work with him wasn't on. They were stuck with Mears.

To persuade the guards of the folly of resisting, McPherson provided Mears and Dugan with a Thompson submachine gun – the favourite heavy weapon of American mobsters brought into Australia in bulk during World War II. It was the sort of weapon that made resistance unwise. McPherson thought that giving the Thompson to Mears would 'steady his nerves'. It didn't.

The plan was to slip in through a hole in the fence early in the morning, dressed in boiler suits so they'd blend in with the workers, and lie in wait in the bicycle shed near the front gate. McPherson would ensure the guns were taken in the night before. Even though there had been a payroll robbery at nearby Cockatoo Island docks back in 1945, security at Mort's Dock was a bit of a joke – the payroll was delivered at the same time, the same day, in the same car and usually with the same pay clerk and guards every week. Planning the robbery was a breeze.

The day was overcast and rain was threatening, which was handy as it kept some of the workers undercover and away from the gate area where they often milled on their breaks. Dugan and Mears took one side each as the car arrived. As Dugan was about twenty-five metres from his target he quickly looked around and saw Mears had stopped and was waving the Thompson. Sid Tuck, the pay clerk with the bag of money, exited the car on Mears' side, and made a break for the pay office. Dugan shouted 'Stop or I'll shoot' and when that didn't work opened fire with his pistol. Tuck stumbled, fell, and, though wounded in the arm, got back up and made it to safety. Dugan's gunfire prompted Mears to fire a few bursts from the Thompson in the general direction of the guards who were going for their pistols – they wisely ducked for any cover they could find. The robbers, plans again shattered, ran through the gates to an old Plymouth sedan for their getaway.

Tuck told police,

> When we got to the dock, we drove in and I got out of the car. Near the bike racks were two men, one with a handkerchief over his face. One had a tommy gun and the other a revolver. I saw them coming at me. I grabbed the bag containing money for the salaried staff. One bandit told me to drop it but I refused and turned to run. As I ran, I heard a bang and down I went. But I got up and ran into the office yelling there's been a hold up.

When one of the guards on the gate tried to intervene, Mears opened up with the Tommy gun, but luckily the bullets he sprayed didn't hit anyone. The broadsheet and tabloid press all agreed that Mears had 'gone berserk' with the Tommy gun and that it was a 'pitched gun battle' as the guards returned fire.

The two hapless crooks jumped into the waiting getaway car with Lennie at the wheel as usual. As they were fleeing, Dugan used the Thompson's butt to break the rear window and sprayed bullets through it to give second thoughts to anyone considering following. Pedestrians jumped for cover.

It's an indicator of Dugan's code of ethics that when writing about the robbery in *Bloodhouse* he never mentioned McPherson's involvement as the getaway driver. Instead, he put Mears in the driver's seat and confected a story that had Lennie well clear of the crime. Contemporary reports on the crime had three culprits. One eyewitness was Beryl Lorentz who'd had a young Dugan as a pupil in her dancing class and denied he'd been one of the robbers, but police had a different view.

Mort's Dock is on the Balmain peninsula and Dugan was worried the location meant police could quickly and effectively seal off the roads, but Lennie was a capable planner and had a cabin cruiser waiting in nearby Snail's Bay. The three headed down the harbour and cheekily moored about half a mile from the scene of the crime. Later that day Lennie took them to his home for safekeeping, but it wasn't that safe as a few hours later the police arrived on the doorstep. The coppers missed finding the two men who were secreted in a hidden compartment. With the inner city far too hot, Dawn McPherson rented a house in Collaroy on the distant northern beaches, an unlikely place to hide two very wanted men. The two tried to disguise themselves, with Dugan dying his hair and growing a moustache, and Mears applying the dye as well, changing his hairstyle and adding glasses.

Their freedom lasted less than a few weeks, until 14 February 1950, when police poured into the house at dawn and found the two men sound asleep in a double bed. What the men didn't know was the source that led police to the house was Dugan's trusted friend, Lennie McPherson. Dugan was headed for a long prison sentence, and McPherson was headed for a long career at the top of Australian crime. Joining him was another Balmain boy, Stan 'The Man' Smith.

26
SQUIRREL GRIP

The Cold War began in 1947 and by the early 1950s its effect was biting – particularly in communities where communism held sway with leaders like Jim Healy. Colin Davis, writing in *Waterfront Revolt,* observed that governments of the West were fearing 'disruption of national economies by communist-inspired agitators, and employer frustration with the union's lack of control over members', and added that 'dock workers stood at the centre of these unfolding dramas and faced the wrath of governments determined to maintain cordial relations with trade union allies and ensure free avenues of trade'.

Davis wrote of a meeting between a militant London dock worker, Joe Bloomberg, who visited New York and had a chat with Joseph 'King Joe' Ryan. Bloomberg probably didn't know that Ryan, life President of the International Longshoreman's Association, had been threatening strikes if the district attorney didn't drop a murder investigation, and had been pressuring shipping firms to drop charges against a gangster caught stealing on the waterfront. And then there was the $20,000 per year cash payments to him from a couple of shipping firms which Ryan said was for a confidential union 'anti-communist fund', but had trouble explaining how it was spent.

Ryan wasn't popular with his own union, who believed he'd regularly sold them out for personal gain, to the point where they held a mock funeral for him. Ryan told Bloomberg, half jokingly, 'You know what we do with a guy like you, don't you? You'd never be sitting here, you'd be buried,' thus making light of the stories of his union being infested with gangsters. On the New York waterfront, that meant murdered and dumped in a lime pit in New Jersey – a method of disposal favoured by Albert 'The Lord High Executioner' or 'Mad Hatter' Anastasia of the Mafia's Murder Incorporated and a man who controlled the dock unions in Brooklyn. Australia was quite genteel by comparison.

In Australia, a key component in conflict within the waterfront was the belief in communism held by leaders like Jim Healy and Tom Nelson. They were out of step with the mood of the nation and many of their members.

Prime Minister John Curtin had died in office before the end of World War II and was followed by Ben Chifley, who scored a decisive victory for Labor over Robert Menzies and his new Liberal Party in September 1946. But the spectre of communism in the union movement and affiliates in Labor was destined to be Menzies' political trump card. The wharfies didn't help the government in 1948 when they joined the Queensland railway workers in a long and bitter strike over pay – other states had received increases, but the Queensland Labor Government declined to follow suit. On 27 February 1948, the Chifley Government declared a state of emergency, and around 2000 wharfies gathered in Brisbane at a 'stop work' meeting and voted to strike. Mr J. H. Conde of the Overseas Shipping Representatives Association pointed his finger straight at the WWF leadership and said the stoppage showed how powerful the 'Communist element has become'.

On 17 March, around 200 protesters gathered outside Brisbane's Trades Hall and began a march through the city. They'd only gone around 200 metres, when around 300 police descended on them, wielding their batons. Fifteen minutes later, the marchers were back at Trades Hall, loudly singing 'Advance Australia Fair' – it wasn't reported if they got to the second verse. Only five were arrested – two of whom were wharfies and one was Max Julius, a barrister and lifelong communist.

Fred Paterson, another barrister and the first communist to be a member of an Australian Parliament – he won the Queensland state seat of Bowen on 13 April 1944 – was beaten about the head by a detective and hospitalised. The detective wasn't disciplined for his actions. The melee only provoked more demonstrations, though with more tolerance and less violence by police. Assaulting a Member of Parliament wasn't prudent, even if he was a communist.

Two days later, around 500 wharfies led by Healy joined a demonstration of around 10,000 workers at Brisbane's Trades Hall. Healy and his men then marched to King George Square, where Healy was hoisted up onto a statue and gave a brief address, exhorting the crowd, which had reportedly nearly doubled in size to 20,000, to march with him back to Trades Hall to hear more speeches. It was a public relations disaster for Premier Hanlon and his government, bringing national focus on both the industrial issues in Queensland and the violence of police. The strike ended in early April when the government capitulated.

In the following year, Lance Sharkey – the secretary of the Communist Party – was gaoled for sedition, and wharfies found themselves in dispute with the ALP over their right to strike. At the end of June, the coal workers went on strike for six weeks, demanding a pay increase, shorter working hours and better conditions.

Chifley lost the next election, and on 19 December 1949, Robert Menzies was again sworn in as prime minister, and this time he was there for the long haul. In his sights were the communists and the unions, preferably both at the same time.

The WWF obliged by having two on its six-member Federal Council.

Menzies' timing to take on communist unions in the early 1950s was ideal – on 29 August 1949, the USSR had successfully tested its first atom bomb; the People's Republic of China, with Mao Zedong as leader, was formed on 1 October 1949; and on 25 June 1950, 75,000 North Korean soldiers had crossed the 38th Parallel in to South Korea, triggering the Korean War. On 28 June 1950 Australia joined the Korean War, with Menzies sending HMAS *Bataan* and HMAS *Shoalhaven*, which were joined at the end of July by the RAAF's 77 Squadron and troops from the army's 3 RAR, all under the ultimate command of Douglas MacArthur who had returned yet again.

Menzies' first major action was to introduce the Communist Party Dissolution Bill – which made the party and any related organisation unlawful and gave the government power to appoint a receiver to dispose of any properties owned. It also flipped the burden of proof from innocent until proven guilty, giving the Federal Government the power for people to be declared communists, and putting the onus on those declared to prove otherwise. A 'declared' person couldn't hold any office in organisations like a trade union. The Bill passed through the lower House in April 1950, but was amended by the Senate, where the Labor Party had the numbers but not the will to reject it. In March 1951, the High Court declared the Act to be invalid, so Menzies used the issue of banking legislation for a double dissolution, with his intent being to gain a majority in the Senate. After getting his wish he took the issue of anti-communism to the people. On 22 September 1951 the question posed in the referendum was 'Do you approve of the proposed law for the alteration of the Constitution entitled "Constitution Alteration (Powers to deal with Communists and Communism) 1951"?'. In the great Australian tradition, the referendum failed but the strongest support in favour came from Queensland and Western Australia.

The waterfront workers continued to flex the muscles they'd developed during World War II. Margo Beasley wrote that 'the WWF had effectively controlled labour supplies to Australian ports since 1942' and hadn't planned for sufficient men to deal with the bumper sugar crop in Queensland in 1953. Harold Holt, then Minister for Labour and National Service, called in the army to load ships with sugar and meat at the port of Bowen in Queensland. On 3 September, 220 troops were flown in to 'help' expedite the loading. Holt said, 'The Army personnel were not sent on a strike breaking operation. No industrial dispute existed at the time. They were sent there to supplement speedily the full waterfront workforce available in order to overcome this immediate emergency.' Holt then asked for support from local wharfies to get the job done so the troops could be withdrawn. His plea didn't work.

The Townsville Branch of the WWF called on the national executive for a stop-work of the 27,000 wharfies in the fifty-two ports across the country if the troops weren't withdrawn in forty-eight hours. Les Louis, in *Labour History*, wrote the use of troops was part of 'Operation Alien' – a secret government military force set up as strike-breakers and under the control of Henry Bland who ran the Department of Labour. When Louis interviewed Bland after his retirement, the former mandarin denied any knowledge of the alleged operation.

The following year, the April defection of the sozzled Vladimir Petrov – a diplomat at the Russian Embassy in Canberra and colonel in the KGB – and his wife Evdokia caused furore resulting in the fractious Labor Party fracturing and the birth of the virulently anti-communist Democratic Labor Party (DLP) with such notable members as B. A. Santamaria and Queensland Premier and later DLP senator Vince Gair.

In November, the waterfront ground to a halt with the cause being an amendment to legislation aimed at breaking the 'closed shop' hiring. The government wanted to shift the right to recruit to the employers and cited the delays, strikes, and slowness of work on the waterfront as key reasons. Holt told a press conference in Canberra that the change was to 'clean up the inefficiency and lawlessness which disfigures our waterfront'.

The strike started on 2 November with workers around the nation walking off the job. They'd prepared for the long haul and were well organised, but as usual, there was an impact on the families. Joan Williams of the Women's Committee in Fremantle, said, 'it looked like being long and hard and the families who hadn't built up their savings began to feel the pinch. We knew a lean Christmas was coming up, so held a Christmas party for the children.' On 4 November, Menzies entered the battle, saying 'the laws are to be made, not by your elected representatives, but by the communist-led Waterside Workers Federation. This is more than a challenge to employers. This is a challenge to Parliament and the whole conception of parliamentary democracy – a precious thing which does not exist in Moscow but is passionately believed in here.'

Fortunately the strike didn't turn into a siege, with the men returning to work on 16 November following discussions between the union and the ACTU. The ACTU announced that 'we declare that the whole resources of the Labour movement, industrial and political, must be mobilized to defeat the operation of the pernicious Menzies recruitment clause', but called for calm from other waterfront-related unions, like the Painters and Dockers, to refrain from striking. During the stoppage, the wharfies had done fine PR work by unloading essential cargoes like medical supplies without pay, and the move by the ACTU took them higher up the moral ground.

The government backed down in February 1955, with the *Sydney Morning Herald* reporting, 'for the time being the Government has no option but to retreat, but nothing can conceal the humiliating terms of the surrender. The Government's handling of this matter must count as one of the worst blunders of the Menzies Government.' Ceding control to the waterfront workers, following a failed confrontation, was appeasement instead of reform – and the waterside workers grew more powerful.

27
IT'S ONLY A CRIME IF YOU'RE CAUGHT

A by-product of this increasing power was the growth and organisation of crime with its roots in the waterfront. The capitulation of the Menzies Government gave a boost to waterfront power at a time of significant change. Communism was on the nose with the public and the smell was deepening as the Cold War became chillier – the 'worker's paradise' of the Soviet Union was beginning to look anything but. The industrial power of the waterfront unions came at a time when their workplace was changing because of modern technology, and what most hadn't acknowledged or planned for was that over the next few decades the need for their skills would diminish and along with it their power. But that was in the future. The Painters and Dockers were feeling the pinch with the decline in shipbuilding since the war – those destroyed had been replaced, the need to swiftly increase fleets to cope with the demands of war had ceased, and the fleets were more modern and less demanding to maintain. In 1958 Mort's Dock, which had once been the largest engineering works in Australia and the largest employer in the colony of New South Wales, was in liquidation and closed a year later. Many of the engineering works around it moved into Sydney's rapidly developing west, where heavy industry was now focused.

Wharfies were heading down a similar route, though not with the same haste as the dockers. In 1951, the first purpose-built container ships went into service.

The use of containers dated back to Britain's coal mines in the late eighteenth century when horse-drawn wagons laden with coal were driven onto barges to move them down the canals to the ironworks. Rail modernised the concept, with coal being carried in containers on both sides of the Atlantic, and in the first part of the twentieth century, rail cars were driven onto ships. World War II and the need for fast, efficient and cost-effective handling resulted in the Australian and US military pioneering the use of a reusable shipping container similar to the ones used today. One stimulus for the Australians was the need for a container that could be swapped quickly from train to train at the state borders when rail gauges differed. During World War II there were twelve locations in Australia where the gauges changed and cargo had to be transferred – around 1.8 million tons were moved during the war, using around 600 military personnel plus civilians to transfer the cargoes. It wasn't until 1962 that people could travel from Sydney to Melbourne without changing trains at the border.

The container brought with it a dramatic change to the working day of a wharfie. The back-breaking and dangerous work mentioned by Dr McQueen in 1945 like lugging sacks to and from the hold of a ship or the warehouse – either on their shoulders or a trolley – and the misery of long days working in the confined space of the hold with often volatile substances declined, along with the danger of cargo swinging from the hook of a crane. Graham Harbord writing for South Australia's *Law Society Bulletin* in 2004 recounted the peril of the pre-container days, recounting wharfies pulling a 6 ton case from a ship using a winch. He wrote,

You hook on your hook. You've got a man out in the square to tell the hatchman when you've got it, then the winch pulls that in. Well, this feller walked in between the side of the ship and the case, he'd just come back from lunch, and it squashed him up against the bloody side. Nobody knew he was there until we heard the scream . . .

Life on the waterfront was changing, but the wharfies weren't frightened to exercise their newfound power from their battles with Menzies. During the 1950s, '60s, and '70s, strikes were frequent and often not with a clear-cut purpose. In the late 1950s, CSR's draught horses – used to haul wagons of sugar bags – were taken out on strike by the wharfies as the beasts had to work 'double shifts'. However, the timing coincided with CSR's unfortunate practice of requiring wharfies to get a ticket in order to use the toilets, and the *Maritime Worker* reported that tickets were given out 'grudgingly'. CSR was making a point to the wharfies, and the wharfies responded in kind.

Despite their increased power, the waterfront communities slowly began to break up. Sydney and Melbourne were growing rapidly westward, away from the suburbs that had started as a cluster around the waterfront. Low-interest war service loans and the rapid construction of new suburbs featuring modern houses of brick or fibro with internal bathrooms and hot water on demand and a quarter acre of their own were tempting to people used to cramped quarters. The growing affluence of the wharfies, and the need for some dockers to follow the work away from the waterfront and to the new industrial suburbs, was changing the communities but not breaking up the loyalties of generations, as attested to by the enduring criminal networks that came to prominence in the following decades.

Along with changes to the working life of the waterfront was the seductive amount of profit to be made from crime. Why go back to a life of long hours of backbreaking, dirty and often dangerous work when other jobs with low risk and high rewards were on offer? Like McPherson in Sydney and Twist in Melbourne, some chose to make it a full-time pursuit, others dabbled to supplement their family's income, and others turned a blind eye.

The promised boost of men to deal with pillaging on the Sydney wharves after the war never happened. The squad of police looking into activities on the waterfront was still only fifteen in number – an almost token number when you factor in shift work, court, days off, sick leave, annual leave and administration – and they were frequently thwarted by the threat of industrial action if they pried.

By 1950, the pillaging problem in Sydney alone was estimated at £100,000 per year. One unnamed 'expert' told the *Sun-Herald* of 2 April 1950 that, 'we know of shops that stock little else than stolen goods, with no questions asked. If we could get evidence against the receivers and get them a solid gaol sentence it would soon stamp out most of the pillaging.' The expert nailed it when he said, 'these thefts were obviously the work of an inside gang and a carefully prepared organization'. The expert concluded that cleaning up waterfront pillaging was 'an impossible task – like trying to put out a bushfire with a child's seaside bucket'. The shipowners were full of rhetoric but little action – they threatened 'all out war', but noted that it wasn't all the wharfies' fault as the problem bore the 'the imprint of large, highly organized gangs working for high stakes'. It was a diplomatic comment but without the pillaged goods the gangs wouldn't have anything to sell.

As a contrast to the expert's comment, Sir Thomas Maltby, Victoria's Minister for Public Works, announced in 1955 that 'losses through pilfering of cargo at the Port of Melbourne are extremely low. Pilferage protection at the port is in the highest world class.' Dockers and wharfies could be forgiven for chortling and ordering another round at the pub.

Lennie McPherson, receiver of stolen goods and graduate to the art of armed robbery, had had a few brushes with the old consorting laws that were still being enthusiastically used by members of the police, but had escaped a prison term. However when he was caught red-handed breaking into an office, by police he didn't enjoy a relationship with, he was charged with 'break and enter' and for possessing house-breaking implements at night. McPherson went back to prison, this time for three and a half years, and while behind bars he was also convicted on three counts of possessing an unlicensed pistol – a signal to police that Lennie was heading for the big time. He got a year on each charge, but to be served concurrently with the burglary sentence. He was paroled in October 1955 and his career was on the ascent.

Joining Lennie's close circle of the time was one of the more intriguing members from the top shelf of crime – Stanley John Smith, popularly known as 'Stan The Man'. Stan was also a Balmain boy, born there on 3 January 1937, and like McPherson, quickly in trouble. One old 'colourful' identity I interviewed in a colourful location – a club for gentlemen featuring pole dancers – knew Stan from childhood. He said,

> he was a wild bloke, but principled. I remember he was in a boy's home as a little bloke, and when he got out we ran together. He wasn't a big kid – just average height and around ten stone wringing wet when he was grown up – but he fought well above his weight. He hated bullies but wouldn't hurt an innocent. Gave a few of the big blokes a big surprise! He fought like a wild bull.

However, his old mate said that 'Stan didn't like being Stan – he'd have been a much happier man if he'd been a professional musician – he was terrific on the tenor sax.'

Stan's first real job was as a wharfie, but a life on the wharves wasn't what he had in mind. He was a good-looking man of average height and wore his clothes well – 'a bit of a dandy, but he knew he looked good, not like the rest of us ugly old bastards,' observed his old friend. Like Lennie, a more lucrative career beckoned.

Stan grew to be a competent fighter in the ring and was the state lightweight champion at seventeen, but it was on the streets of Sydney that his abilities were legendary. The warning sign was when he removed his glasses – Smith had terrible eyesight – and you knew it was 'on'. He was 'fast and hard, and never fazed by the size of his opponent – he was fearless,' said one of his old mates. Smith was modest about his abilities, saying, 'I can't fight, but I keep knocking up mugs who think they can.'

One of Smith's early criminal exploits was to try and crack the safe at Balmain's West End Hotel.

Smith may have been adept as a fighter, and was a fine shoplifter – then a highly lucrative and well-organised criminal venture – but he was a lousy 'tank man'. Instead of using finesse to open the safe, he used too much gelignite, rumoured to be provided by Lennie McPherson who had a penchant for explosives. The explosion was so great it brought part of the roof down, and police came running from their station a short distance up the hill, but it didn't get the safe open. Stan departed empty-handed and fortunate to be unscathed and not under arrest. He gave up safe breaking and resumed his work on the doors of illegal gambling establishments like the Kellett Club and Golden Nugget, as well as his shoplifting and protection work.

The firm of McPherson and Smith put themselves on the map in May 1963 when they had an altercation with Robert 'Pretty Boy' Walker, a ship's steward and an aspiring criminal. The two were planning on 'sorting out' Walker over some issue that was never quite clear, but unfortunately for Smith what might have been a 'solid flogging', with him doing the flogging, went wrong when Walker shot him in the chest with a .303 rifle. Smith survived the attack and Walker was arrested for the shooting and allowed bail – but he was on borrowed time. He decided that heading back to his flat in Paddington might not be too smart, and instead took refuge with a female acquaintance in Alison Road, Randwick – but it seems someone couldn't keep that a secret. In July that year, Walker left his refuge just after dusk, and a stolen Holden sedan cruised along beside him. It's likely his last living glimpse was of a machine gun poking out of the car's back window. He was hit six times and died at the scene.

In the fit for the murder were Smith and McPherson, with some pundits asserting McPherson had left his new bride Marlene at their wedding reception to 'attend to business', then returned and calmly resumed the celebration. Another prime suspect was Raymond 'Ducky' O'Connor. Heading the investigation was the legendary Ray Kelly who'd arrested Dugan and Mears after the tip-off from McPherson. Premier Askin said at Kelly's retirement party at the swanky Chevron Hotel in Potts Point in 1966 that Kelly was a 'close personal friend that no fictional detective could hold a candle to'. It wasn't until a generation later that the depths of Kelly's corruption became apparent.

At the inquest into Walker's murder, police offered the team of Smith and McPherson as culprits, or Ducky O'Connor. When O'Connor was called he declined to answer questions. In the absence of any decent evidence, the inquest could only find the manner and cause of Walker's death but not who did it. The coroner noted his 'abhorrence at the thought' of death by machine gun in NSW, and hoped for 'ruthless measures' to 'combat this type of crime'.

Three years after the Walker killing, McPherson proved his worth as an informant when he tipped off Kelly about the whereabouts of Pentridge prison escapees Ronald Ryan and Peter Walker. Kelly led the team that arrested both men at the Concord Repatriation Hospital on 6 January 1966.

Ducky O'Connor – standover man, gunman and general pest – had his career brought to an end at around 3 am on 26

May 1967 in the Latin Quarter nightclub in Sydney's Pitt Street. At the time of his murder, O'Connor was on bail for the murder of Shirley Bowker in Richmond, Victoria, on 1 May 1967.

The Latin Quarter was one of the nightspots where you could get a drink at any time provided you confirmed you intended to dine – a neat way of getting around the still onerous liquor laws – and was popular with police, politicians and criminals. Along with O'Connor at the club that night was the Abe Saffron confidant 'Sir' Wayne Martin, lawyers, business types, a sprinkling of socialites, a few members of the NSW Police – including Brendan 'Jack' Whelan who'd rise to the rank of superintendent before retiring at an opportune time – and Lennie.

On stage that night was Norman Erskine, son of a wharfie, who'd grown up tough in Newtown, had a few menial jobs after leaving school and when he reached eighteen he got what journalist Norm Lipson writing in the *Sun-Herald* on 30 May 2010 described as 'an inner-city boy's dream job – working on the wharves'. Erskine counted Sydney's criminal glitterati, including Smith, McPherson, and casino king and former wharfie, Perc Galea, as mates. Galea had won the lottery, left the wharves and gone into the baccarat business in Kings Cross with Dick Reilly. Erskine said, 'The crooks would often come along to the nightclubs where I was performing and at times I'd go out with them. I knew who they were but I always found them to be good blokes.'

Sir Wayne Martin recalled that the lights in the Latin Quarter dimmed, which he took as an opportunity to move a little closer to the girls he was with that night, but his amorous intentions stopped when a single shot rang out and he and the girls dived under the table. When full light returned, Ducky O'Connor was dead on the floor beside McPherson's table. Erskine recalled that a thug walked up to him and said, 'Get to the dunny and you didn't see anything'; he complied and found around twenty other men inside with a similar lack of memory. The crack investigators from the Criminal Investigation Branch didn't see anything either. McPherson later told detectives that O'Connor had approached his table, pulled a gun and said to him, 'Here's yours', but after a short scuffle O'Connor 'sort of shot himself'. No one was ever charged with the death. Crime and punishment Sydney style.

28

THE UNDERBELLY

During the 1960s, a difference in attitude between the Painters and Dockers and other waterfront workers emerged. For the dockers, particularly in Melbourne, the union was the heart of the Melbourne crime world, but the wharfies took a different route – men like McPherson and Smith left the docks and went into crime full-time. Those working on the wharves settled into what was becoming a well-paid life. The union's outflanking of the government, shipowners and stevedoring companies had left them with what was still often a hard job – improved significantly by containerisation and modern cargo handling – but one in which they controlled the size of the workforce, hiring, work hours and rosters and money when overtime and allowances were factored in. Growing up in Sydney's northern beaches in the 1960s, I remember wharfies forsaking the waterfront communities and moving into comfortable middle-class suburbs like ours. While they became my father's mates he muttered about their new Holden or Ford every three years while he had to make do with an old banger leaking oil on our driveway.

Trouble from employers, or nosey police and Customs officials resulted in the threat of a stop-work or strike. The wharfies knew they had the country by the balls and weren't averse to giving them a squeeze. It was accepted as an annoying, but inevitable part of Australian life in the '60s and '70s. Jim Beggs, a one-time WWF Victorian President said, 'we could literally sever the lifeline of Australia if we wanted to. Sometimes we did that – and sometimes not on the right issues, but most of the times the issues were right.' But unlike Melbourne's dockers, one wharfie said, 'we kept our head down and got on with our business – it was a good job and we ran our own race, so why fuck it up?'

They weren't pristine though and some of the business they got down to was the selective pillaging of cargo. The old black market still ticked over with shoes, 'luxury spirits' like Johnnie Walker Black Label and Chivas Regal, and televisions, preferably German or Japanese. I can remember helping my father struggle with a large box containing our first colour television from the back of the Holden HR wagon. The set was 'straight off the boat, son', but hadn't passed through Customs, the importer's warehouse or a retailer. With a lifetime of working around the docks, and a trusted face in the pubs that were still dotted around, the old man was quite capable of getting a deal on a little bit of luxury for the family.

A few years later he worked for a 'pillage squad' privately operated by a consortium of shipowners, but they were quite ineffectual. At the time, wharfies would complain or strike if the police tried to investigate crimes on the docks – even though there was a NSW Police Pillage Squad, that was hampered by the union's stance. The idea behind a group of men employed by the shipping companies was they could operate in the space between the police and the wharfies, liaising with both in the hope crimes could be effectively investigated without industrial strife, or crimes prevented. That was the theory, and it didn't work. Investigate and the threat of industrial strife loomed – and then there was the problem of compromise. The private squad lasted about eighteen months and achieved very little – aside from our new colour television of course. Jim Beggs said of the time, 'sure there were professionals down there – one bloke had a false bottom in his car and was always taking things out. It was a working class attitude of "I'm not taking this out of another bloke's pocket, I'm taking it out of an insurance company of a shipowner's who is making too much money anyway".' It was similar to the attitude of some professional criminals who considered theft to be a victimless crime if they stole from the well-off or a business.

In Melbourne, while there were plenty of Painters and Dockers who weren't criminals, there weren't many serious criminals who hadn't been a member of the Painters and Dockers. Melbourne media crime pundits have described the dockers as the 'outlaw bikers of their day', which is a fair call – except the bikers were part of a far more sophisticated and profitable criminal enterprise. The dockers played hard, fast, and without much planning for the present, let alone the future.

They weren't discreet – one senior Labor politician recalled sharing his union office on the Melbourne docks with the Painters and Dockers. He'd had to duck for cover one day when he heard gunfire in the car park, followed by warring dockers running through his office. He also recalled standing at the bar of his regular pub when a docker he knew dropped something heavy in his pocket just as a pair of detectives walked into the bar. When the police had gone, his docker acquaintance came back and removed a pistol from the man's pocket. 'I'm a bit hot,' he said, 'but you're a cleanskin.'

Men like John Twist, now grown into a criminal of some ability, were the key players in the dockers' criminal enterprises in the 1960s – with standover, assaults and robbery as their stock in trade rather than crimes requiring any planning or subtlety. Darryl Clarke, a homicide detective in Melbourne said, 'the senior management [of the union] were bloody hoodlums, thugs and murderers who stood over people for money! That was the best

I could say about them, they were just drunken, bloody lazy, brawlin', murderin' thugs.'

WWF's Jim Beggs believed the change in the dockers could be traced back to World War II when they were 'infiltrated – mostly from the underworld. This bloke went up to Pentridge and started recruiting.' When men were released from prison, the man was offering them the chance to run an SP bookmaker's business and other criminal endeavours while enjoying access to the docks and the cover of a legitimate job – but working only a day or two per week.

One emerging talent was Bill 'The Texan' Longley, a man who'd carry on the tradition of internal violence in the union as well as external. His nickname probably had its origins in the US TV series *The Texan*, a popular western in the flickering black and white of Australian television in the late 1950s, starring Rory Calhoun as Bill Longley, a man who was fast with his guns.

Longley was one of the new generation of dockers not born into a waterfront community. Instead, he was the son of law-abiding Scottish migrants who'd settled in middle-class Moonee Ponds – the home of Dame Edna Everage. Longley eschewed the dull and predictable future that his parents would have preferred, and instead gravitated to wild young men with roots in the waterfront. He had a patchy work record and was regularly sacked – blaming his termination on police who'd been harassing him for petty theft and brawling. He was on the police radar and they made a point of letting him know it.

His wharfie mates urged him to join them – the money was good and it was a place not frequented by police. Longley's first step toward work was to join the union, which required being nominated and seconded by members – no problem there. Longley was a late starter, joining at the age of twenty-seven in 1952, when the Melbourne waterfront was already a 'closed shop'. Rochelle Jackson wrote in *In Your Face*, 'it was easier getting a job in the bank than getting a job on the Melbourne wharves'. Longley said of the selection process, 'they didn't want undesirables – so if you were a police informer, a child molester or a debt collector you didn't stand a chance! You'd have to come pretty well recommended to get a job on the wharf – they were men's men, the cream of the crop.'

Longley found sanctuary and opportunity on the waterfront. He had an apprenticeship on the wharves, starting as a 'floater' and working where needed until he finally got a gang, 'made up of blokes who would stand by you, watch out for you and not dob you in to any authorities', he said, and rose to be a 'gang leader' – an honorary position elected by the members and tasked to speak from the gang on any issues arising in their workplace. He was also one of the union's tough guys with a reputation for hitting first – the king hit – in any disagreement. Theft, according to Longley, was small time and endemic.

In 1961, he was charged with the murder of his wife who'd been shot in the back. At trial, he was found not guilty of murder, but guilty of manslaughter. After a successful appeal he was retried and found not guilty of the manslaughter charge as well. He then married Barbara who when interviewed by Jackson for *In Your Face* said of her husband that he was 'the perfect family man – unassuming, a man who neither smoked nor drank'. Barbara and her family were from the waterfront and had known Longley for years, 'a very nice person' according to his wharfie brother-in-law Eric Martell. Contrary to Barbara's rosy view, Longley did like a drink or two, and his right to work on the wharves was terminated by the Stevedoring Authority for enjoying his vice while at work – one sin that not even the WWF could tolerate if you were caught on duty.

He wasn't out of work for long. The Painters and Dockers had an eye for talented, tough men, and in 1967 offered Longley membership of their union. He readily accepted and observed of the recruiting process, 'the only reason I was invited to join the Painters and Dockers was because I was a gunnie [reputed gunman] and I could look after their backs'. But he also believed, 'you could get work there when you couldn't get it anywhere else'. His wife Barbara was pragmatic about the career change, saying, 'I wasn't that happy; I don't think he was over-keen to start with' but with a family to feed and not much choice, Longley signed up. As Rochelle Jackson observed, 'waterside workers stick like shit to a blanket' and so Longley felt quite at home.

His old friend Frank Flannery, a wharfie, said in *In Your Face* that Longley was joining an organisation of 'hoods and bastards – not all of them, most of them, 95% of them. They'd rob their grandmother, pinch her pension!' He also believed they 'made their own justice. Billy was the Sheriff – he made himself the sheriff anyway!'

Longley would also prove the accuracy of the dockers' unofficial motto 'We catch and kill our own'.

The sheriff ran into serious legal troubles in 1973 when charged, then convicted, for ordering the murder of union secretary and his bitter rival in union politics, Pat Shannon. In May 1972, when the violence in his union was attracting plenty of publicity Shannon had issued a statement to the press which included the phrase 'Remember, no stray bullet or bomb has harmed a non-unionist.' It was an aimed bullet that killed Shannon when making his inaugural visit to the Druids Hotel in South Melbourne. It was 17 October and a pleasant spring evening. Shannon was sitting in the public bar, facing the door, which was propped open by a chair to let in the breeze. John Loughnane, a fellow docker, said he'd met Shannon at O'Connell's pub in South Melbourne around six thirty, with Loughnane noting that he'd started work with a meeting at nine that morning and had repaired to another pub at 11 am, where he and his docker cronies had spent the afternoon – working hard on union issues presumably. Loughnane and Shannon had then headed to the nearby Druids where they were enjoying a cleansing ale with Loughnane's de facto Noella Jansen and Joan Hosking, the wife of docker Lawrie who'd recently been badly injured and was in hospital. The pleasant evening came to an abrupt end when Kevin Taylor – a minor criminal until that point – stepped through the open door carrying a rifle. Shannon uttered 'you cunt', upon which Taylor took aim and fired three shots, hitting Shannon in the heart, the right shoulder, and the wrist. He was dead by the time he hit the floor.

Shannon had been a publican in Adelaide and about twenty years before his abrupt departure had switched careers to work on the waterfront. However, he'd managed to attain a drinker's vibrant red-veined nose which was in contrast to how journalist Evan Whitton described him in his book *Can of Worms* (1986) as 'an impressive looking, square jawed man, whose grey business suit was of faultless cut'.

Shannon had taken over the role of secretary in 1971 at a time when some union members were busy supplementing their incomes with armed robbery (both in Sydney and Melbourne). This was also the time of a fraud involving 'ghost' employees – the Phantom Dockers – and a 'letter of credit' scam targeting the Commercial Bank of Australia. A later royal commission reported the fraud was worth A$2 million and was a 'crime that required a simultaneous and complex operation both in Melbourne and Sydney' and 'relied heavily on Painters and Dockers from the Sydney wharves'. The dockers were smart, creative and brutal.

There were power struggles within the union and Shannon was in conflict with Longley and his faction. Longley was about to do time for receiving some of the proceeds from an armoured car robbery and Shannon was seen as a man keen to reform the union's erring ways – he was notably unsuccessful. After his death, the members were levied fifty cents from each weekly pay for the following eighteen months to support Wilma Shannon and her children – the levy ceased after she wrote to the union telling them it was no longer needed.

Union internal violence was common: members had been murdered, 'disappeared' and viciously assaulted.

Crimes had also been committed against non-members. Six months before Shannon's murder, Nicholas Kolovrat, a ten-year-old boy, was sipping lemonade with his father Zlatko, a hospital cleaner, in the Moonee Valley pub in Fitzroy, when a gunman walked in and opened fire with a handgun. Zlatko was wounded, the gunman's target – docker Lawrence Chamings – was killed, as was Nicholas who was accidentally shot between the eyes. Zlatko told the Coroner's inquest, 'nobody wanted to call the police', and no one saw anything. The catchphrase from Sergeant Schultz of TV's comedy *Hogan's Heroes* that 'I see nothing' was as popular with Melbourne crims as it was with Sydney's. Police were finally coming around to the notion that the dockers were out of control.

Later that year, commenting on the Shannon and Kolovrat killings, the *Herald* editorialised on 18 October 1973 that 'the State Government should not defer any longer a confrontation with the criminal elements of this union who have been spreading murder, wounding and terror – Chicago Mafia style – for far too many years. These criminals are not just amusing tough boys playing a terrible game among themselves. They poison the community and are a constant danger to it.'

The situation didn't improve when Longley was arrested and charged thirteen months later for ordering Shannon's murder. He'd been on the run, but finally returned to Melbourne and gave himself up – with his lawyers present. He was later convicted and served thirteen years of a life sentence.

There were plenty of other dockers around to keep the mayhem happening including Graham 'Munster' Kinniburgh, a former shoplifter with the Kangaroo Gang led by New South Welshman Arthur 'Duke' Delaney – one of the police force's favourite criminals when I was a young detective because of his élan. The gang plundered the boutiques of London's Mayfair and

Knightsbridge in the 1960s then returned to Australia. 'Munster' then turned to drug trafficking. He was a good friend of Sydney shoplifter and SP king, George Freeman. Others included Lewis Moran, the patriarch of the murderous clan pivotal in Melbourne's gang war of the 1990s.

29
OCEANS OF CASH

In 1967, Sydney became an official Rest and Recreation (R&R) destination for US troops fighting in Vietnam. The troops brought piles of cash with them to spend in the bars, brothels and strip clubs of Kings Cross and Sydney's inner east, and they also brought with them a taste for heroin, which changed crime in Australia forever.

Heroin was available for medical use in Australia until 1953 when the Menzies government banned both its manufacture and import, but the problem of addiction hit Australia in great volume during the 1960s when the nation's involvement in Vietnam brought more back than just the troops.

The first place to change was Kings Cross, which had recovered from being party central during World War II, and was back to being home to Sydney's arts or 'bohemian' community as well as home to well-to-do country families with an apartment to use during the Royal Easter Show, the gay community who kept low key to avoid a beating by the less than sensitive NSW Police Force, and older affluent couples who'd moved from the family pile into something more convenient and manageable. It was also home to the city's great restaurants, nightclubs, after hours drinking spots, and the art of strip tease introduced by Abe Saffron at his

'Staccato Club'. 'Sir' Wayne Martin ran strip clubs for Saffron and saw the change. He told *Time Out* magazine that in the pre R&R days, 'the Cross was beautiful then – no heroin or cocaine. It was movie houses, bands at Surf City, supper club shows at the Chevron or Silver Spade – a real swinging scene.'

Prostitution, soon to be a conduit for the spread of heroin, was still in East Sydney, and Martin recalled 'all the brothels were on or around Stanley Street, and the streets were packed with guys and gals, five quid, bang, bang, bang. But when the police shut it down we invited the molls and hoons up to the Cross where we could keep an eye on 'em.' And along came the US soldiers shortly after.

The timing was one of the many accidents that have characterised crime in Australia. Heroin came at a time when the nation was liberating after the cultural straitjacket of the 1950s and there was a lack of recreational drugs thanks to the destruction of supply lines during World War II. Shortly after the beginning of the Vietnam War, heroin laboratories were set up along the Thai–Burmese borders by enterprising Chinese producers, and their finished product transported into Vietnam and sold to the US soldiers who either smoked or injected it – a brief, cheap and readily available respite from war. Nearly one third of US servicemen were using the drug within a short space of time, and when they arrived in Sydney, they shared their pursuit with sex workers and the 'bohemians' who called Kings Cross home.

Heroin spread through Australia with a similar haste to its spread through the US troops, and as the war came to an end, it was making its mark in Australia's cities, suburbs and regional areas. It became a driver of crime from large-scale imports down to burglaries, shoplifting and minor frauds that supported the user's habit.

Supply was easy. Australia's border protection was focused on people bringing in dodgy wood, fruit or meat products – but not large packets of powdered problems. Heroin walked through the airports and off cruise ships packed in suitcases along with Speedos, T-shirts and safari suits, and through Australian ports, either handed over to wharfies and dockers by seamen on arriving ships or secreted in pre-arranged places on the ship. Containers made smuggling even easier, less risky because of the low rate of search by Customs, and with the potential for greater volume. All you had to do was mark the container so it could be identified then it could be opened on the docks by the wharfies and the contraband removed, in transit to or at the final destination. With a network that started on board ship and included the wharfies, waterfront clerks and drivers, it was a smooth operation.

Heroin brought a need for criminals to organise on a grander scale – the high profit crime of the 1960s was armed robbery which was relatively straightforward and needed only some basic logistics, weapons, a getaway route and a car, and if the crooks were sensible, a disguise. The old black market pillaging from the wharves was 'small beer' in comparison to profits from heroin supply but did lay the groundwork for smuggling and distribution. Given the size of the market, crooks had to organise themselves to optimise their profits, and reduce their risk of being caught or ripped off by their suppliers, dealers or competitors.

Sydney was the ideal base for the new boom industry. Alfred McCoy wrote in his 1980 book *Narcotics and Organised Crime in Australia* that only Sydney and Melbourne 'had enough population to sustain vice sectors in their local economies' – though the later Fitzgerald Commission in Queensland would suggest Brisbane was trying to stake a claim for inclusion – and that 'Melbourne manufactured and Sydney imported'.

McCoy was on the money, and while he was writing, the Hells Angels were setting up the first amphetamine manufacturing labs in the rolling hills outside Melbourne. He also wrote that 'Sydney's convict past and port city present have combined to create a cynical political climate open to systematic corruption and ideal for the growth of organized crime'. With Southeast Asia's heroin syndicates having difficulty pushing into the Mafia-dominated North American market, Australia had become a target, and 'the effect of their [the Southeast Asian syndicates'] decision was soon felt'. He noted that by the end of the 1970s, heroin was moving from being a drug of 'middle-class youth' and was 'growing most rapidly among unemployed youth in the poorer sections of Sydney and Melbourne. Bored and without prospects, unemployed youth were turning to heroin to make time go away.'

Around the time McCoy was writing, some NSW Police had finally tumbled to the profits from drugs, with some of their number profiting from pillaging cash or product or both during drug raids. They worked on the assumption that dealers would keep quiet in fear of reprisals, a cost of doing business or the perverse logic that the less product and cash seized then the lesser the penalty. The drug squad's long-time boss Cec Abbott, who became commissioner in 1981, had overseen a doubling in the size of the squad during his tenure, but hadn't quite come to grips with the problem he was supposed to be policing. When asked by a journalist 'How seriously do you think we are threatened in the future with large scale drug addiction in this country?', he replied, 'I'm not greatly worried about the position. I feel that Australians are not generally drug conscious.'

The lie to Abbott's views came in 1979 when the CIB squads were rallied to support their drug squad colleagues in major raids on heroin syndicates at various locations on Sydney's north shore. When the detectives crashed through the doors, the first tasks were to round up the occupants and make sure the products weren't being flushed down the toilet. The second was to do a comprehensive search to find cash and drugs – and then decide what to do with it. One honest detective on the raids recalled some of his colleagues finding bundles of cash in high denomination notes and the collective comment was 'How good is this!' With coppers earning A$30,000 a year, finding a chunk of cash that exceeded their salary was too much of a temptation.

The raid was another of those moments that was providentially timed – if you were one of the coppers who looked to supplement their salary first and practise the art of policing second. The traditional cash cows like vice, gambling and after hours drinking were still supplying regular 'quids' to bent coppers and an assortment of 'hangers on' that may have included members of the judiciary and government, but the revenues were dropping as R&R came to an end and the local market couldn't continue to drive the level of graft they'd enjoyed.

Crimes like robberies were more occasional opportunities rather than regular and corrupt officials liked their payments to be predictable – the Friday brown envelope stuffed with cash was born of observation rather than imagination. Abortion had been a great money-spinner for decades – one senior copper from the ongoing 'Abortion Squad' in the early 1960s had curled a lip when £10,000 was given to him to keep his men away from the doctor, and told me, 'Next time guineas, son', but Dr Bertram Wainer, the Victorian campaigner for abortion law reform, had turned his sights on New South Wales and in 1971 District Court Judge Aaron Levine made a ruling that effectively meant abortions could be performed in NSW, thus killing a police cash cow. When you've lived beyond your means for years, it's hard to change, so the arrival of drugs as a major criminal enterprise was timely.

The only cloud on the horizon was that the public were slowly waking up to the fact that all was not necessarily rosy in law enforcement and that crime might just be organised.

One of the catalysts for this change in public perception was Lennie McPherson and his mate Stan Smith. In 1968 Stan and George Freeman had headed to the US on a holiday where they caught up with Joseph Dan Testa – a gentleman alleged to be involved with the Mafia and the Bally poker machine company that was then eyeing the Australian market. The following year, Testa came to Sydney and it wasn't a low-key visit. He was interviewed by *People* magazine, wined and dined at Chequers nightclub with Lennie and the guys, and photographed pig shooting with Lennie near Moree in northwestern NSW. The Australian public was getting the uneasy feeling that the American-style organised crime they'd seen in movies and television was about to arrive.

Lennie's hospitality inadvertently launched a decade of royal commissions starting with one stimulated by an old Mort's Dock employee and ending with one targeting the Painters and Dockers.

30
HERE COMES THE JUDGE(S)

The 'Royal Commission of Inquiry into certain matters relating to allegations of organised crime in clubs' began in 1973 with Justice Athol Moffitt in charge. It was prompted by media reports that the Bally poker machine company, with its links to the Mafia in America, was eyeing Australia as a profitable new market. Bally started in Chicago in 1932 making pinball machines then moved into slot (or poker in Australia) machines. By the late 1960s it was one of the world's largest manufacturers of gaming machines and reportedly provided 90% of the slot machines to the mecca of gambling – Nevada.

Until the media campaign, both the NSW Premier Bob Askin and his Commissioner of Police Norm Allan had denied that NSW had any organised crime – an assertion reminiscent of J. Edgar Hoover who'd made similar denials in the face of overwhelming evidence, until the Mafia dons and their minders were sprung en route to a crime summit in sleepy Apalachin in New York State.

Assisting Moffitt were some crack NSW detectives including one who once warned me about the consequences of 'poking my nose' into places like the notorious gay bordello Costello's and a nearby brothel in Kellett Street, Kings Cross; and Doug Knight.

McPherson was described in the commission as a 'well-known Sydney criminal and standover man' and given his title as 'Mr Big'. According to Moffitt, 'some of the senior police were inclined to accept McPherson's claims of departure from the criminal scene', however the judge wasn't buying it and made pointed reference to Lennie's 'substantial source of income' that the police couldn't quite explain. Lennie was really in mid-career and the coppers weren't about to derail him.

The commission was also told what has become the popular story of the founding of organised crime in Australia. According to Detective Sergeant Brian Ballard, Lennie McPherson, Stan Smith, George Freeman, Arthur 'Duke' Delaney, Frederick 'Paddles' Anderson (a major force in the underworld with a long career in both Sydney and Melbourne), Milan Petricevic (better known as 'Iron Bar Miller'), and State Labor MP Albert Sloss, met on three occasions at the home of Karl Bonnette at 44 William Street, Double Bay. Bonnette had a few convictions on his record and was Bally boss Jack Rooklyn's driver. Ballard told the commission they met nearby and 'usually have drinks until 11 pm when they move to the William Street address. A male person in an old Holden car is alleged to act as cockatoo during these meetings.' The informant told him the meeting was 'to organise crime', but hadn't actually seen the Labor MP at the meetings. Ballard's story was backed up by Federal Police, who had the house under surveillance on an inquiry of their own and had recorded the comings and goings.

In a move that confused and annoyed Moffitt, the police didn't follow up the information –'to discard this material from the police inquiry without further inquiry is almost beyond belief'. The judge was getting first-hand knowledge of policing NSW style.

While Moffitt was highly critical of his investigators, none of them suffered a career setback. The lead investigator, Jack McNeill, did penance in uniform – the usual penalty for a detective who'd had a public scrape – and a few years later was back at the CIB as Chief of Staff, where he was welcomed by Assistant Commissioner (Crime) Jim Black with a glass of Johnnie Walker Black Label, and the toast, 'Here's to you, Jack, we all knew you'd be back.' Like the waterfront communities that spawned the major criminals, the police were close-knit and protective of their own.

Karl Bonnette told me the meetings to organise crime were 'all bullshit, mate – the coppers made it up. There was no meeting.' The truth is probably somewhere in the middle, and while the men gathered – supported by the Federal Police assertions rather than the assurances of Ballard – the jury is out on whether they were organising crime or just having a late night drink and bragging about their exploits and plans. With the benefit of time passing, no evidence of nefarious schemes emerged. McPherson kept an interest in gaming machines – a good money-spinner whether in licensed clubs or illegal gambling dens – and Stan didn't help his reputation by being caught on tape in 1976 saying to illegal casino operators over lunch that, 'we [presumably Lennie and he] run it because we put in the right men, the right business administrators in to fucking handle it, with our brain power behind it and so on'.

The royal commission didn't achieve a great deal. Moffitt sagely recommended that police look at how other countries deal with organised crime – which in reality endorsed senior police taking overseas trips that achieved very little aside from a good time – and recommended a special squad of police be formed to tackle the issue. The latter didn't happen until over a decade later. What Moffitt didn't mention was that McPherson was a paid informant for the commission. The most significant achievement of the commission was to take organised crime off the front page and, with that done, it was back to business as usual for both crooks and coppers – for a few years.

•

Victoria had a run at problems with criminals and police in 1975 when the government appointed Barry Beach, QC to chair a board of inquiry. Beach's inquiry followed the William Kaye, QC, inquiry into the involvement of police in abortion rackets – an inquiry prompted by Bertram Wainer. In a 2004 article referring to an editorial at the time (1970), *The Age* said of Kaye's findings that police were indeed up to no good and 'it would have been naive to suppose that responsible ministers and officials, and successive police chiefs, had no inkling of what was going on'. The Bolte Government called in Colonel Sir Eric St Johnston, a former UK copper, to advise and restructure.

However, five years later, that pesky Dr Wainer was at it again, this time producing a tape of a copper being offered and accepting a bribe. Beach focused on traditional policing methods like verballing (fabricating admissions of guilt and the like), loading (giving the allegedly criminal things like a gun or a bag of drugs), false charges, assaults and so on. After fifteen months, Beach found that the force had serious problems. Fifty-five police were named in the report and thirty-three were charged, but all were acquitted. As with Moffitt, adverse mention wasn't a bar to promotion, and some achieved lofty ranks. A subsequent review of the inquiry was prompted by the threat of 4200 coppers going on strike – and the review overturned all but four of Beach's recommendations. Many of the allegations made against police involved cases with members of the Painters and Dockers. Inquiry done and back to business.

In October 1977, Prime Minister Malcolm Fraser appointed Justice Edward Williams of the Queensland Supreme Court to lead the first ever royal commission focused on the importation of drugs into Australia and the connection with organised crime. The commission found that only between 1 and 15% of imports were detected – probably because the inspection regime was focused on inbound passengers rather than large shipments arriving by air or sea. One witness, a Mr Mitchell from the Narcotics Board, gave evidence that 'methods used in the illegal importation of drugs are restricted only by the imagination of the importer'. Mr A. Besley, the Secretary of the Department of Business and Consumer Affairs, told the commission, 'Against the traditional importation of illicit drugs by Asian crew of merchant vessels plying between Southeast Asia and Australia, the constant development of more sophisticated techniques indicates the probability of a higher incidence of undetected importations,' and that 'methods of importation always tend to be designed to exploit the more vulnerable areas of the Department's [Customs] control system'.

The most useful evidence came in a submission from the Administrative and Clerical Officers Association, who nailed the real problem, saying,

> we believe that any person with even a limited knowledge of commercial cargo procedures will be aware that the enormous volume hopelessly outweighs the limited resources assigned for examination and control purposes.
>
> The significant feature of importation by ship or air cargo is the opportunity available to import large quantities of drugs with the minimum risk.
>
> However, the emphasis is placed on the prevention of drugs through passengers' baggage, and the baggage of crewmembers of ships and aircraft. We consider that this avenue of importation offers the greatest risk of detection and nets significantly smaller quantities of drugs per seizure than the commercial cargo area.

In his report, Williams noted that criminal activities funded the imports, but the financiers, who were in businesses like gambling and vice, didn't involve themselves in the import and distribution. Funding was fine, but they didn't want the risk or stigma of actual participation. Williams also found there wasn't a drug kingpin sitting on top of a criminal hierarchy, no Mr Bigs but 'plenty of Mr Big Enoughs'. He made a point about the lack of communication between the states and Commonwealth that led to the 'wasteful deployment of resources, duplication of effort and sub-optimal performance'. What should have set off alarm bells was he named Sydney as the heart of the heroin trade, and estimated it at around A$59 million per year – a tantalising figure for any enterprising criminal. His report didn't stimulate the NSW Police to swing into action.

As noted earlier, NSW Police had their own Pillage Squad which didn't do a great deal – if the coppers tried to investigate crime on the waterfront they were greeted with a wall of silence from the workers, and if they pushed, then the wharfies pushed back with the threat of industrial action. In the politics of policing, investigation came a distant second to the commercial reality of the nation's trade. Drugs came in regularly and easily through the waterfront secreted in containers or in packages slipped from seaman to trusted workers then walked off the docks and into the networks as they had for decades. It was a time when policing was locally focused so tip-offs and coordinated operations involving other states or internationally were quite rare – a global approach to policing, and in particular the drug trade, is growing but still way behind the slick operations of the major traffickers and their international businesses.

The disappearance of Donald Mackay – a Griffith anti-drugs campaigner and proprietor of a furniture store – on 15 July 1977 prompted the NSW Drugs Royal Commission run by Justice Woodward. However, the commission was inward-looking and focused on cannabis growing and trafficking in Australia. It blamed the 'men in grass castles' – the Griffith branch of the Calabrian Mafia-style organisation 'Ndrangheta that are still very active in the global drug trade today.

The Painters and Dockers did, however, make an appearance in the aftermath of the commission when James Frederick Bazley was convicted in 1986 of conspiring to murder Mackay. Bazley was a docker, and a fan and breeder of poodles, who had the nickname 'Machine Gun' – because of his use of a machine gun in a 1964 bank robbery. He was also a long-time associate of Bill Longley.

Like many of his colleagues, Bazley had started out working on the fringe of the law as a bookmaker's clerk, a bouncer at a casino then slipped into bank robbery, at which he didn't excel, and ended up in prison. After being released in 1969, he used the connections he'd made in prison to get a job on the Williamstown docks and membership of the Painters and Dockers. Without a hint of irony, he stood on Longley's ticket in the blood-spattered 1972 union elections as 'vigilance officer'. In his career as a docker he'd been shot twice, ambushed by gunmen, and his brother had been shot in the knee allegedly as a warning to Bazley.

With union business getting rather dangerous, Bazley told a source, 'I was getting too old for this kind of work'. He returned to armed robbery with an equal lack of success as his earlier attempt. In February 1975 he robbed a bank in Gardiner, Victoria, of A$10,000. While the robbery was a success, his escape wasn't, and he was captured by a one-legged butcher who owned the shop next door. At trial, Bazley's barrister described him as 'the Maxwell Smart of bank robbers'.

After arrest, he was allowed bail and disappeared – becoming successful as a hitman, with the Mackay disappearance and presumed murder, plus the murder of Douglas and Isabel Wilson, heroin addicts involved in the Mr Asia drug trafficking syndicate. Bazley was caught in 1980 in Sydney while driving a stolen car and eventually convicted for his role in Mackay's disappearance and presumed murder, and for the murder of the Wilsons.

As the Williams and Woodward inquiries were coming to an end, Australia's waterfront was about to become the focus of an investigation that would drive a stake through the heart of the Painters and Dockers.

In 1981, Malcolm Fraser followed up with the Williams Royal Commission into Drug Trafficking conducted by NSW's Justice Donald Stewart – one of the few former police officers to make the judicial big time. Like Woodward, his inquiry was focused on the internal players, not the methods, and featured the activities of Terry Clark. The commission led to the formation of the National Crime Authority – rebranded on 1 January 2003 as the Australian Crime Commission.

In NSW it also spawned a response by the police about the rise of heroin and how best to deal with it. The report echoed Williams' findings, and noted, 'efforts should be made to evolve integrated drug enforcement programs with other States and the Commonwealth' and that 'during the past six months [1983], a State/Commonwealth task force along the lines suggested has been effectively operating in New South Wales'. The report recommended priority to 'high level and organisational trafficking' and that 'at least 65% of the drug law enforcement effort is spent in attempting to intercept traffickers above street level'. The clincher was 'various law enforcement authorities must gear themselves to combat an almost inevitable emergence of more highly organised crime than has hitherto been present in this state'.

The report read well, but if you were a NSW detective, you'd snigger into your schooner. Arthur 'Neddy' Smith was then Australia's biggest heroin trafficker and his occasional colleague, wharfie Daniel Chubb, was using his knowledge of the waterfront, and contacts, to make sure Neddy's supplies were slipping through unfettered.

An indicator of the size of Smith's business was the 1978 arrest in Bangkok of two of his couriers – former Double Bay hairdresser and barman Warren Fellows and Neddy's brother-in-law and former rugby league player Paul Hayward. The pair were caught with 8.5 kilos of heroin destined for Australia when Thai police raided their rooms at the Montien Hotel. Both men were convicted and spent long sentences in the less salubrious 'Bangkok Hilton' – the Bang Kwang prison. Police sources, though unable to pinpoint just how much Smith was importing said, 'Mate, there were a few in the game but Neddy was the top dog. They were walking it in through the airport, or picking it up from his contacts on the wharves. He had more connections than the Water Board.' However there was no evidence to suggest he was doing bulk imports via shipping containers – Neddy was more of the old-style 'hands on' crim – a highly successful small business operator rather than a large franchise.

Chubb's career came to an abrupt conclusion on the morning of 8 November 1984 near his mother's home at 36 High Street, Millers Point where he'd been living since separating from his wife. Chubb's morning got off to an early start with allegedly a meeting with a few Chinese gentlemen who were staying at the Cliveden Hotel in Bridge Street in the Sydney CBD. Police believe that at the meeting his contacts gave him around two million dollars worth of heroin. The system, according to police, was that Chubb would then have the supply checked for quality and if okay, he'd then have the payment made by a person trusted by both sides of the deal. Chubb then slipped back home and at around 10.30 am drove to the Captain Cook Hotel – then a pub where locals drank and only a short walk but Chubb wasn't a fan of physical fitness. He drove his new Jaguar, bought just a month before for $55,000 and without finance – an interesting choice of car for a middle-aged waterfront worker living with his mother in a house that had been rented by his family from the government for generations.

Chubb met with Neddy and his colleague Graham 'Abo' Henry – a nickname courtesy of his complexion rather than indigenous roots – who were having a heart starter (mid morning beer) at the hotel. The conversation was brief, then Chubb drove home, stopping at the local fish and chip shop to buy an early lunch. Smith and Henry headed to the Star Hotel in Alexandria, a favourite pub in which police, according to a source of mine, suspected they 'carried out drug transactions'.

Danny had just parked when he was hit in the face by a shotgun blast. His killer then shot him four times with a handgun just to make sure. At the time of his death Danny's wealth was estimated at around $7 million, including cash in a Swiss bank, investment properties, and a 21-foot cabin cruiser. One motivation for the murder was speculated as a dispute between Middle Eastern drug dealers and their 'heavy police' protectors and Chubb and his associates in the Southeast Asian heroin trafficking gangs. No one was arrested for the killing.

Once the various reports were tabled very little happened.

But the commission to have the greatest impact came on 10 September 1980 when Prime Minister Malcolm Fraser commissioned Melbourne barrister Frank Costigan, QC, to have a hard look at the 'activities of the Federated Ship Painters and Dockers'. The first hearings were appropriately at the Williamstown courthouse.

It was an own goal for the union. With the stirring interest in drugs and corruption, the union's decades of public violence, internal and external battles, and a conga line of dockers convicted of everything from petty theft to armed robbery and murder made them obvious targets. Historian Jim Stokes, commenting in *The Australian* on 2 January 2012, added that, 'for the public, the painters and dockers, with their bizarrely murderous culture and strange nicknames, provided a little colour in a generally dreary political and economic landscape'.

The dockers' lethal blend of arrogance, violence and insularity didn't bode well for their long-term future. What they lacked was the objectivity to step back and consider the way the public might be looking at them. *The Australian* in January 1972 had reported in an article headlined 'Death Feud in Dockland' that 'the war on the wharves no one wants to talk about – the most intriguing, and shameful aspect of Melbourne's waterfront war is the casual acceptance of the situation by the unions, the police and the State Government. And the people.' The article noted 'behind the violence is the struggle for control of the Melbourne wharves. And the key to that power lies with the Ships Painters and Dockers Union – an organisation that has grown since the war into an uneasy alliance between the union movement and the underworld.'

James Ramsden, writing in the *Financial Review* on 8 March 1976, said 'no other industry has appeared so unfavourably in the public eye, so consistently as our waterfront industry. Everyone wonders if there is to be any more honest perspiration on our waterfront.'

The dockers hadn't noticed that times were changing fast.

The Age, with commissions of inquiry humming away, said the dockers were engaged in a 'Little World of War Without End' and reported on 11 October 1979 that 'a seventy-year-old crane driver was shot on the docks this week with 100 workers close by. The crime had a familiar stamp – it was in the open but no-one saw what happened including the victim Mr Joseph Francis Stone.'

Police speculated part of the trouble on the wharves was because of the recent acquittal of three men – Raymond Bennett, Victor Mikkelsen and Laurie Prendergast – charged with the machine-gun murder of docker Les Kane the year before. Kane, his wife Judy and their three children had returned to their home in the upwardly mobile outer Melbourne suburb of Wantirna, and allegedly found three men with 'silenced machine guns' lying in wait in the matrimonial bedroom for Les, who they promptly murdered. They allegedly loaded his body into the back of a waiting pink-coloured Ford Futura – not the ideal choice of getaway car if you were planning on a discreet departure. Mrs Kane didn't call the police and instead called a family conference – after she'd mopped up the blood in the house. She later told the coroner that she wanted time to arrange protection for her family. The less trusting speculated that she knew the killers and her brother-in-law Brian wanted time to flush them out and deliver 'summary justice'.

One of the reasons speculated for the murder was the reputation of the Kane brothers – Les, Brian and Ray. Brian had recently lost a brawl in a pub in Richmond during the course of which a chunk of his ear had been bitten off by one of his assailants. With the arcane ways of Melbourne dockers in general, and the thoroughly unpleasant Kanes in particular, it was believed the brothers would be out for revenge. Police sources believe Les Kane was the 'maddest' of the three brothers – unpredictable and violent.

Bennett and Prendergast had long and unpleasant reputations for violence and, in Bennett's case, a long-standing dislike of Les Kane. Bennett had been the mastermind of the 'Great Bookie Robbery' at Melbourne's Victoria Club in April 1976 in which the thieves had escaped with A$6 million in cash. He'd been the target of standover men, like Kane, who thought he should share the wealth.

Bennett was shot to death on 12 November 1979 at the Melbourne Magistrate's Court while being transferred to a courtroom by police officers. Journalist Andrew Rule, who was there at the time, recalled in *The Age* of 7 February 2009, 'it reeked of an inside job'. The two leading suspects were Brian Kane and Mr Rent A Kill – Chris Flannery – but no one was ever arrested for the killing and no one on the waterfront was talking. One docker commented, 'nobody's saying nothing. Even the dogs at Port Melbourne are barking out of the sides of their mouths.'

Prendergast, whose forebear John 'Snowy' Prendergast was shot dead by Kate Leigh in Sydney, was a long-time partner in crime of Flannery with the two involved, allegedly, in murder and rape among other crimes. He disappeared in 1985 – probably murdered – and as for Flannery, who also disappeared the same year, the queue of potential killers was a long one.

Brian Kane was shot to death at the Quarry Hotel in 1982. Ray Kane survived this fight, and the Melbourne gang war of the 1990s, and was close to the Moran family of former dockers. In 2009, he commented on the late 1970s in an interview in *The Age,* saying, 'we were in the midst of a war. My brothers tried to shield me from it as much as they could. I was the spoilt one in an underprivileged family, if you know what I mean.'

The nation's high-rating *Willesee* current affairs program targeted the dockers in late 1979, and in January 1980 *The Bulletin*, published in Sydney by Kerry Packer's Consolidated Press Holdings, joined the media chorus. Longley was happy to chat, and told *The Bulletin* that his union mates had 'knocked off' around thirty people, which was probably conservative, and made it a national problem by adding, 'they have either been killed for money or simply their mouths. This is not just in Melbourne, but in Sydney, Brisbane, Perth.' Longley, enjoying his media moment, also said, 'don't let anyone kid you that there is not corruption on the Australian waterfront. It is rife. The private sector is open slather to graft and corruption. You can simply name your price.'

Bob Hawke, the ACTU leader at the time, commented in a 2011 interview in *The Australian*, 'to me the practices of the Painters and Dockers was something that I found appalling. We made it quite clear that as far as the ACTU was concerned there was no support at all for those practices.'

While the dockers had a flair for crime, their public relations skills were dismal. They should have taken heed of Ken Stone, Secretary of the Victorian Trades Hall Council who said in 1972, 'I don't think the other unions look down on these men [the dockers] but there is an opening for a bright young lad to handle their public relations.'

Costigan began the commission by looking at thirty-eight violent events – a figure that included fifteen murders – involving the dockers from 1970 to 1979. The commission got results quickly and by March 1981, the investigators broadened their scope and uncovered massive tax evasion by dockers – a topic that would later cause the commission to broaden its remit and look into the entrails of corporate Australia. One docker had been arrested in the Queen Victoria Market, which would later be 'outed' as a popular spot for crooks to launder money and broker deals. Police found $1 million in cash in the boot of his car. Overtime was plentiful for dockers but not that much.

In May, Longley made the first of his appearances at the commission and pointed the finger at the current executive of the union, claiming they were a 'bunch of crooks'. His evidence may have prompted Jack 'Putty Nose' Nicholls into revenge. Terry Gordon, the union's federal president, said of Longley's accusations, 'if we can be slandered by a convicted murderer responsible for the death of a union official then it's a pretty sad state of affairs'. Costigan didn't let Gordon get away with assertions, and listed the deeds of the dockers going back as far as Freddie Harrison's murder in 1958. It was a very long list.

Nicholls, also responding to Longley, offered to give the commission the ballot papers of what Costigan described as 'a critical union election, which he asserted, demonstrated he had defeated Billy Longley in a fair ballot.' Nicholls didn't make it to court and was found dead in a pale blue Falcon a few kilometres south of Albury on 16 June 1981. The cause of death was a bullet wound to the head, and the coroner found he'd committed suicide. The view on the street was very different – Nicholls had been murdered and it had been done well. *The Sun* interviewed a 'burly docker' who in the days following Nicholls' death said, 'No way. For two reasons. Jack was under no pressure. He was the same as he always is. And secondly he loved life too much to commit suicide. It was murder. Any other story is just bullshit.'

Longley later confided to a member of the Federal Police that while he knew it was murder, it wasn't one he'd had his hands in. 'Yes, mate, I've been in a few but not this one. Not me,' he said.

Nicholls had started his day with breakfast at the Viscount Hotel in Albury where he'd spent the night. He'd been keeping a low profile in the lead-up to his evidence and there was speculation he'd already been murdered, but the night before his death he'd been seen by the doorman at the Commercial Club in Albury, who'd made a joke, saying, 'Hey Putty Nose, you're supposed to be dead', to which Nicholls replied, 'You can't believe what you read – newspaper rubbish!' Twelve hours later it wasn't.

At the funeral, Terry Gordon said of the late 'Putty Nose', 'he was a man of great ability and energy' and taking a swing at Costigan and the media, said, 'he was tireless in his efforts; above all he was an humanitarian. He believed that if a man made a mistake and paid the penalty for it, then he should be helped to re-join the mainstream of society, join a union and go to work.'

Bob Dix, who became the union's Victorian secretary, dryly observed of the commission that 'the only thing they haven't got is thumbscrews and the rack. They do it mentally, not physically these days. We believe our past secretary was driven off his crumpet and blew his brains out.'

The day after Nicholls' death, the union's lack of PR skills were obvious when the executive met at the Council Club Hotel in South Melbourne and passed a resolution pointing the finger of blame for the death at the commission, and recommending that no further co-operation be given, not that they'd rushed to help earlier, unless it was in their interests. From then on, members turned up to the commission, were sworn in and then refused to answer. The maximum penalty for refusal was $1000 – not enough to nudge a change of mind. Costigan described their actions in lawyerly terms as 'the justification advanced for the flagrant breach of the law was not one recognisable in law. By all other measures, it was humbug.' For Costigan, humbug became a well-used term of derision, and the commissioner learned that his witnesses, on the occasion they did speak, 'dissembled and admitted nothing until it was demonstrated that the truth was known'. Costigan the lawyer was learning what police have known for generations.

Phillip Adams offered a softer view of the union, writing in *The Age* on 11 July 1981, that

> I've come to the conclusion that to apply middle-class morality and legality to the painters and dockers is rather like superimposing British law on Aborigines in the Northern Territory. Just as the blacks have their perfectly efficient tribal laws, the painters and dockers have their peculiar code of ethics, with the depths of the Yarra awaiting anyone who breaches etiquette. In any case, is the odd burst of gunfire on the wharves all that different from the back-stabbing in corporate board rooms?

Mr Adams had overlooked the occasional murder of both dockers and innocents. He concluded his insight with 'it smacks of hypocrisy to tut-tut about Puttynose and his painters when they are, in a sense, dealing with the detritus of social inequality and buck passing'. In the great tradition of opinion writing, never let reality get in the way. Costigan gave Adams a mention in his report under 'The Image, As Propounded By Apologists For The Union'.

Within eighteen months, the Costigan Commission was looking at the broader issue of tax evasion outside the union and corporate skulduggery. He later said, 'to the Commission's surprise, the inquiry turned from an investigation into multi-murders to white collar crime and tax evasion'.

Though the catalyst for the commission was the bloodthirsty ways of the Victorian Branch of the Painters and Dockers, Costigan didn't neglect the rest of the nation. He said in a 2003 speech to the Victorian Bar, 'it was an immensely exciting time, but I have never worked harder. Most weeks were six days and, often towards the end, seven. In one year I spent 165 days in hotel rooms. In one week I flew to Perth for a few days hearing, then to Singapore for two days, then back to Perth. I woke up the next morning in a hotel room and didn't know what city I was in. So I decided it was time for a short break.'

He found that 'the union, at least in Victoria, Newcastle, Queensland and South Australia (if not Sydney as well) was an organised criminal group following criminal pursuits'. Aside from the earlier mentioned Sydney frauds, the New South Welshmen had been involved in armed robbery, allowed 'transfers' of dockers from other states using false documents – often from dead men – and doctoring of the union's books to give them access to work on docks in other states, providing alibis if police came asking questions, giving workers the ability to work under another name if they'd just been released from prison, and for a few, the chance to work under a false name while on the run from police or other thugs.

In South Australia, the membership had dropped from around 200 in 1975 to twenty-five by 1980 – the closure of shipbuilding was the cause – and Costigan found that extortion was rife with some unionists 'extorting' employers for pay whether they worked or not.

Queensland was a favourite place for displaced Victorian dock workers with its pleasant climate, and in those pre-Fitzgerald days, certain members of a government and police force that were accepting of both their aberrant behaviour and envelopes of cash. Costigan found it was a fine place for dockers to keep off the radar and he described it as 'an escape route, which involved – from time to time – harbouring escapees in the union rooms'. Their route involved false identities, clothes, transport and work. The commission found social security rorts involving ninety-eight dockers.

Costigan's commission finished in November 1984, and the union stumbled along in name only until being de-registered in 1993 because of legislation by the Hawke government that required at least 1000 members for registration.

While Costigan's commission had moved from its original brief on the Painters and Dockers, it put the final nail in the coffin of a union that contemporary maritime technology and offshore shipbuilding and repair had made pretty much redundant. But with crime, there is always an opportunity, and the nature of criminals doesn't allow a vacuum when there's money to be made.

31
DEMISE OF THE DINOSAURS

Costigan had exposed criminal enterprises, organisations and opportunities on the waterfront, but not a great deal happened – the scalps could be shown, the dockers were a spent force – the core problem of the waterfront's vulnerability to crime wasn't on the agenda. Likewise, the crooks that'd been part of the problem were used to a lifestyle that had to be maintained.

Brian Murphy, the hard man of the Victorian CIB who'd investigated plenty of docker crime over the years, and had also been close to quite a few dockers, said of their post-Costigan career progression, 'they've already been credited with violence with the painters and dockers when they were young and they had that name and they've gone from there into the drug scene, a lot of them'. Some, like Flannery, headed to Sydney where a magnificently corrupt core of detectives were reaping in the profits from organising crime and drugs in particular. Like Melbourne in the decade before Costigan, Sydney had become the wild west of crime, while the southern capital was relatively quiet – at least it seemed that way.

The early 1980s were a strange time – the politicians, the judiciary and police were under close scrutiny. Costigan, Woodward and Stewart's inquiries had put corruption on the front page, and the media, driven by publications like *The Bulletin* and *National Times,* had awakened from its torpor and was finally asking some questions rather than accepting what was fed through sources in policing and politics.

In 1984 *The Age* reported on illegal phone tapping by NSW Police that resulted in 'The Age tapes' in which High Court Judge Lionel Murphy was allegedly trying to 'pervert the course of justice' by attempting to influence the Chief Magistrate of NSW, Clarrie Briese. It wasn't the best choice of magistrate as Briese was not only honest, but had followed an old rogue, Murray Farquhar, into the top job and was trying to rebuild the sullied reputation of the lower courts. Around the same time, Farquhar was under investigation, along with NSW Premier Neville Wran, who had stepped aside while another royal commission examined his role in allegedly trying to influence a magistrate (Farquhar) who was hearing committal proceedings for a fraud allegedly committed by rugby league notable Kevin Humphreys. Rex Jackson, Wran's Corrective Services Minister, was also in strife following allegations he'd accepted bribes to secure an early release for some prisoners. Wran was exonerated and Farquhar and Jackson both ended up in prison.

Still in NSW, the police were on the front page for the wrong reason when Roger Rogerson shot drug dealer Warren Lanfranchi in June 1981. Rogerson said it was in self-defence.

In Melbourne, the dockers proved Brian Murphy correct and moved into drugs. Families like the Morans had such great success that Graham 'Munster' Kinniburgh, a Moran ally, moved from the traditional dockland suburbs to Kew – where Billy Hughes had lived.

Rolling along on top of all this national activity, the Queenslanders made their bid for infamy. Phil Dickie, a journalist from the *Courier-Mail,* investigated corruption in the police force and government, and took his investigation to the ABC's *Four Corners*. The result was Chris Masters' piece, 'Moonlight State'.

The show was aired on 11 May 1987, and so dazzling were the allegations that Bill Gunn, the deputy premier running the state while Sir Joh Bjelke-Petersen was running his Joh for Canberra campaign, commissioned Tony Fitzgerald, QC, to investigate. Joh never made it to Canberra as member of either Federal house, but a few of his colleagues did make it to prison.

One further addition to the mix of corruption, crooks, coppers and commissions was the arrival of the National Crime Authority in 1984 that had men like Abe Saffron, Karl Bonnette, 'Paddles' Anderson, Stan Smith and Robert Trimbole as primary targets. It was a rather odd list – Abe was all rumour but no evidence and was finally done in for tax issues after being given up by his former trusted lieutenant James McCartney Anderson, who'd literally got away with murder when he'd shot Donny 'The Glove' Smith outside the seedy Venus Room in Kings Cross in 1970. Though he'd shot Smith in the back, the charge of murder didn't proceed. Anderson later enjoyed a career as an NCA informant and his lavish, government-funded lifestyle prompted a Senate inquiry into the handling of informants. Bonnette continues to claim he was more of a bystander than a player and 'Paddles' keeled over from natural causes in 1985.

Stan was more intriguing. By the time the NCA arrived he'd almost retired from crime, a departure prompted by the death of Stan Jnr, and a brief stint in prison in Victoria for amphetamine possession. He'd had a hard time before the Woodward Royal Commission where his job as supervisor at Balmain Welding was described by the commissioner as 'his role in this enterprise was one of protection whereby his name and reputation could reasonably guarantee that drug transactions could be effected without interference or rip-offs'.

Balmain Welding was run by NSW ALP figures, and as Alfred McCoy wrote in 1980, in Labor's birthplace 'the criminal milieu has continued to dominate a number of local Labor Party branches through to the present day, giving elements of the

NSW Labor Party overtones of a corrupt and violent machine'. Though Stan's name was often used to put a scare into some, and he did keep in contact with men he'd known for decades, his criminal career was over. He became a Baptist lay preacher. As one old mate told me of Stan, 'I wasn't surprised when he got religion – even as a kid he was frightened of going to hell.'

Lennie McPherson's grip on his title of 'Mr Big' was slipping with the changing face of crime. Standover was still profitable, illegal gambling was on the decline thanks to the popularity of the TAB and the rumoured arrival of legal casinos – two events that were accompanied by yet another police crackdown – armed robbery was slipping out of fashion, and drugs were flavour of the month but not quite Lennie the traditionalist's cup of tea. In 1984, Sydney crooks started shooting at each other in what was played up as a gang war but, according to Labor power player Tom Domican, was a 'three page script' allegedly crafted by Rogerson and Lennie McPherson to give them control over Sydney's underworld. Mr Big and his consigliore. However, they were too late.

Lennie was a dinosaur; the old school were either dead, too old to change or, like Stan, had headed into legitimate business. For Lennie, old habits were hard to shake, and in 1994 he was convicted for his role in the beating of a rival in legitimate business – as Karl Bonnette observed, 'Lennie was a hands-on bloke'. He died in Cessnock prison on 30 September 1996 while serving his sentence. Justice Athol Moffitt – who'd formally bestowed the title of 'Mr Big' on him – outlived him by nine months.

Costigan's hopes to clean up the waterfront and make sure it didn't resume its role as finishing school, haven, and opportunity for criminals were substantially ignored.

With the docks now off the target list, enterprising criminals began to organise and seize the opportunity. To shift the drugs, they needed 'on side' players on the wharves plus transport infrastructure to move their goods. It was the birth of the current criminal problems that beset the nation. Gangs – with an ethnic basis or kindred spirits like the bikers – began to either network or insinuate people into the docks. Crane operators, cargo handlers, drivers, tally clerks, security and so on became sought after contacts.

Moving containers packaged with staples like heroin or weapons – Australia has long been a favoured transhipment place for weapons – was easy as there was a high volume of traffic and a low inspection rate so it was low risk. Problems only occurred if there'd been a tip-off, either in Australia or overseas, or if you were just out of luck and the container was opened for inspection.

As one detective from the Federal Police told me, 'Mate, it was open slather. A lot of coppers were "in the know", and kept us all clear.' He also observed the docks weren't the only place suffering from a lack of formal interest, planes loaded with heroin were island hopping their way to Australia, but waiting for Sunday to cross the northern coastline. He said, 'It's a joke – the crooks know the radar is turned off on Sundays. We can't afford the penalty rates!'

In the decades following Moffitt's commission, crime organised, but the men in sharp suits and Italian sounding names people had been worried about weren't at the heart of the problem. The new regime came in a variety of shapes, sizes, backgrounds and fragrance choices – but they all had one thing in common – a passion for the oceans of cash from drug trafficking.

32
SKULDUGGERY

Paul Houlihan of the National Farmers Federation (NFF) had been busy on the phone and over lunches with journalists, telling them something big was on the cards and to 'stay tuned'. It was early 1998, and Australia was just re-awakening after a summer of cricket, tennis, surfing and a good time. It was also the time when journalists were heading back to work and hungry for big stories.

The issue on the boil was the productivity on the waterfront – for a country that relied so heavily on its ports, Australia was falling behind the rest of the world. Prime Minister Bob Hawke had put the issue on the agenda in 1989 when his government formed the Waterfront Industry Reform Authority and it reported in 1993 'the Australian waterfront needed to change. It was known for high costs, poor performance, bad work and management practises, industrial strife and unreliability.' It also found the average age of the waterfront workforce had dropped from around fifty years old in 1989 to around forty-one by 1992 – suggesting a generational change.

The Productivity Commission in 1998 followed with a report that Australian ports had problems with co-ordinating the offloading from ships and transport from the docks, and that the speed of unloading was 'lower than overseas'. The Productivity Commission reported that in Hamburg the number of containers was around 1600 per employee per year, around 3000 in Singapore, and in Australia it was between 500 and 800. Sydney, the busiest port, was among the worst. With unloading running at an average eighteen containers per hour, the joke around businesses who relied on getting their products off the wharves was it sometimes took longer to unload than to make the sea journey to Australia.

After years of militancy, union bosses were being exposed by the media and government inquiries as fatter cats than some of their opposite numbers in the corporate world. With the introduction of workplace agreements, unionism was a bit on the nose, with the number of members in the workplace plummeting from around 50% in 1976 to around 28% in 1998, and it was still travelling south. One old wharfie recalled that when he joined in 1948 there were around 25,000 members and by the late 1980s when he retired it was down to around 6000.

As usual, pillaging from wharves and multi-million dollar illicit drug imports weren't on the agenda and hadn't been since Costigan had wrapped up his report. Law enforcement was playing the man not the ball by targeting specific criminals but not paying attention to their methodology. There isn't a photo opportunity for politicians and police in a system that dramatically increases vigilance, but a bloke in handcuffs with packages of powder gains plenty of media interest.

By 1998, the Painters and Dockers were history, but the WWF had grown to absorb other maritime unions and become the Maritime Union of Australia (MUA) – and it still had a stranglehold on the docks. Journalist Michael Duffy described them in the *Sydney Morning Herald* as 'the aristocracy of the working class'.

Paul Kelly in *March of the Patriots* wrote 'the MUA ran a closed shop that dictated poor waterfront productivity', and poor productivity came at a high price with the workers collecting an average yearly income in 1990 of $75,000 to $100,000 per year – more than many experienced police, nurses and teachers get in 2015. The old days of lousy conditions and miserable, erratic pay were ancient history. The old communities had largely dispersed, and places like Balmain and Williamstown were sought after places to live but the nature of the MUA's workplace meant the old ties remained strong. The members still socialised together with their families, holidayed together, drank together.

A few still lived in government-owned housing around Pyrmont and The Rocks, but most made the move toward the dream of the great quarter acre in the suburbs in the 1960s and '70s. A modern spacious home in a new suburb, with an onsite van or weekender near the beach, or a Gold Coast home unit was not uncommon. Wharfies had gone from dirt poor to quietly affluent in the space of a few decades, primarily because of their grip on the maritime sector and the unwillingness of either corporate Australia or the government to upset the nation's ability to export. As Kelly wrote, the union had 'sacrosanct status'. However, as one senior MUA member told me, 'Mate, we knew the good times weren't going to last. Trouble was, none of our top blokes wanted to acknowledge the fact.' Like Lennie McPherson, they were dinosaurs.

The recently arrived Howard Government and Chris Corrigan of Patrick Stevedoring, then the most powerful dockside company in the country, decided it was time to get some balance – there had never been 'balance' before so restoring it was impossible. Corrigan had been trying for reform and failing. He said in an unsourced interview, 'I assumed reasonable people would reach reasonable compromises', but by the time the Howard Government arrived in 1996, Corrigan knew that 'there was not a chance in hell that would happen without upheaval'. Peter Reith led the government on the issue, with support from the NFF to complete the trifecta. Their plan was for Patricks to lease

Melbourne's Webb Dock to a stevedoring company set up by the farmers and break the MUA's grip.

In late 1997, the new 'wharfies' had been recruited from former military personnel to train in Dubai on dock operations. As operations go it wasn't a great success. The MUA got wind of the scheme and threatened industrial action. The United Arab Emirates withdrew the visas for the men. On 28 January 1998, Patrick locked the MUA out of Webb Dock – game on, and Houlihan's promise of something big was fulfilled. The only problem was the union had been expecting a move as a member involved in a crane hire company had received a phone call a few days before asking about equipment for Webb Dock.

When the story broke, I was sent by Channel Nine's *Sunday* program to Melbourne and the next morning I did a preliminary interview with Greg Combet, then the ACTU's Assistant Secretary, at Trades Hall. Combet struck me as being deeply shaken over the events and in a quandary over what to do next. MUA National Secretary John Coombs declined a chat – no surprise given the escalating unpleasantness on the docks. Unionists were confronting the 'blacklegs', with reports of spitting on the men, and threats to their families along the lines of the old and very unpleasant 'we know where you live' threat. For an organisation that had prior knowledge of what might be coming, the union's preparation was as flawed as the other side.

In the cast of this epic was Australian businessman Richard Pratt's security consultant, Stephen Zagon. Zagon had been a lieutenant colonel in the Australian Army and liked to be referred to as 'The Colonel'. I'd known him for around a decade.

A chat with Zagon followed my meeting with Combet. As usual, the Porsche-driving colonel arrived in a light-coloured, immaculately pressed safari suit, his flowing white hair perfectly in place, twinkling eyes, tan, sparkling white teeth and bristling with bonhomie. The colonel was amazed at the developments on the docks, and though he didn't know much, offered to ask around his army and corporate connections to give me a hand. But I soon found that I'd been given the finger. Along with Stephen Webster, another Pratt consultant, Zagon had been a key player in Patrick's strategy.

The dispute dominated the news cycle, spurred on by industrial action by the MUA in Melbourne, Fremantle, Brisbane and Sydney. Scenes of picket lines, scuffles between picketing wharfies and security guards with slavering dogs, and riot police poised to intervene were made for television. Industrial action by the MUA, followed by the Australian Workers Union who threatened to close down oil refineries, was targeted to get Patrick to back down. They didn't.

On 7 April Patrick sacked its workforce of around 1400 permanent workers and 300 part-timers, and announced it would be outsourcing – thus breaking the hold the waterside union had enjoyed for decades. The following day, Reith proclaimed the government's support for Patrick, spurring on the picketers at ports around the nation. It was confrontation rather than diplomacy. In the ensuing fortnight, police and protesters clashed on the docks in Fremantle and Melbourne – though without the fatal outcome of clashes in the past.

Justice Beach, who'd presided over the inquiry into Victoria's Police, intervened on 20 April, when he granted Patrick an injunction that meant the entrance to the Melbourne docks could be cleared of protesters so the port could operate. That same day, the ACTU endorsed the picketers but declined to support strikes by other unions who wanted to show their solidarity. The following day, Justice North of the Federal Court ordered the reinstatement of Patrick's union workers, which like most decisions in tempestuous cases was immediately appealed and a stay granted. Meanwhile in Brisbane, the vigorous Queensland Police showed they hadn't learned greatly from history and arrested 186 dock workers, some of who had chained themselves to rail tracks. There wasn't a Member of Parliament among the arrested this time, and the charges against the wharfies were later dropped.

In an interview in *The Age* of 12 May 2007, Combet commented that 'I think what we really learn from the waterfront dispute is that a negotiated way of achieving change can work. It's been a far more sustainable outcome than trying to smash people.' The dispute divided the nation. A few days after it began a Bulletin-Morgan poll found 47% supported Patrick, and that support rose to 50% in the following week. On the picket lines, wharfies were joined by their families, friends and supporters.

Getting cargo into or out of the country was a major problem and neither side was backing down. Wharfies in Japan and South Africa had offered to strike in support of their Australian colleagues, adding some spice to the dispute, and the further problem of longer lead times to get products here when the dispute was over. Mass rallies and picket lines continued around the nation but, as with any protracted dispute, both sides were haemorrhaging cash – the only people profiting from the situation were their lawyers – which was pushing them closer to a solution.

The High Court gave both sides a hefty shove on 4 May when it upheld Justice North's decision to reinstate the union workers. Two days later, the wharfies had reclaimed their jobs. By the end of the month even the hardiest of picketers had gone home. Over the next few months, the docks returned to 'normal' and on 5 September the MUA and Patrick reached a deal. Helena Trinca and Anne Davies wrote in *Waterfront: The Battle that changed Australia* that 'the real loss however, was the union's day to day power on the dock'. Within two years, productivity had improved, with the wharfies shifting around twenty-five containers an hour.

When interviewed by the *Sydney Morning Herald* in May 2007, Chris Corrigan said of the outcome of the dispute that 'Productivity per man was approximately five times higher than the mid-90s. We have successfully negotiated three new agreements in those nine years without disputation and on each occasion efficiency has been improved.' Tom Bramble in *War on the Waterfront* in 1998 observed that in the deal between Patrick and the MUA, the union 'signed away nearly fifty percent of the permanent Patrick's workforce.' He went on to say, 'the deal is also a setback for union power on the waterfront. Alongside further casualisation, the MUA agreed to management control over the allocation of workers.'

Trinca and Davies' book was aptly named – but for other reasons that had little to do with industrial relations. The breaking of the union's grip on the waterfront opened up the opportunity for other non-traditional criminal organisations to build a presence – capitalising on existing relationships, and building their own small, close-knit communities of waterfront workers. Some of the names and backgrounds reflected the multiculturalism of modern Australia but the purpose was still the same. These new people skipped the development phase of decades of hard work and misery, and were intent on the main prize – guaranteeing a large, low risk and consistent supply of drugs and precursor chemicals.

33
SOME THINGS CHANGE, SOME REMAIN THE SAME

Michael Hurley – called Mikel by most – was one of the last and probably one of the most successful crooks to emerge from the traditional Australian waterfront. He grew up in a housing commission flat in Pyrmont – just a stumble, via the numerous waterfront pubs now lost to gentrification, from the wharves where his forebears had worked. While he could have laid claim to the title of Mr Big of drug trafficking, Hurley was a man liked by everyone he'd come to know on both sides of the law.

He was born in Pyrmont in 1945, into a family of eight children. His first venture into crime was allegedly as a poultry thief – stealing chickens from the chook runs that were a feature in many homes back in the 1950s and selling them to his cash-strapped neighbours for eggs and the table. He got a basic education and left school at fourteen and went to work at the Swift and Moore distillery putting labels on bottles. At eighteen he was working on the waterfront.

Hurley had an agile mind, the ability to 'read' people, an eye for an opportunity and a healthy disregard for the law, and so when he was old enough to drink in hotels, he put those talents to work and became an SP bookmaker. Working men of the time loved a 'punt' and in those pre-TAB days, an SP or someone connected to an SP could be found lounging over a beer and the form guide in most pubs around the country. The profits were good, the risk was low, and blokes like Hurley always made sure their clients didn't overextend. One 'colourful' chap who knew him, and who ran casinos around the city told me, 'We'd take the bloke's money on payday – they knew it and we knew it. If he was pissed, then we'd put him in a taxi to get him home and give him enough dough to get breakfast when he sobered up. If the bloke had a family, you'd give him a loan to make sure they had food for the week. If he was a real dill, then we'd slip past and give his missus the cash direct. Good for them, and good for return business.'

Hurley was involved in other traditional businesses like shoplifting, break and enter, and masterminding robberies on the waterfront – products rather than payrolls – before moving into drug trafficking. In a busy career, he'd spent time in prison for stealing and later for break and enter, but had avoided conviction for possessing a forged passport and for his alleged role in the 1980 theft of the diamond Golconda d'Or, stolen in broad daylight from its glass display case in the Sydney Town Hall.

Police sources described Hurley as 'a leading figure in NSW organised crime'. Unlike his predecessors, Hurley preferred charm to leg breaking, and was old school with his refusal to be an informant. For him, the cat and mouse game with law enforcement was part of the fun. He stayed in Pyrmont and one of his vices, which singled him out from a crowd of ordinary-looking middle-aged working males, was a taste for fine clothing. One Sydney importer of expensive menswear said of him, 'I'd met him through mates in the business – he often popped by a client's store to pick up a few things, and to use their phone. We had lunch a few times and he was always great company – funny, genuine and oh the stories he'd tell. I didn't know he was a crook until I read it in the paper. I had wondered why he didn't use a mobile phone.'

The immaculate Mr Hurley is a shining example of the change in criminals with waterfront links. When asked about what he did for a living he'd either call himself a 'wharfie' or his favourite line 'just a garbage collector'. On the money he spent on clothing or his chic waterfront apartment in Refinery Drive, Pyrmont – just a short walk from his childhood home – if anyone asked him where his wealth came from he claimed to have 'won the lottery twice'. The truth was Hurley was a superb networker who brokered deals with criminal cartels in Southeast Asia to bring in amphetamines – in one instance thirty-four kilograms of ecstasy – and with the Mexican cocaine cartels who now supply around 85% of the drug.

His last big deal brought together the old wharfie and his colleagues, corrupt baggage handlers at Sydney Airport, and the Bandidos outlaw biker gang. The major outlaw biker gangs in Australia – the homegrown Rebels and Comancheros and the US imports the Hells Angels, Bandidos and very recently the Mongols have long-term involvement in the global and local drug trade. The Australian Crime Commission describes them as 'one of the most high profile manifestations of organised crime' with an 'increasing prevalence of international connections'. They also have strong links to the waterfront, with members and associates working on the docks and in transport companies with access to the waterfront. In January 2015, law enforcement belatedly acknowledged the depth of the problem with Customs' Roman Quaedvlieg telling the *Herald Sun* 'the insider threat is real'.

Hurley and his gang's downfall wasn't thanks to brilliant investigation or heightened awareness, but a confidential informant to the NSW Crime Commission who reported to the now imprisoned drug-dealing copper Mark Standen. Hurley and his mates Les Mara, a former first grade league player, and Shayne Hatfield, a former professional surfer from Bondi, were doing a brisk business in cocaine. The product arrived on commercial flights, but didn't make it to the carousel to be collected and walked through – too much risk for too little. Instead, bent baggage handlers would remove the bags that had been tagged by the syndicate, unpack them and remove the cocaine before any Customs inspection, and walk the drugs to their cars. Another variation – for added security – was the handler would drop the package into a garbage bin, and it would be removed by another bent employee and then walked out of the airport.

The cocaine then went to the late Rodney Monk and the late Russell Oldham of the Bandidos to supply their thriving inner city network of dealers and snorters. It was delivered either discreetly packed in with the take-away pizza; handed over while sipping a cocktail in the living room; or sold on the floor of the nightclubs. In major Australian cities getting amphetamines or cocaine is as challenging as getting a litre of milk. Between June 2004 and May 2005, police estimated Hurley and his crew had imported 200 kilograms, which when 'stamped on' [diluted with other substances prior to sale] by the dealers in the chain sold for around A$400 per gram, with adjustments for low and peak seasons – or volume.

In December 2004, 'Tom', who arranged the financing for some of the deals, and was allegedly one of the baggage handlers, became an informant. He told police he'd 'had a gutful of my involvement with one particular person' in the operation and decided to blow the whistle – a decision stimulated by allegedly being caught in a drug deal. He knew Standen was leading the investigation into Hurley's band – which suggests a number of reasons, one of which was someone at the Crime Commission was leaking to the bad guys – and approached Standen offering inside information. Five months later, the police swooped on Hurley's syndicate.

In late April 2005, they intercepted calls from Hurley in which he said he thought there might be a 'rollover' in the syndicate.

Tension went up a few notches when some of the members found their homes were bugged. The operation against Hurley was in peril of falling apart. On 4 May, Hurley confronted 'Tom' and demanded to know if he was working with the police – he denied it, but it prompted the police to act. Five days later, in synchronised raids across Sydney, they arrested thirteen people including Shayne Hatfield, but not Hurley or Mara who'd gone into hiding after allegedly getting a tip-off.

The shipment the men had been planning had a street value of $24 million, from which the syndicate made a little over $4 million – all for an outlay of around $100,000 in South America.

Hurley and Mara were the subjects of a global search, with Mara believed to be lurking in Rio de Janeiro, but in February 2006, Hurley was arrested in Glebe – a little over a kilometre from his home, and Mara in Callala Bay on the NSW south coast at the end of November 2006. Hurley died in prison from cancer in January 2007.

In Hurley's place, and building on generations of crooks on the waterfront, were what the Australian Crime Commission said are the 'range of people with access to information, infrastructure, government services, knowledge of institutional weakness or access to specialist skills. These individuals or groups are referred to [by the Commission] as facilitators or trusted insiders.' The commission also noted that the maritime and aviation sectors 'are the key link to the international illicit economy'. It wasn't news. With organised crime revenues estimated at around $15 billion per year – with drugs the biggest money-spinner – the market is too compelling.

The strength of the Australian market was shown in recent years by the arrival in the market of the Canadians. While the nation has a reputation for being polite and good natured it's also been deeply involved, particularly through its outlaw bikers and Mafia, in drug trafficking. Commenting on the Canadian arrival, the Australian Federal Police said in an August 2014 statement that, 'even though it may be logistically complex to get illicit drugs to Australia traffickers feel the expense is worth it because of the high prices they can obtain if successful'. That price is usually around five times that of Canada. The Australian Crime Commission around this time acknowledged that the Canadian drug traffickers have 'significant connections' with Australian outlaw bikers and other criminal organisations. One Canadian police source of mine told me, 'You guys have a great market for drugs. The guys here have the connections to get things like cocaine and ice, and the bikers in particular are the world's best logistics managers. Get it across your border and their contacts downunder have got the networks going back years. It's easy, pretty low risk and profitable.'

The facilitators and trusted insiders haven't changed much from the black market days of World War II. They're family members or friends of people working in the nation's docklands and with connections to crime syndicates; or people who get an offer they can't refuse, usually in large bundles of cash. They hold the appropriate maritime security card which gives them access to most of the docks – the background check is cursory.

A prime example of how this operates is the cocaine trade that has been expanding since the 'greed is good' days of the late 1980s. While Australians' passion for the stuff is world beating, the profits are equally stunning. A kilogram from Colombia is worth around US$2500. When it arrives in Australia, you add a zero. Once it is cut and bagged for distribution that same kilogram is worth up to $1 million. Mexico's virulent Sinaloa Cartel are the leading supplier in Australia with an estimated 85% share. A source in the US Drug Enforcement Agency confirmed that fees of up to $500,000 were paid to pilots to fly 500-kilogram shipments to Australia. So brazen are the cartel that they agreed to replace any shipment intercepted at no cost to the Australian buyers – probably a first in the drug business where there is no such thing as a warranty. Preferred landing places are small airports without Customs officials. Albion Park near Wollongong was the scene of one recent successful seizure operation, but as a source told me, 'little places like Wedderburn [in southwest Sydney] are perfect – you're in, unload, refuel and get in the air before anyone really notices'. To add to the problem, sources in Mexico believe that 70 to 80% of all the various cartels' exports go by sea – Australia with its porous border and passion for drug use is seen as an important market.

The cartel's primary distributors are alleged to be the outlaw motorcycle gangs and their networks that have been humming since the 1980s. The cartel has also branched out and joined the Asian warlords in the amphetamine business. It may be a coincidence that the arrival of the Mongols – the biker gang who are the most dangerous and violent in the United States according to the Bureau of Alcohol Firearms and Tobacco – arrived in Australia around the time the cartel was becoming the supplier of choice. The two have a long history of successful operations in the US, particularly in California.

The waterfront remains the easiest and lowest risk way to import drugs – no precarious flights across the ocean or an unwelcoming welcoming committee when you land. Around seven million twenty-foot shipping containers pass through the docks every year – with 102,288 inspected and 14,788 examined in 2013–2014. Technology to prevent accessing them on the docks – to remove drugs or other contraband – is about as useful as the wire recommended back in the 1920s. One source told me that as soon as the new technology to prevent containers being opened had arrived, his band of crooks had devised technology to beat it. They can crack the container open, get their product, and reseal it without the authorities having a clue.

At the time of writing, the prime minister has just announced a task force, this one to focus on the use of crystal methamphetamine 'ice'. The action has been a long time coming, and just like the failure of law enforcement leaders and their political masters to deal with the arrival and spread of heroin in the 1970s and 1980s, their actions are too little too late. In 2010, 22% of amphetamine users admitted that 'ice' was their preferred form of the drug. Three years later that figure has jumped to 50.4%. It's a drug that infects rural Australia as well as our cities, and it doesn't respect age or social standing. While some is made here, most of it is imported, particularly from Southeast Asia. We haven't learned from our experiences with heroin a couple of decades ago. We've invested more time, effort and money in stopping boats full of people rather than gathering intelligence on, and penetrating the organised crime syndicates bringing in drugs like ice – labelled by the prime minister when announcing the task force as 'a dreadful scourge' and going on to state that 'massive quantities of this pernicious and evil drug are coming into our country all the time'.

EPILOGUE

In 2009, Australia's law enforcement leaders were finally realising that there was a very serious problem on the waterfront. It wasn't rocket science, but it wasn't on the front page either so those who control the budgets weren't all that interested – operational police usually don't get a say in such matters.

A Chinese drug syndicate in Queensland had been found to be recruiting on the waterfront and a little bit of probing found the outlaw bikers were doing the same thing. The bikers added to their woes by escalating their inter-gang wars over drug turf and put themselves firmly in the public gaze with the March 2009 melee at Sydney airport. Finally, police took notice. Their report revealed organised crime had infiltrated ports on the east coast and it was likely they were using their influence to smuggle drugs and weapons. While it was close to stating the obvious, it did stimulate the politicians. The government announced a task force, and the Opposition claimed the problem was the government's fault – blithely ignoring decades of bipartisan failure.

Paddy Crumlin, the head of the MUA, stepped in to defend his members and claimed the task force shouldn't just target Australia workers, but should also have a look at 'foreign seafarers and cover container parks and all areas in the freight-forwarding industry'. The latter part was a fair call as it was highly likely that some product could slip through the docks without need of workers' intervention, and be collected from the container storage yards. Crumlin had a crack at rewriting history and said in a media statement on 27 July 2010 that the 'Costigan Commission most notably, found that criminality on the wharves was largely white-collar controlled and executed rather than pointing to wharfies and seafarers', which was half clever as he omitted the terms 'painters and dockers'. But there was a slight credibility problem when Dean Summers, the MUA organiser looking after security issues, commented in the *Sun-Herald* on 9 September 2012, 'it's ridiculous. This bagging, this trying to suggest we're all crooks and gangsters and, in the past, terrorists, just doesn't wash. The wharves are largely a sterile environment. It's boxes moving across the tarmac. To suggest it's a dark and dingy festering den of criminality is just off the page.' His comment came shortly after the arrest of four Sydney waterfront workers, a former wharfie and two men who police believed had dockland connections on drug charges in four unrelated cases.

Since then, politicians have regularly banged on about crushing the well-entrenched drug syndicates; improving co-operation and communication between law enforcement bodies; beefing up laws; increasing funding and so on. Unquestioning media outlets give the political spin doctors space for their press releases and media opportunities and then move on.

To give law enforcement credit, there has been some terrific recent work that showed both co-operation internationally, nationally and locally – if only we'd started decades ago.

In 2013, legislation changes brought in new offences for the use of 'restricted information; the ability to suspend a worker's maritime security card if they're charged with a serious crime'; and 'new obligations on cargo terminal operators and cargo handling companies including the reporting of unlawful activity and to check that their employees were fit and proper persons'.

The following year, the government announced $88 million to add eight more intelligence officers and improve cargo screening. Another boost of around 1500 more container inspections is the target. While it's a step in the right direction – it's a small one. It's thirty years since Costigan exposed the criminal antics of the Painters and Dockers, and a serious look at the problems on the waterfront and how best to combat them hasn't been done since the 1920s.

In 2012 the Australian Research Council Centre of Excellence in Policing and Security reported one issue in dealing with crime on the waterfront was the relationship between government and the 'industry stakeholders'. They noted 'many government authorities on Melbourne's waterfront reported having somewhat problematic engagement with their industry counterparts', and 'not being content with the level of commitment of industry stakeholders appeared to hold towards securing their facilities/workplaces or complying with reporting requirements'. On the flip side the industry 'encountered substantial difficulties when it came to broaching public/private partnerships, perceiving their ties to be strained and problematic'. Trust between both parties, 'was generally perceived to be quite weak'.

Australia faces a couple of major problems. The Australian Crime Commission reported that organised crime on the waterfront was 'helped by a small number of criminally influenced individuals employed in the legitimate workforce'. These 'trusted insiders share information with external criminal groups'.

Detective Superintendent Gary Ryan of Victoria Police had a more depressing view when he said in late 2013 that around 90% of the state's leading criminals had ties to the wharves – a figure that not only reflects the depth of the penetration but also the diversity of criminals on the waterfront, with mobs like the survivors of the 1990s gang war, outlaw bikers, Southeast Asia and Middle East influenced gangs and the recruits they're targeting in the Sudanese and Somali communities.

A year later police arrested members of a gang who were importing thirty kilograms of 'ice' through the Melbourne docks. The 'ice' was believed to have been manufactured in the USA and shipped to Australia via China by a gang that included Albanians and a Spaniard, and had, according to police, 'flown under the radar for years'. It's a story that can be repeated with only a change of cast and setting.

The biggest issue is that, as Justice Lukin observed in the 1920s, 'crime is rife' – and we're applying band-aid solutions to a haemorrhage caused by years of neglect, corruption and the insatiable demand for products we're not allowed to have. The risk to criminals remains low and the profit is extraordinarily high. Over two centuries since the first crooks arrived on the waterfront it remains our greatest and most vulnerable asset. To draw even with the crooks is as the unnamed expert of the 1950s said, like 'trying to put out a bushfire with a child's seaside bucket'.

A NOTE ON SOURCES

With most of my books, sources start with memories of conversations had and stories told by family members – helped by growing up in a slightly eccentric multi-generational family home – and friends and colleagues who've led long and intriguing lives. The two combine to provide motive, opportunities and the beginning of an investigation into the subject. And then you start to dig.

Working on a book that spans Australia's European settlement means your dig is more diverse than usual and begins with some book buying – Margo Beasley's *Wharfies* was a fine resource. And then the contemporary writer's new best friend, Google, and libraries and archives both in Australia and the United Kingdom – the number of documents that have survived never ceases to astound me. Online collections are terrific but there is a great pleasure in thumbing through the pages – or maybe I'm just a bit old-fashioned.

My research physically took me to the state libraries in Brisbane, Melbourne, Sydney, the National Library of Australia and the Australian War Memorial in Canberra and the British Library and National Archive in London. The early days of Australia were great fun to hunt through – a time when people documented their days and their adventures and libraries inherited them. It also provided fantastic source material for many of the books I later used, with Herbert Evatt's *Rum Rebellion* a standout – an informative and entertaining read. Unfortunately, the diarists dwindled as the nation became more established. I wonder if social media may be a replacement?

For any writer not dealing with today, the National Library of Australia's online Trove is remarkable. When you're hunting around subjects like crime and politics, seeing a contemporaneous report rather than a view filtered by other writers over decades is both handy for accuracy and an insight into the time. One of my favourites was the writings of Hugh Buggy on crime in

Sydney and Melbourne during the 1920s and 1930s. His prose was purple, lurid and compelling – the sort of writer who could put his arm around your shoulder and take you with him into the crime scene.

One of the sad things about writing about the waterfront is that so few first-hand accounts of life in that community exist – which I guess attests to the lack of opportunities they had and the sheer grind of their days. Unlike the diarists of the early days of the colony there wasn't much adventure or variety to be had, or to warrant writing about. My great finds in the library were the works of unionists and writers like Rupert Lockwood, who interviewed community members and committed the results to print.

Crooks are a rather different breed. While it's become fashionable for ne'er-do-wells to have a carefully written book about their exploits, the truth often becomes a victim. Old-style crooks are much quieter – unless they're sitting around bragging with their fellow crooks, or talking to someone who comes with the right introductions – something I'm fortunate to have. They tell wonderful stories, but even then they're circumspect on a few details! Old coppers are a little more talkative and it's intriguing to find that often the old crooks and their nemesis catch up regularly for long lunches – policing in Australia has long been one of blurred lines.

Throughout the book there is reference to both metric and imperial measures, and pounds and dollars – I've done a conversion for some to give a sense of the amounts.

Prologue
Australian Crime Commission Illicit Drug Report 2010/2011

Chapter 1
John Howard, *State of the Prisons in England and Wales*, 1777.
Memoirs of the First Thirty-Two Years of the Life of James Hardy Vaux, A Swindler and Pickpocket; Now Transported for a Second Time, and For Life by James Hardy Vaux published 1819.
Horrors of Transportation by William Ullathorne, 1837
Account of the English Colony in New South Wales by David Collins, 1798

Chapter 2
Journal and Letters of Lieutenant Ralph Clark
Rum Rebellion by Herbert Evatt, 1938
Early Australian History by Charles White, 1889

Chapter 3
Notes on the sealing industry in early Australia by J.C.H. Gill, 1967
Biography of Sydney: a city by Lucy Turnbull, 1999
Studies in Scottish Business History by Peter Payne

Chapter 4
New York Times
The Sydney Gazette

A chronological account of crime, public order and police in Sydney by Bruce Swanton, 1983

Chapter 5
State Library of NSW, *1808, Bligh's Sydney Rebellion*
Australian Dictionary of Biography
The Coming of the Strangers: Life in Australia 1788–1822 by Baiba Berzins, 1988

Chapter 6
Thomas Bigge reports to the UK Government, 1822–23
A Colonial Autocracy by Marion Phillips, 1909
A Peaceful Army by Dymphna Cusack and Flora Eldershaw, 1938

Chapter 7
Police in Victoria, 1836–1980 by Victoria Police Management Services Bureau
Chronicles of Early Melbourne, 'Garryowen', by Edmund Finn, 1888
Picture of Sydney by James Maclehose, 1839
Chronicle of Port Phillip from 1770 to 1840 by Henry Gurner, 1876

Chapter 8
Boom – the underground history of Australia by Malcolm Knox, 2013
Sojourners by Eric Rolls, 1992
Rush to be Rich by Geoffrey Serle, 1974

Chapter 9
A History of Australia by Marjorie Barnard, 1962
Opportunity and Exile by Marjorie Harper, University of Aberdeen, unknown date.
My Union Right or Wrong, Issy Wyner, 2003
Emigration and the labouring poor by Robin F. Haine, 1997

Chapter 10
Pall Mall Gazette
Gangland Sydney by James Morton and Susanna Lobez, 2011
Peeps into gaols, police courts and opium dens by Charles Woodward, 1933

Chapter 11
The Origins of the ALP – A Marxist Analysis by Jim McIlroy, 2004
They Called Him Billy, by Frank C. Browne, 1946

Chapter 12
Lords of the Ring by Peter Corris, 1980
Wharfies by Margo Beasley, 1997

Chapter 13
W. M. Hughes and the Waterside Workers by L. F. Fitzhardinge, 1957
The Hungry Mile by Tom Nelson, 1957
In Search of Billy Hughes by Donald Horne, 1979

'Bubonic plague comes to Sydney', University of Sydney Medical School
Plague in Sydney by Peter Curson and Kevin McCracken, 1989
Living in Cities edited by I. Burnley and J. Forrest, 1985

Chapter 14
The World After The War by Isaac Marcosson, 1916
Brief History of the Australian Waterfront and Waterside Workers by Jim Healy – undated
Australia's Prime Ministers – National Archive
Australian War Memorial WW1 Collection.

Chapter 15
Australian Dictionary of Biography

Chapter 16
The Australian Century by Robert Manne, 1999
Untitled documents, State Library of NSW
University of Sydney Medical School – The Flu Pandemic – undated

Chapter 17
Report of Royal Commission into Industrial Troubles on Melbourne Wharves (Dethridge)
Report of Royal Commission into the Evil of Cargo Pillaging (Macfarlane)

Chapter 18
Darkest Sydney by S. D. Yarrington, 1914
Australian Journal of Pharmacy – date not known

Chapter 19
Razor by Larry Writer, 2011
Shotgun and Standover by James Morton and Russell Robinson, 2010
Gangland Sydney by James Morton and Susanna Lobez, 2011

Chapter 20
Wharfies by Margo Beasley, 1997
Meet the Ship Painters and Dockers by Lew Hillier, 1981
The Hungry Mile by Tom Nelson, 1957
NSW Police News – various

Chapter 21
Tough men – Hard times – Policing in the depression, Historic Houses Trust, 2007
Restless Waterfront by James Gaby, 1974

Chapter 22
Australia's War 1939–1945 edited by Joan Beaumont, 1996
Report of the Stevedoring Industry Commission (Foster)
Profits over Patriotism by Timothy Blum, 2011

A NOTE ON SOURCES • 329

Chapter 23
Ship to Shore by Rupert Lockwood, 1991
Judges in Industry by Mark Perlman, 1954
Various collections, Australian War Memorial

Chapter 24
Australia in the War 1939–1945 by Paul Hasluck, 1952–57
Lives of Crime: Melbourne Gangland Murders and other Tales of True Crime by Gary Tippet & Ian Munro, 2008
The Case for the Waterside Worker by Tom Nelson (date not specified)

Chapter 25
Mr Big by Tony Reeve, 2007
George Freeman: An Autobiography, 1988
Catch Me if you Can by Darcy Dugan, 1992

Chapter 26
Waterfront Revolts by Colin Davis, 2003
The Story of Jim Healy by Rupert Lockwood, 1951

Chapter 27
The Box by Mark Levinson, 2007

Chapter 28
In your Face by Rochelle Jackson, 2005

Chapter 29
Narcotics and Organised Crime in Australia by Alfred McCoy, 1980

Chapter 30
Report of the Royal Commission of Inquiry in respect of certain matters relating to allegations of organised crime in clubs (Moffitt)
Report of the Royal Commission into Drug Trafficking (Woodward)
Royal Commission of Inquiry into Drugs (Williams)
Report of the Royal Commission into the Federated Ship Painters and Dockers (Costigan)

Chapter 31
Outlaw Bikers in Australia by Duncan McNab, 2013

Chapter 32
The Battle that Changed Australia by Helen Trinca and Anne Davies, 2000

Chapter 33
Snapshot of crime prevention partnerships on Australian and American Waterfront, Russell Brewer, Australian Centre of Excellence in Policing and Security, 2012

Epilogue
Australian Crime Commission, 'Organised Crime'
www.crimecommission.gov.au

ACKNOWLEDGEMENTS

This is book number eight and none of them would have happened without the guidance, support (which includes application of wine as required), and sheer common sense of my agent, Lyn Tranter. Writing is a rather odd business and a fine agent is as necessary as a laptop . . . or typewriter.

My thanks also to the editors from Hachette who take my occasional segues into gibberish and turn them into something cohesive, package it up beautifully and take it to print. Without them I'd still be labouring over grammar and use of the apostrophe (thus neatly avoid using one of the damn things . . . I hope).

Gathering such large swag of information is made much easier by the great libraries of Australia and the National Library of Australia's Trove – like any story, history can change dramatically with the retelling, and access to the contemporaneous reports in Trove give a writer both accuracy and a glimpse of the time. It was terrific when researching Sydney mid century to read the stories written by Hugh Buggy – lurid, saucy, and in a rollicking style. Finally, I'm as usual in the debt of the band of old friends, new friends and sources who give a marvellous insight into our recent history.

While not quite a note of thanks, I should mention the rather large number of more formal bodies involved in the waterfront, such as the AFP, ACC, NSW Police and Customs – who drew my attention to various reports but declined to chat further. In prior books I've complained about the poor communication between Australia's law enforcement bodies but it seems to have improved – at least in one instance.

INDEX

A
Abbott, Cec 280
Abbott, Tony 319–320
ABC *Four Corners* 302–303
Aboriginal people 9–10, 15, 63, 138
abortions 234–235
abortion rackets 281, 286
Adams, Phillip 298
Adelaide 86
AE1 145
Afghanistan 103
Albion Park 319
Allan, Dawn 243, 250
Allan, Norm 283
Amalgamated Shearers Union 95–96
Amalgamated Society of Engineers 79, 88
Amalgamated Stevedores Union 93
American Revolutionary War 1, 73
amphetamine ix, 279, 315, 316, 319–320, 324
Anderson, Blanche 248
Anderson, Frederick 'Paddles' 284, 303
Anderson, James McCartney 303
Antony, Ernest 207–208
Argentina 109
Argo (ship) 26
Argyle Cut Push 112
armed robbery 279
Asian immigrants 133–134

Askin, Bob 265, 283
Associated Chambers of Commerce 170–171
Atkins, Richard 32–33, 37–38, 39
Aubrey, Father 125
austerity drive 225–226
Australia, HMAS 145
Australian Agricultural Company 57
Australian Army 256
Australian Council of Trade Unions 215, 257, 295, 309, 310
Australian Crime Commission viii, 290, 315–317, 323
Australian Federal Police 159, 317–318
Australian Labor Party ix, 122, 254
   1893 conference 108
   1916 split 154–155
   1954 split 256
   caucus 107–108
   first federal parliament 141–143
   as Labour Electoral League of New South Wales 100–101, 105–107
   trade unions relationship 135
Australian Naval and Military Expeditionary Force 145
Australian Research Council Centre of Excellence in Policing and Security 323
Australian Steamship Owners Federation 139–140

Australian Workers Union 123–124, 150, 310

B
B, George (strike-breaker) 157–158
baccarat 234
baggage handlers 316–317
Baldwin, Clifford 197
Baldwin, Joseph 197–198
Ballarat 70–71
Ballard, Detective Sergeant Brian 284
Bally poker machines 281–282, 283, 284
Balmain, Sydney 66, 83–85, 88, 104, 241
Balmain, William 66
Balmain Labourers Union 83, 101, 126
Balmain Welding 303
Balmain Workers Union 91
Bamford, F. W. 135
Bandidos 315, 316
Bangkok Hilton 291
Bank of Australia 111
Bank of England 109
Bank of New South Wales 55
Banks, Joseph 2–3, 28, 34
Bannon, M. J. 180
Barbaross family 198–199
Baring, Sir Francis 19–20
Barings Bank 109, 110
Barker, Tom 149–150
Barrett, Thomas 11–12
Barton, Edmund 133
Batman, John 60, 62–64
Battle for Kushka 103
Battle of Pozières 152
Battle of the Somme 152, 157
Baudin, Nicolas 62
Bayer 175–176
Bazley, James Frederick 288–289
Beach, Barry, QC 286
Beach, Justice 310
bed bugs 140
Beeby, Justice George 195–196, 198, 218
Beeby Award strike 1928 196–202
Beggs, Jim 269–270, 271
Bendigo electorate 155
Bengal 172
Bennett, Raymond 293–294
Berrima, HMAT 145
Bertram, Captain 5
Besley, A. 287

BHP 215
Bigge, John Thomas 58–59
Bird, Sarah 47
Birt, Colonel 89
'Bishop's Court,' Darling Point 84–85
Bjelke-Petersen, Sir Joh 303
black 198
Black, George 106, 107
Black, Jim 285
black market 228–234
Blacket, Edmund 84–85
blacklegs 92, 309
blacklisting 98
Blackmarket Act 1942 235
Blamey, Thomas 200
Blanch, Constable 187
Bland, Henry 256
Blaxcell, Garnham 48
Bligh, William
  Campbell and 35–36, 55
  films about mutiny 30–31
  as governor 31–34, 44–45
  Macarthur and 36–42
  port regulations 37
Blisset, Ray 230–231, 232
Bloody Sunday, Fremantle 161
Bloomberg, Joe 252–253
Blue Mountains 17, 128
boat building 21–22
Bobbs, Cecil 238
Boer War 138–139
Bolte, Sir Henry 286
bombing campaign 198–199, 201–202
Bonnette, Karl 284, 285, 303
Boorara, HMAT 144
border protection 278–279
Border Security: Australia's Frontline viii
Bounty, HMS 30–31
Bourke, Governor Richard 57, 60, 63
Bowen 254, 256
Bowker, Shirley 266
Boyd, Constable 148
Boyd, J. A. 170
Bradley, Lieutenant William 9
Bradshaw, Norman 237
Brando, Marlon 31
Briese, Clarrie 302
Brisbane, Sir Thomas 59
Brisbane Wharf Labourers Union 94
Brisbane wharves vii, 86
Britain
  Australian cargo pillaging 171
  Australian penal colony 1–6, 17
  Boer War 138–139

cocaine use 191
dock workers 89–90
Great London Dock Strike 1889 91–95, 97
Kangaroo Gang 275–276
Opium Wars 172–173
Pacific War 216–217
ten pound poms 78
trade with Australia 147
World War I 142–143, 151
Britannia (ship) 19–20, 22
brothels 177, 178, 234, 283
Brotherton, Cecil 148
Brown, Arthur 207
Brown, John 204
Brown, Leslie 'Lair' 238
Brown, Malcolm 241
Brown, Norman 209
Browne, Frank C. 102
Bruce, Stanley 196, 204–205
Bruhn, Irene 185
Bruhn, Norm 182, 183–189
Brunel, Isambard Kingdom 73
Bryant and May 91–92
bubonic plague 127–132, 136–138
Buggy, Hugh 185–187, 191
'bull' system 124, 195–196
Bunning, Walter 84
Burke, Edmund 3
Burn, John 94–95

C
Caesar, John Black 14–15
Caines, Mr 178–179
Calabrian Mafia 288
California Gold Rush 69
Callan Park 195
Camden, Lord 25–26
Cameron, Nellie 185
Campbell, Clarke & Co. 23
Campbell, Eric 210–212
Campbell, Robert
 career in New South Wales 23–29, 35–36, 42, 47
 Harrington 43–44
 Macquarie and 55–56
Camperdown, Sydney 32
Canada 191, 317–318
cannabis growing 288–289
cargo pillaging vii, 162–171, 180, 223–224, 228–232, 236, 262, 269–270, 288
Caroline Islands 145

Carter, Godrey 174
Carters & Drivers Union 198
casinos 304
Castlereagh, Viscount 44, 45
Catchpole, Margaret 54
Catholic Church 158–159
Central Police Station, Sydney 246
Chamings, Lawrence 275
Champion, Harry 93–94
chemists 175, 178–179
Chicago, USS 227
Chifley, Ben 253, 254
child sexual abuse 242
China 26
 Japanese aggression 214–215
 Opium Wars 172–173
 People's Republic formed 255
Chinese drug syndicates 321
Chinese heroin traffickers 291
Chinese immigrants 80–81, 133–134, 173–174
Christian, Fletcher 30, 31
Chubb, Daniel 290, 291–292
Churchill, Winston 216
Circular Quay wharves 97
Clark, Lieutenant Ralph 9, 10, 12
Clark, Manning 126
Clark, Terry 290
Clarke, Darryl 270–271
Clarke, William 68
Clarkson, A. E. 171
class war 209–210
Cleveland, Grover 110
clipper ships 73–74
closed shop 86–87, 256–257
coal discovery 24
Coal Lumpers Union, Melbourne 90, 96
coal miners 204
coal miners strike, Hunter Valley 208–209
Coal River 42
coal transport 82
coal workers 1948 strike 254
Cobb & Co 140, 146
coca leaf 176
cocaine 172, 176–181, 191
cocaine runners 185–187, 190
cocaine supply 316
cocaine syndicate 315–317
cocaine trafficking 318–319
Cockatoo Island Dock 82, 219, 243, 249
Cold War 217, 252, 259

Collins, David 5–6, 8, 10, 14, 15, 45, 62
Colonial Sugar Refinery 231, 261
Combet, Greg 309, 311
Commancheros 315
Commercial Bank of Australia 111, 274
Commercial Banking Company of Sydney 111
Commonwealth Bank, Ultimo 247–248
Commonwealth Court of Conciliation and Arbitration 162, 204–205
Commonwealth Investigation Service 159
Commonwealth Line 152
communist influence 252–258
Communist Party Dissolution Bill 255
Communist Party of Australia 208–210, 221
communist revolution 165
company unions 98, 123
competition for jobs 138–140
Conde, J. H. 253
Connolly, Pierce 87
conscription 99, 152–155, 158–159
Consorting Act 190–191
constitutional referenda
  1916 conscription 154–155
  1917 conscription 158–159
  1951 banning communism 255
container shipping 260, 279, 305, 319
convicts
  barracks 50
  on First Fleet 4–5, 8
  labour 13, 50–51
  punishment 10–13
  rum thefts 20
  seal trade and 26
  on Second Fleet 16–17
  seize *Harrington* (brig) 43–44
  in Thames hulks 2
  on Third Fleet 17
  ticket-of-leave 51
  women 5
Cook, James 5
Cook, Joseph 142, 154
Coolgardie, SS 137–138
Coombs, John 309
Corby, Schapelle viii
Corio 229
Cork, Sidney 186
Corrigan, Chris 308, 311–312
Costigan, Frank, QC 292–293, 295–300
criminal gangs 15
Croft, Peter 237–238
Crossley, George 42

Crumlin, Paddy 321–322
crystal meth *see* amphetamine
Curtin, John 154, 212, 216, 219–221, 225–226, 253
Customs 167, 279, 287, 315
Cutmore, John Daniel 181, 185
Cutts, Elizabeth 104

D

Dalfram (ship) 214
Dame Edna Everage 271
Darlinghurst Gaol 117
Darwin, Japanese bombing of 217
Darwin port 221
Davidson, Elsie 197
Dawes Point 24
de Brosses, Charles 1
de Groot, Francis 211
de Largie, Hugh 135
De Laurentiis, Dino 31
Deakin, Alfred 106, 133–134, 141, 142
Delaney, Arthur 275–276, 284
Delaney, Francis 202
Democratic Labour Party 256
dentists 179
Depression (1890s) 109–111
Dethridge, George 162
Devine, James 182–183
Devine, Matilda 'Tilly' 182–183, 185, 186, 192
Dibbs, George 105–106, 107
Dickie, Phil 302
Direct Action 150
disabilities 222–223
Dix, Bob 297
Dixon, Francis 87
dock labourers 79
dock work 79, 83, 89–90
dockers 193–194
dockland strikes 80
Dog Collar Act 196–197, 214, 215
the Domain 104
Domican, Tom 304
Doohan, Henry 119
double dissolutions 142
draught horse strike 261
Dray, George 199–200
drought 136
Drug Enforcement Agency (US) 318
drug importation 286–288
drug laws 173
drug raids 280–281
Drug Squad Bureau, NSW 180

drug trafficking 172, 290, 312, 317–318
drugs viii–ix
Dugan, Darcy 245, 246–251
Dunn, John 40

E
Eadie, Robert 234
early closing 177
East Asiatic Squadron 144–145
East India Company 19–20, 27, 28–29, 48
East Sydney brothels 234, 278
Ebden, Charles 64
ecstasy ix
Edwards, Tom 161
Eliza (brig) 44
emancipists 50
Emden (raider) 146–147
Erskine, Norman 266
ethnic gangs 305
Eureka Stockade 95
Eveleigh 155
excise tax on alcohol 47, 48
executions 11–13, 14, 117

F
Fanesi, Joe 237–238
farming at Sydney Cove 9
Farquhar, Murray 302
fascist salute 211
fashion 226
Faure, Les, Keith and Noel 190
Faure, Noel Ambrose 184, 189–190
Fawkner, William 63
Federal Bank of Australia 111
Federated Painters and Dockers *see* Painters and Dockers Union
Federation 124, 133, 139
Federation Drought 136
Fellows, Warren 290–291
Fielding, James 164
First Fleet ix, 3–8, 13, 24, 138
Fisher, Andrew 135, 141–143, 151
Fisk, Arnold 43, 44
Fitzgerald, Tony, QC 279, 303
Flannery, Chris 294, 301
Flannery, Frank 273
Flinders, Matthew 61–62
Flynn, Errol 30
Foley, Larry 113–114, 115
Fort Denison 12
Fort Nepean 144

Foster, Justice 120
Foveaux, Lieutenant Colonel Joseph 44
Fox, Norman 171
Foxcroft, Henry 171
France 1, 7
Franki, James 84
Fraser, Malcolm 142, 286, 290, 292
Free Traders 141
Freeman, George 243, 276, 281
Freeman, John 12
freight-forwarding industry 321–322
French Revolution 21–22
Freud, Sigmund 176
Fulton, Mr 40

G
Gable, Clark 31
Gaby, James 194–195
Gair, Vince 256
Galea, Perce 266
Gallipoli 151, 200
gambling 212–213
gambling clubs 264
gaming machines 281–282
gang system 222–223
gang wars 177, 323
Garden Island 15
Gardiner bank robbery 289
Garrard, Jacob 88
Geelong 70, 90
Gellibrand, Sir John 166
General Strike 1917 155–158
George III of England 26
German Australians 146
German waterside workers 147–150
Germany 143–147, 216
Gibson, Mel 31
Gietzelt, Dawn 206
Gilchrist, John 66
Gipps, Sir George 68
Glebe Push 112
gold rushes 68–76, 111, 140, 173–174
Gordon, Daniel 12
Gordon, Terry 296, 297
Gore, Mr 40
government, first in Australia 10
Government House, Sydney 8, 42
Government Wharf 13
Grafton Gaol 244
Great Bookie Robbery at Victoria Club 294
Great Britain, SS 73
Great Circle Route 73–74

Great Depression (1930s) 203,
    205–208, 212
Great London Dock Strike 1889 91–95
Greek Club bombing 201–202
Griffin, Mr 40
Griffiths, Albert ('Young Griffo')
    114–116
Grimes, Charles 62
Grose, Major Francis 17–20, 21, 24–25
Gunn, Bill 303

H
Haldane, Bob 200
Hall, Joseph 11–12
Hall, William 70
hangman 12–13
Hanlon, Premier 254
'happy as Larry' 114
Hargraves, Edward 68–69
Harrington (brig) 43–44
Harris, John 14
Harrison, Freddie 237, 239–240, 296
Harrods 177–178
Hartley 68
Hatfield, Shayne 315–316, 317
Hawke, Bob 295, 299, 306
Hawkesbury River dockyard 22
Hawkesbury River floods 36
Hawkesbury River settlers 33, 34
Hayes, Bobby 239
Hayes, Jack 185
Haynes, Thomas 51
Hayward, Paul 290–291
Heagney, Muriel 90
Healy, James 'Big Jim' 208, 212, 217,
    218, 220, 221, 254
Hells Angels 279, 315
Henley, Sir Thomas 179
Henry, Graham 'Abo 291–292
heroin 175–176, 277–282
heroin syndicates 280–281
heroin trade 288
heroin trafficking 290–292, 305
Hicken, Abe 114
Hickman, Mary Jane 116–117
Higgins, Justice 146
Higgs, William 135
High Court of Australia 255, 311
Hill, George 114
Hillier, Lew 220
Hills, Tom 218–219
Hoddle, Robert 64
holey dollar 48

Holland, Sydney 92–93
Holman, William 101–102, 104, 105,
    107, 108, 174
Holt, Harold 256–257
Holt, Joseph 18–19, 34–35
Hong Kong 216
Hoover, J. Edgar 283
Hope, Bob 231–232
Hopkins, Anthony 31
Horne, Donald 122, 125
Hosking, Joan 273
Hosking, Lawrie 274
Hospital Wharf 13
Houlihan, Paul 306
housing 129
Howard, John (prison reformer) 2
Howard, Trevor 31
Howard Government 308–312
Howitt, William 74, 75
Hughes, W. M. 99, 122
    as attorney-general 141–142
    background 101–105
    Boer War 138
    bubonic plague 130–131
    conscription 152–155, 158–159
    in federal parliament 133
    Labour Electoral League of New
        South Wales 105–108
    Legislative Assembly 123
    Maritime Industries Bill 204–205
    as prime minister 151, 196
    Waterside Workers Federation
        134–136, 139, 142, 154
    Wharf Labourers Union 124–126
    White Australia policy 134
    World War I 150
Humphreys, Kevin 302
Hungry Mile, Sydney 206–208
Hunter (ship) 23
Hunter, Captain John 7, 9, 15, 21
Hunter River 53
Hurley, Michael 313–317

I
ice *see* amphetamine
Illawarra 52
Illicit Drug Report 2010/2011 viii
immigration 77–78
Immigration Restriction Act 1901
    133–134
India 17, 25, 28
industrial disputes 9, 87, 217, 221
industrial revolution 26, 78

influenza pandemic 159–160
Inman, Noel 189
Innes, Justice 120
International Longshoreman's
   Association 252–253
International Workers of the World
   (IWW) 149
IRA 198
Irish political prisoners 18–19
Isaacs, Sir Henry 94
Isaacs, Sir Isaac 214
Italy 216

J
Jackson, Rex 302
Jansen, Noella 273
Japanese attack on Pearl Harbor 216
Japanese immigrants 133–134
Japanese in Pacific 214–217
Japanese in Sydney Harbour 226–228
Japanese wharfies 311
Jeffs, Phil 'The Jew' 182
Johnston, George 18, 32, 37–42, 45
Joseph, Roger 247
JP Morgan 110
Julius, Max 254
justice system 11, 19, 24–25

K
Kable, Henry 27
Kane, Brian 294, 295
Kane, Judy 293–294
Kane, Les 293–294
Kane, Ray 294, 295
Kangaroo Gang 275–276
Kaye, William, QC 286
Keane, Senator Richard 229
Kelly, Ray 232, 265
Keltie, James 9
Kemp, Captain Anthony Fenn 34–35
Kenny, Sergeant 159
Kent Group 27
'Kicking Their Livers Out' (poem) 113
Kiely, Jack 200–201
Kilberg, John 124
King, Anna Josepha 32
King, Governor Philip Gidley 24,
   27–28, 29, 31, 62
Kings Cross 66, 182, 233–234,
   277–278, 283
The King's School, Parramatta 68
King's Town 24

Kinniburgh, Graham 275–276, 302
Klondike Gold Rush 111
Knight, Doug 283
Kolovrat, Nicholas 275
Kolovrat, Zlatko 275
Korean War 255
Krahe, Fred 232
Kuhiken, Captain W. 143–144
Kuttabul, HMAS 227

L
La Trobe, Charles 65, 70–71
Labour Council of Sydney 85
Labour Electoral League of New South
   Wales 100–101, 105–108
Lady Barlow (ship) 28
land grants
   Duntroon 55, 56
   illegal leases 37
   to Macarthur 26
   in New South Wales 17, 18, 19, 25,
      32
   to New South Wales Marine Corps
      42–43
   Wurundjeri land sale 63
Lanfranchi, Warren 302
Lang, Dr John 19
Lang, Jack 210, 211, 212
Langley, John 124, 125
Laperouse, Comte de 7
larrikinism 113
Latin Quarter, Sydney 266
Laughton, Charles 30–31
Laycock, Lieutenant 40
Lea, Canon Howard 209–210
League of Nations 172
Lee, Sammy 234
Leigh, James 183
Leigh, Kathleen 'Kate' 182, 183, 185,
   192
Leighton, John 24
Leo XIII, Pope 177
letter of credit scam 274
Levine, Judge Aaron 281
Liberal Party 142, 253
lime washing 194
Lister, John 69
Logan Downs Station 98
London's port authorities 28
Long Bay Gaol 246
Longford, Raymond 30
Longley, Barbara 272, 273

Longley, Bill 'The Texan' 271–273, 274, 275, 289, 295, 296
Lord, Simeon 27
Lorentz, Beryl 250
Loughnane, John 273
Louis XVI of France 7
Lovell, Henry 11–12
Lukin, Justice vii, 171, 324
Lyell, Lottie 30
Lyne, William 125, 131
Lynton, Mayne 30
Lyons, Joseph 214
Lytle, Wellington 203

M

MacArthur, Douglas 219, 255
Macarthur, John
  Bligh and 32, 36–42
  land grants to 26
  Macquarie and 45, 56–58
  in New South Wales 19–20
  in New South Wales Marine Corps 16–17
  wool industry 16, 25–26
McCarthy, Senator Joseph 217
McCarthy, 'Young Bull' 115–116
McCoy, Alfred 279–280, 303–304
McCredie, George 128–129
MacDougall, Harold 184
McElroy, Errol 179
Macfarlane, William Macpherson vii, 166–170
McGregor, Lancelot 185
McIver, Alexander 202
McIver, Norman 202
Mackay, Donald 288–289
MacKay, William 208–209, 211–212
MacMillan, Alan 233
McNeill, Jack 284–285
McPherson, Dawn 243, 250
McPherson, Leonard Arthur 241–251, 263–267, 281–282, 284–285, 304
McPherson, Marlene 265
McPherson, Sir William 201
Macquarie, Governor Lachlan 42, 45–51, 52, 55–59
Macquarie Street 235
McQueen, Dr Ronald 222–223
Madden, Dr Cawley 160
Mafia 176, 253, 280, 281–282, 283, 284, 288
Mahony, Robert 194
Malaya 216

malingering 222
Maltby, Sir Thomas 262
mandatory penalties 1, 170, 190
the manifest 231
Manne, Robert 155
Mannix, Archbishop Daniel 159
Mann's Hotel, Sydney 124
Mansion House Committee 94–95
Mara, Les 315–316, 317
Marco Polo 74
Margarot, Maurice 34
Maritime Industries Bill 204–205
maritime revolution 72–74, 79–80
maritime strike 95, 96–98, 110
maritime trade 24
Maritime Union of Australia 307–312
Marsden, Reverend Samuel 31–32, 34
Marsuo, Lieutenant 227
Martell, Eric 272
Martin, 'Sir' Wayne 266, 278
Masters, Chris 302
match girls strike 91–92
Matra, James Mario 2–3
Mauritius 130
Mears, William 246–251
media bias 105–106
media investigation 302–303
medical cocaine 191
medical practitioners 179
medicinal opiates 174
Mei Quong Tart 173–174
Melbourne 62, 70, 72, 163
  Depression (1890s) 110–111
  ganglands wars 184, 190
  underworld 237–240, 268–276
Melbourne Cup 225
Melbourne Harbour Trust 170
Melbourne waterfront
  Americans and 218–219
  cargo pillaging 162, 167, 170–171
  dock workers 86
  docklands 75–76
  Federated Ship Painters and Dockers 292–293, 295–300
  gelignite charges during war 228
  Webb Dock 309
Melbourne Wharf Labourers Union 90, 111, 134, 139–140, 149, 155–156
Melon, Andrew W. 203
Menzies, Sir Robert 162, 214–216, 253, 254–258
Mercantile Marine Officers Association 95, 96–97, 98

Mercury (ship) 11
Mexican cocaine cartels viii–ix, 315, 318–319
Middle East 216
Middle Eastern drug dealers 292, 323
Mikkelsen, Victor 293
military service avoidance 236–237
Miller, Robert 188–189
Miller, William 184
Millers Point 24
Millers Point Push 112, 118–120
Millwall docks, London 89
Minchin, Lieutenant 40
Mitchell, James 180
Mitchell, Mr 287
Moffatt, Able Seaman 145
Moffitt, Justice Athol 283–285, 304
Mongols 315, 319
Monk, Rodney 316
Moody, Captain 26–27
Moore, Lieutenant 40
Moore, Thomas 22
Moran, Lewis 190, 276
Moran family 295, 302
Moreton Bay 81
morphine 175
Morris, Joe 135
Mort, Henry, James and William 81
Mort, Thomas Sutcliff 81–82, 84–85, 87
Mort's Dock, Balmain 81–82, 87, 91, 126, 219, 243, 248–250, 259–260
Mt Penang juvenile detention 242–243
Mount Rennie outrage 116–117
Mr Asia drug trafficking syndicate 289
Mullins, Barney 221
multiculturalism 72
Munro Ferguson, Sir Ronald 154
Murdoch, Keith 151
Murdoch, Rupert 82
Murphy, Billy 115
Murphy, Brian 301, 302
Murphy, Lionel 302
Murray, John 60–61
Mussolini 199

N
Nagel, Jim 199–200
Nalder, Leslie 247–248
Napoleonic Wars 25, 36–37, 44
Narcotics Board 287
National Crime Authority 290, 303
National Farmers Federation 306, 308

National Labor Party 154, 204–205
National Service Bureau 156
Nauru 145
Nelson, Tom 236
Neville, Richard 241–242
New Guard 210–212
New Guinea 145
New South Wales 70
New South Wales Commissary 24–25
New South Wales Marine Corps *see also* Macarthur, John
   Campbell and 29
   commercial activities 20, 33–35
   establishment by Grose 18–19
   Harrington (brig) 44
   as Rum Corps 18
   Rum Rebellion 39–42
New South Wales marines 9, 10, 13, 14, 18
New South Wales Painters and Dockers 299
New South Wales penal colony 1–22, 17, 45–46
New York Stock Exchange 203
New York waterfront 252–253
New Zealand 171
Newcastle 24, 42, 52–53, 227
Newcastle Harbour 57
Newcastle Wharf Labourers Union 134
Newman, Keith 229
Newport Beach 227
Nicholls, Jack 'Putty Nose' 296–297
Night Watch and Row Boat Guard 14
nightclubs 234, 316
Nordeutscher Lloyd 143–144
Norfolk Island 12, 15, 44
North, Justice 310, 311
nuclear tests 255
Nugent, Harold 237–240

O
O'Connell, Jack 221
O'Connell, Timothy 202
O'Connor, Raymond 'Ducky' 265–267
oil *see* sealing; whaling
O'Keefe, David 136
Old Guard 210
Oldham, Russell 316
Oliver, Pearl 237–238
Operation Alien 256
Ophir 68, 69, 70
opium black market 175
opium import ban 174

opium trade 73
Opium Wars 172–173
organised crime 176, 177, 283–285, 321–324
O'Shannessy, Les 197, 205, 228
outlaw bikers 270, 305, 315, 318, 319, 321
overfilling 140
Overseas Shipping Representatives Association 253

P

Pacific War 216–219
Packer, Robert 179
Page, Earle 196
Paine, Arthur 127
Paine, Daniel 21–22
Painters and Dockers 91, 159
painters and dockers 83
Painters and Dockers Union 126, 184, 190, 194, 220, 236, 237–240
   1917 General Strike 155–158
   1980 Royal Commission 288–289, 292–293, 295–300
   deregistration 299
   Melbourne crime world 268–276
   organised crime 259–260
Palmer, John 24–25
Palmer, Sophia 24
Park, Thomas 72
Parkes, Henry 81, 105, 106, 107, 110–111
pastoralists 96
Paterson, Fred 254
Paterson, William 44
Patey, George 145
Patrick Stevedoring 308–312
Peakes, Nipper 115
Peisley, A. J. 179
penal colonies 1
Pentridge Gaol 190, 265, 271
Perlman, Mark 217
Perry, Detective Inspector Charles 240
Perry, John 'Black' 113
Pert, Robert 119
Pert, Thomas 118–120
Petricevic, Milan 284
Petrov Affair 256
Pfalz, SS 143–144
Phantom Dockers 274
Pharmacy Board of NSW 175
Philadelphia (merchant ship) 17
Phillip, Captain Arthur 3–9, 17, 26
   powers as first governor 10–13
Phillip Island 61
Phillips, Marion 58
pick-up system 195–196, 221–222
pig iron exports to Japan 214–216
Pius X, Pope 177
Pockley, Captain 145
policing
   abortion rackets 281, 286
   black market 230–231
   cargo pillaging 223–224
   coal miners strike, Hunter Valley 208–209
   cocaine sting 178
   consorting powers 190–191, 208
   Criminal Investigations Branch 232, 266–267, 280–281
   Light Brigade, Sydney 120
   against New Guard 211–212
   in New South Wales penal colony 14
   Pillage Squad 262, 269, 288
   police corruption 232, 280–282
   police districts 48–49
   police informers 244, 316–317
   Port Melbourne riot 199–200
   sly grog trade 212–213
   State and Federal Police vii–viii
   Webley Scott pistol 248
Port Adelaide Working Men's Association 86
port duties 49
Port Fremantle 111
Port Jackson ix, 5–6, 89
Port Kembla 215
Port Melbourne viii, 71–72, 199–200, 205, 262
Port Phillip Bay 60–65, 74, 79–80
Port Phillip Pilots 144
Port Phillip Stevedores Association 90, 111, 134, 135, 147–150
Port Stephens 52, 57
Power, Anne 15
Pratt, Constable Michael 190
Pratt, Richard 309
Premier Permanent Building Association 110
Prendergast, John 192
Prendergast, Laurie 192, 293–294
Price, Tom 97
Prince of Wales, HMS 216
Privy Council 25
Productivity Commission 306–307
prostitution 76, 179–180, 278
Protectionists 105–106, 107, 141

INDEX • 341

punishment in colony 10–13, 31–32, 51, 67
the pushes, Sydney 112–121
Pyrmont, Sydney 313
Pyrmont docks 88

Q
Quaedvlieg, Roman 315
Quantock, James 137–138
Quarantine Station, North Head 127–128, 131
Queen Mary 219
Queen Victoria Market 296
Queensland 1948 wharfies strike 253–254
Queensland as moonlight state 302–303
Queensland Defence Force 103
Queensland Painters and Dockers 299
Queensland Police 310–311
Queensland Supreme Court vii

R
racing industry 225
railway gauges 260
railway workers 155, 158, 198, 253
rat trapping 129–130
rationing 225–226
Razor Gang 181, 186–187
Rebels 315
red-light district 233
refugees ix, 218, 320
Reibey, Mary 53–55
Reibey, Thomas 53
Reibey, Tom 54–55
Reid, George 141, 151
Reid, Thomas 120
Reilly, Richard Gabriel 234, 244, 245, 266
Reith, Peter 308, 310
Repulse, HMS 216
Returned Sailors and Soldier's Shop and Wharf Worker's Union NSW 158
returned servicemen 161–162
Rich, Edward 120
Riley, Alexander 42–43, 48
Roach, E. C. 214
Robertson, Sir John 88
Robinson, Captain 144
Rogers, Will 203
Rogerson, Roger 302, 304
Rooklyn, Jack 284
Ross, Major 12

Ross, Sandy 113–114
rotary system 222
Rothbury coal miners strike 208–209
Rothschild family 110
Rowntree, Captain Thomas 82, 84
Royal Australian Navy 144–145, 147
Royal Commissions
　1919 returned servicemen labour 161–162
　1921 cargo pillaging vii, 166–170
　1973 organised crime 283–285
　1977 cannabis growing 288–289
　1977 drug importation 286–288
　1980 Federated Ship Painters and Dockers 292–293, 295–300
　1981 drug trafficking 290–292
　2015 child sexual abuse 242
　uses of 161
Royal Sydney Yacht Squadron 36
rum currency 15, 20, 33–35, 47
Rum Rebellion 16, 18, 39–42, 45
rum trade monopoly 48
Russia 103, 165
Ryan, Gary 323
Ryan, John 11–12
Ryan, Joseph 'King Joe' 252–253
Ryan, Ronald 265

S
Saffron, Abe 266, 303
St Johnston, Colonel Sir Eric 286
St Marks, Darling Point 85, 209–210
Santamaria, B. A. 256
scab labour 91, 97, 198
Scandinavian Australians 148
Scotch whisky 229
Scottish immigrants 77
Scottish Martyrs 21–22, 34
Scullin, James 154, 205, 211
sealing 26–27, 29
seamen and wharfies 231
seamen's strike (1931) 211
Second Fleet 16–17, 18
security industry 168–169
Serturner, Friedrich 175
sex trade 76
Shannon, Pat 273–275
Shannon, Wilma 274
Sharkey, Lance 254
shearers strike 97–99, 110
shearers union 95–96, 108
shearing sheds 95
Sheerman, William 12

shipowners 156, 165, 196–197, 269
shipping routes 73–74
ships officers 96
Shipwrights Society of Sydney 78
Shireham, Charlie 130
shonks 222
Shortland, Lieutenant John 24
Sinaloa Cartel viii–ix, 315, 318–319
Singapore, fall of 216–217
six o'clock swill 177
slavery 4–5
Sloss, Albert 284
sly grog trade 48, 177, 212–213, 225–226
smallpox 81, 138
Smith, Arthur 'Neddy' 243, 290–292
Smith, Donny 'The Glove' 303
Smith, Stan 'The Man' 251, 263–265, 281, 284–285, 303–304
Smock, William 148
Sofala 70
Solidarity Group 107
Somalian drug dealers 323
Sorrento 62
South African wharfies 311
South America 180, 317
South Australian Painters and Dockers 299
South-East Asia 216
  amphetamine labs ix
  amphetamine trafficking 315, 319–320
  heroin labs 278, 279–280
  heroin trafficking 292
Southwell, Daniel 10
Soviet Union 212, 221, 255, 256, 259
SP bookmaking 177, 314
Spanish Civil War 198
Spee, Graf von 144–145, 146–147
Spence, William Guthrie 95–96, 99
Spigelman, James 47
Standen, Mark 315, 316
Stanley Street brothels 278
Steamship Owners of Victoria 95
steamships 80, 82, 83, 140
stevedores 90, 156, 165
Stevedoring Authority 272
Stevedoring Industry Commission 221–223
Stevens, Lorna 190
Stewart, Justice Donald 290
Stewart, Michael 43–44
stock market crash (1929) 203
Stone, Joseph Francis 293

Stone, Ken 295
stonemasons 80
Street, Able Seaman 145
strike-breakers 157–158
Stuart-Jones, Reginald 234–235
Sudanese drug dealers 323
sugar crop (1953) 256
sugar industry 81
Sullivan Bay 62
Summers, Dean 322
Suttor, George 39
Swanton, William 198
Sweetman, Charles 116–117
Sydney 13, 29, 37, 72, 173, 180
Sydney, Lord 3, 6
Sydney Airport 315
Sydney Chamber of Commerce 163
Sydney Chamber of Manufacturers 164
Sydney Cove 6, 8
Sydney Cove (ship) 23
Sydney Harbour ix, 5–6, 9–10, 226–228
Sydney Harbour Bridge 132, 211
Sydney Harbour Trust 132
Sydney Hospital 46, 47–48
Sydney Town Hall diamond theft 314
Sydney waterfront
  cargo pillaging 164, 167–168, 171, 223–224
  dockyards 22, 36
Sydney Wharf Labourers Union 85–86, 94, 96, 97–98, 134
Sydney–Lang electorate 123

T
TAB 304
tarpaulin musters 165
tax evasion 296, 298
Taylor, Joseph 'Squizzy' 180–181
Taylor, Kevin 274
Taylor, Mrs 138
television sets 269
temperance groups 116, 174
ten pound poms 78
Tench, Watkin 11, 15
Testa, Joseph Dan 281–282
Thailand 216
Thargomindah, Q'ld 102–103
The Age tapes 302
The Rocks 20, 46–47, 49–50, 65, 80–81, 206
The Rocks Push 112, 113–114, 115, 117
Therry, Robert 66–67

Third Fleet 17, 26
Third International 209
Thomas, Drummer E. 143
Thompson, Eliza 63
Thompson, Jack (jockey) 246–247
Thompson submachine gun 248
Thomson, Sir Edward 69
Three Jolly Settlers 47
Thursday Island 103
Tillett, Ben 89–95
Tom brothers 69
tombstones 75
Townsville 166
Trade Union Act, 1883 91
Trades and Labour Council 87, 101, 106
Trades Hall Committee, Melbourne 85
Trades Hall Council, Melbourne 96
Tradesman's Arms hotel, Darlinghurst 183
Transport Workers Act 196–197, 214, 215
Transport Workers Union 134
transportation 1, 3–6, 66–67
Triads 72
Trimbole, Robert 303
Trolley and Draymens Union 134
Tschudi, Johann von 176
Tsuzuku, Petty Officer 227
Tuck, Sid 249
Tunks, Mr 138
Turkish waterside workers 149
Turner, Joseph 237
Twain, Mark 109
Twist, John Eric 237, 239, 240, 270

U
U boats 147
Ullathorne, William 4–5, 11
Underwood, James 27
Union Bank 111
union membership 78, 95, 307
union movement ix, 78, 85–86, 135
United Arab Emirates 309
United States 17
    American mobsters 248
    American sealers 26–27
    American servicemen on leave 228, 231, 233–234, 237–238, 277–278
    cocaine use 191
    Depression (1890s) 109–110
    heroin addiction 176
    Japanese attack on Pearl Harbor 216
    Pacific War 218–219
    World War I 157

V
Van Diemen's Land 25, 26, 44–45, 49, 52, 63
Vaux, James Hardy 2
Victoria 70
Victoria Club, Melbourne 294
Victoria Police ix, 310, 323
Victorian Mounted Rifles 97
Vietnam War 277
Vin Mariani 177

W
Wainer, Dr Bertram 281, 286
Walker, Able Seaman 145
Walker, Peter 265
Walker, Robert 'Pretty Boy 264–265
Wallace, George 185
Walsh, Constable 148
War Risk Insurance Scheme 147
war service loans 261
Ward, Eddie 220–221
Warner, Charles 109
Water Board 88
waterfront crime 162–171, 259–267, 304–305
Waterfront Industry Reform Authority 306
waterfront productivity 306–307, 311–312
waterfront unions 78, 80–81, 94
Waterloo Push 112, 116–117
waterside workers affluence 308
waterside workers conditions 85, 140, 147–150, 193–196, 222–223, 260–261
Waterside Workers Federation 185
    1902 federated unions 134–136
    1917 General Strike 155–158
    1919 Royal Commission 161–162
    1921 Royal Commission 171
    1928 Beeby Award strike 196–202
    1948 Queensland wharfies strike 253–254
    1953 stop-work 256
    1954 closed-shop strike 256–258
    Australian Steamship Owners Federation 139–140

ban on pig iron exports to Japan 214–216
becomes MUA *see* Maritime Union of Australia
black market 232, 236
conscription 154
formation 85–86
gang system 223
Healy as General Secretary 212
log of claims 145–146
during World War II 217–220
Watson, Chris 141
Watson, Dr Frederick 4
weapons, wildlife and cash ix, 305
Webster, Stephen 310
Wedderburn 319
Wentworth, D'Arcy 17, 48, 49
Wentworth, William Charles 17
West End Hotel, Balmain 264
West Sydney electorate 133
Western Australia 111
whaling 26, 29
Wharf Labourers Union 124–126
Wharf Labourers Union of Victoria 90
wheat crop 152
Whelan, Brendan 'Jack' 266
White, Tommy 116
White Australia policy 133–134
White Horse Hotel, George Street 114
Whitlam, Gough 142
Whittaker, Allan 199–200
Whittle, Serjeant Major 39
Whitton, Fred 83
Williams, Able Seaman 145
Williams, Justice Edward 286–288
Williams, James 199
Williams, Joan 257
Williams, John 12
Williamstown 64, 90, 219
Wilson, Douglas and Isabel 289
Wilson, Senior Constable P. B. 223–224
Wimbow, John 15
Windeyer, Justice 117
Windsor, Sergeant 44
wine 177
women 201, 206, 230
Woodward, Justice 288–289
wool broking 81
wool exports 70
wool industry 16, 25–26, 56–58
Woolloomooloo 22, 25, 65–66
Wootton, Charles 240
workplace agreements 307
World War I 141, 142–150, 151–154, 157, 159, 177–178
World War II 191, 212, 216–220
Wran, Neville, QC 241, 302
Wright, Charles Alder 175

Y

Yampi Sound 214
Yandra, HMAS 227
Yarra Stevedoring Company 162
Yarrington, S. D. 173
Yarroma, HMAS 227
York, Duke of 133

Z

Zagon, Stephen 309–310
Zedong, Mao 255

www.ingramcontent.com/pod-product-compliance
Ingram Content Group UK Ltd.
Pitfield, Milton Keynes, MK11 3LW, UK
UKHW041307180426
11947UKWH00009B/742